Therapeutic Practice in Volume Two The Conte Adolescent

In common with *Therapeutic Practice in Schools: Working with the Child Within* (Routledge, 2012), this second volume serves as a practical handbook for school-based counsellors, psychotherapists, arts therapists and play therapists working with young people. Written in accessible language, it is eminently applicable to the practice of both qualified and trainee therapists.

Therapeutic Practice in Schools: The Contemporary Adolescent begins with an overview of key psychoanalytic ideas informing our understanding of adolescence before moving on to focus on life circumstances and issues that commonly bring young people to the therapist's consulting room in the school. Dedicated chapters on key themes including identity, relationships, sex and sexuality, anger issues, self-harm, bereavement and bullying aim to deepen our understanding of the adolescent experience while also providing the therapist with invaluable insights into what one might say in the 'here and now' of the session. Chapter authors, all with considerable experience in the field, discuss approaches to sustaining the therapeutic relationship in the face of ambivalence or defiant resistance as well as thinking about the impact of social media on all aspects of adolescent development. The advantages and limitations of working with adolescents in the educational setting, where school staff will have their own reasons for referring students for therapy but the young people themselves might come with a very different agenda, are also covered.

It is widely acknowledged that engaging troubled or troublesome adolescents in therapy can make an enormous difference to their lives. This book ensures that both trainee and qualified therapists are supported in the often daunting yet ever stimulating and enlivening task of working with young people in the school setting.

Lyn French is an art therapist, counsellor and psychoanalytic psychotherapist. As the Director of A Space for Creative Learning and Support, Hackney, East London, she supervises trainee and qualified therapists and manages school-based services. She is also on the staff of the MSc in Counselling and Psychotherapy with Children and Adolescents at Birkbeck, University of London.

Reva Klein is a psychodynamic counsellor and psychoanalytic psychotherapist supervising emerging and established counsellors working in London schools. She also sees parents/carers and teachers for consultations in school and has a private practice. She has written extensively on children's mental health issues.

Therapeutic Practice in Schools Volume Two The Contemporary Adolescent

A clinical workbook for counsellors, psychotherapists and arts therapists

Edited by Lyn French and Reva Klein

Routledge
Taylor & Francis Group

LONDON AND NEW YORK

First published 2015
by Routledge
27 Church Road, Hove, East Sussex, BN3 2FA

and by Routledge
711 Third Avenue, New York, NY 10017

Routledge is an imprint of the Taylor & Francis Group, an informa business

© 2015 Lyn French and Reva Klein

The right of Lyn French and Reva Klein to be identified as the authors of the editorial material, and of the authors for their individual chapters, has been asserted in accordance with sections 77 and 78 of the Copyright, Designs and Patents Act 1988.

British Library Cataloguing-in-Publication Data

A catalogue record for this book is available from the British Library

Library of Congress Cataloging-in-Publication Data

A catalog record for this book has been requested

ISBN: 978-0-415-85816-8 (hbk)
ISBN: 978-0-415-85821-2 (pbk)
ISBN: 978-1-315-75714-8 (ebk)

Typeset in Times
by Apex CoVantage, LLC

Contents

PART II
Common themes   69

PART III
Using creative approaches and applied therapies 175

Contributors

Myra Berg initially worked as a teacher in secondary and special schools. She became increasingly interested in the emotional experiences underlying teacher–pupil interaction and consequently enrolled on the Psychoanalytic Child and Adolescent Psychotherapy training at the Tavistock Clinic, London. During this training she worked as a school counsellor in an inner-city secondary school. On qualification, she worked in Child and Adolescent Mental Health Service outreach services in schools, integrating her previous experience as a teacher and counsellor with her training as a child and adolescent psychotherapist. Myra currently works at the Tavistock Clinic in a community team treating children, adolescents and their parents both in the clinic and in schools. She also teaches and supervises on a number of post-graduate courses at the Tavistock, particularly those focusing on therapeutic work in community settings.

Tamsin Cottis (UKCP) is an Integrative Arts Child Psychotherapist. She has over 25 years experience of working with people with learning disabilities and other diagnosed special needs, including autism. She is a co-founder and former Assistant Director of Respond, the UK's leading provider of psychotherapy to children and adults with learning disabilities. She is a founding member of the Institute of Psychotherapy and Disability. Currently Consultant Clinical Supervisor at Respond and a teacher at the Bowlby Centre, she also works as a therapist in schools and in private practice. Her publications include *Intellectual Disability, Trauma and Psychotherapy* (Editor) (Routledge, 2008). She is a published author of short fiction.

Margery Craig is a Design Consultant with her own practice. Margery worked with creative teams on architectural, retail and museum projects as well as taking on a Visiting Assessor's role on post-graduate courses in the field. Alongside this first career she gained experience as a volunteer counsellor at a national helpline for children and young people, which motivated her to go on to study for the MSc in Psychodynamic Counselling and Psychotherapy at Birkbeck. Since graduating, Margery has combined her role as a trainer and supervisor of telephone and online counsellors in the same children's charity with working as a sessional counsellor for A Space, seeing both primary and secondary school pupils. She is currently training in psychoanalytic psychotherapy at the Guild of Psychotherapists.

Angie Doran works as a counsellor in both secondary and primary schools for A Space for Support. She completed an MSc in Psychodynamic Counselling and Psychotherapy with Children and Adolescents at Birkbeck, University of London, before taking on the role of lead researcher on a joint PhD research project set up by A Space with the University of Essex (Centre for Psychoanalytic Studies). In her work at A Space, she has been responsible for setting up new services in the primary sector and in a sixth form college. She also had a lead role in establishing staff counselling as an A Space service.

Jenny Dover is a senior educational psychotherapist who has worked in Child and Adolescent Mental Health Service in inner London for 24 years since training as an educational psychotherapist at the Tavistock Clinic. She also teaches on the MA at the Caspari Foundation, and as well as contributing to a range of journals, she co-authored, with Gillian Salmon, *Reaching and Teaching through Educational Psychotherapy*, published in 2007.

Jo Evans. Following on from an earlier career in West End/Touring and Repertory theatre, film and television and voluntary work as a literacy tutor, Jo Evans trained as a child and adolescent school counsellor and psychotherapist on the Birkbeck MSc course. Since qualifying, she has worked for A Space, setting up new services in both the primary and secondary school settings, developing Year 6/7 transition support projects and seeing school staff for counselling (and supervising Birkbeck trainees on placement at A Space). Her background in the performing arts feeds into her creative approaches to working with difficult-to-reach adolescents; she continues to pilot the use of the A Space/Iniva emotional learning cards in her sessions as well as in workshops with Iniva artists and is contributing to A Space research on their applications.

Lyn French is an art therapist, counsellor and psychoanalytic psychotherapist. She was one of the original team members contracted in 1997 to set up A Space for Creative Learning and Support, a partnership between Alex Sainsbury (Sainsbury Family Charitable Trusts), the Social Science Research Unit (Institute of Education, University of London) and Hackney Education. She has been the Director since 2000 and continues to oversee service delivery across Hackney schools as well as taking a lead on research, most recently a three-year study conducted with the University of Essex (Centre for Psychoanalytic Studies) funded by the Glass-House Trust. A long-term partnership with the Institute of International Visual Arts (iniva) brings artists into A Space to work in collaboration with therapists. Out of this work, Lyn co-developed sets of emotional learning cards with iniva which feature contemporary art and psychologically resonant commentary and questions. The sets, entitled *What do you feel?*, *Who are you?*, *Where are you going?* and *How do we live well with others?*, are sold internationally through www.iniva.org and www.inivacreativelearning.org. Lyn is also a sessional lecturer on the Birkbeck MSc course in Counselling with Children and Adolescents.

Norma Gould is Assistant Headteacher at Bacon's College, London, with responsibility for Student Support Services while also being a member of the therapeutic counselling team. Previously she has taught on the MSc in Psychodynamic Counselling and Psychotherapy with Children and Adolescents at Birkbeck College, University of London, and taken up the role of Associate Director and Consultant at the Birkbeck College Group Relations Conference. Before her present position, she worked at Forest Hill Boys School, London, where she set up and managed the counselling service for four years and worked as a counsellor with 'Just Ask', a therapy service for homeless young people. Prior to training to be a therapist, Norma was a secondary school teacher and head of department for 12 years. She has also worked with young people in Ireland in a variety of contexts including those who were homeless and in the prison system.

Melissa Jones completed post-graduate studies in communication, culture and society before enrolling on the Birkbeck MSc in Psychodynamic Counselling and Psychotherapy with Children and Adolescents. Her work has included commissioned research with the National Children's Bureau, telephone and online counselling for ChildLine and various roles within Kids Company, where she now works as a Team Leader in the Schools Programme. Melissa also provides counselling for adolescents and staff in an A Space secondary school on a sessional basis. She has a particular interest in thinking about cultural and societal influences on contemporary adolescents as well as working with school and life-cycle transitions.

Sue Kegerreis is currently the Director at the Centre for Psychoanalytic Studies at the University of Essex, where she is also the Programme Lead for the Foundation Degree in Therapeutic Communication and Therapeutic Organisations. She trained as a teacher, as a child and adolescent psychotherapist at the Tavistock Clinic and later as an adult psychoanalytic psychotherapist with the Lincoln Centre. She has practised in a range of settings: hospital, Child and Adolescent Mental Health Service and privately, and she worked for many years as a school counsellor, as well as teaching on many courses, both clinical and applied. She has published widely in professional journals, and her book *Psychodynamic Counselling with Children and Adolescents* was published in 2010. She originated and was course director of the MSc in Psychodynamic Counselling with Children and Adolescents at Birkbeck College.

Reva Klein is a child and adolescent counsellor and adult psychoanalytic psychotherapist who supervises trainee therapists at A Space. Previously a freelance journalist, writer and editor, Reva taught journalism at Goldsmiths College for many years. She is the author of three books on education: *Defying Disaffection, Citizens by Right* and *We Want our Say* and is the co-author of *Reluctant Refuge: The Story of Asylum in Britain*. She twice won the Commission for Racial Equality's Race in the Media Award for her writing in the *Times Educational Supplement*, and she founded and edited the *International Journal on School Disaffection*, an Anglo-American publication now in its second decade. In the 1990s Reva sat on the Secondary School Reform Committee of UNESCO. A Birkbeck MSc graduate and a professional member of the Association of Group and Individual Psychotherapy, she has a private practice.

Sue Lund's first career was in teaching; she then took on a Headship, which she held for 20 years. Her interest in the social and emotional aspects of teaching and learning led to her completing the Tavistock MA in Observational Studies before taking a place on the Birkbeck MSc in Psychodynamic Counselling and Psychotherapy with Children and Adolescents. In addition to working as a school counsellor for A Space in both the primary and secondary school settings and providing staff consultations, Sue has continued to develop her thinking around the emotional aspects of the learning relationship and has created projects on this theme for A Space. Her earlier professional experience has led to providing consultations for emerging and experienced school staff on all aspects relating to working in a pressurised environment with pupils who have challenging circumstances and complex needs.

Akin Ojumu is currently in the final phase of his training as a child and adolescent psychotherapist with the British Psychotherapy Foundation. Prior to this, he completed the MSc in
Child and Adolescent Counselling and Psychotherapy at Birkbeck and was a sessional counsellor at A Space while also working as an arts editor for *The Observer*. Akin has a long history in journalism and has published many articles, including one on the role of black fathers
('As a Father, Why I Fear for My Son', *Observer*, 2008). He continues to write and publish
as a freelance journalist while working as a therapist and training in child psychotherapy.

Stefania Putzu-Williams completed her first degree in psychology at Rome University before
receiving an MA in Psychoanalytic Observational Studies at the Tavistock Clinic and University College London and an MSc in Psychodynamic Counselling at Birkbeck. After writing a thesis on child abuse in the UK, she began specialising in the care of children and
young people and has worked therapeutically since 1989. From in-depth experience including residential assessment of high-risk families prior to Family Court decisions, she has
developed expertise as a counsellor in community and school-based projects (since 2003
within Child and Adolescent Mental Health Service) and, in more recent years, as a counsellor at Bacon's College in Southwark, where she also coordinates a team of four counsellors.

Tara Richards' first degree was in Classical Studies, specialising in drama. As well as acting in theatres in London, Edinburgh, Italy and India, she has worked extensively as an
arts practitioner in the theatre, developing educational and therapeutic programmes for
children and young people on themes such as crime prevention, bullying and peer relationships using forum theatre puppetry and role play. Following her post-graduate training in dramatherapy at Roehampton University, she has facilitated individual and group
sessions in mainstream schools, in the National Health Service, Adult Services and private practice. She currently works for A Space providing services in both the primary
and secondary school settings. Her specialist interests remain rooted in using drama as
an expressive and exploratory tool, and she continues to perform in improvised theatre.

David Trevatt is a child and adolescent psychotherapist and a former director of Open Door, a
psychotherapy service for young people aged 12 to 24 and their parents in Haringey, North
London. He was the clinical manager of 'Hear and Now', an adolescent counselling service in the North East London Foundation Trust of the National Health Service and clinical
consultant to A Space. He trained at the Tavistock Clinic and previously worked as a social
worker in different settings, including several Child and Adolescent Mental Health Service
teams. He has worked as a psychotherapist in mainstream and special schools and supervises
the work of therapists delivering counselling services in educational and community settings.

Camilla Waldburg has been the Development Officer for support services at A Space
since 2001. Following on from a degree in psychology, she trained in play therapy at
Roehampton and has developed the play therapy service at A Space, where she continues to supervise trainees. She gained an MSc in Systemic Psychotherapy with Families
and Couples and worked for many years as a clinical practitioner in a social care team
based in the London borough of Hackney. More recently, she has taken up a part-time
role as a family therapist in a Greenwich under 5's Child and Adolescent Mental Health
Service team. In parallel, she continues to develop the family consultation service at
A Space and oversee trainees on placement. She is also a visiting lecturer on the MA
course in Play Therapy at Roehampton University.

Foreword

Adolescents are busy people. This, for some, may come as a surprise – beleaguered parents, for example, who are bemused by the wiles and ways of some of their teenagers, well bedded as they can be for more than half the day, if not the week, or well loafed within the muddled privacy of their bedrooms and fascinations of their sacred screens. But, however it looks on the outside, inside there is an awful lot going on. Adolescents just do have a lot on their minds. Pubertal preoccupations with their newly changing bodies take up a lot of mental time; so, too, do ever perplexing wonderings about what it's going to take to become an independent man or woman, on the big, wide road to adulthood, whatever that might be. All this takes place in the midst of the fast-changing rush and complexity of our contemporary society with its mind-blowing technology and cultural diversity. The internet opens wide, the knowledge swells, the music booms, the dance floors flash, the drugs float – living ain't boring even though being bored is one way of dealing with it.

Is it all too much? For the majority, no, not really. There is an irresistible energy in most young people and an alert curiosity and willingness to do, find out, have a go – enough, in other words, to face the many pressures and demands of the day. But, and this is a big but, there is a minority too – not an insignificant group of young people who are indeed finding things too much. In their essential isolation and too often without the essential emotional backup they need, they can become overwhelmed by what is expected of them and by what they find within themselves that is disturbing and frightening. And then they 'fail': they lose confidence, and they don't learn as well as they might.

Attention needs to be paid – and by all kinds of people, not least of course by those working in schools. Schools are such remarkable places, such complex communal places in which, under the right circumstances, so much can be realized and brought forth. Teachers and school staff are there to help make a difference to all sides of development – the academic, intellectual, social, spiritual and emotional. In the ordinary daily life of school, much can be done to foster learning in its full sense.

Most head teachers and school staff these days know that they can't contend alone with the mass of challenge that presents itself every day. They value extra help of different sorts, and this book is about one such support, something very important, that of counselling and psychotherapy. The book is in fact a second volume of *Therapeutic Practice in Schools*, which was published two years ago. Much of the spirit – the psychoanalytic understanding and approach and the readiness to work in school and alongside school staff – of Volume 1 shines brightly through these pages too, but this time with more focus on the adolescent and the specific task of working in a secondary school.

Secondary schools by and large are big, with a thousand or so pupils of different ages, different abilities, different developmental levels, different cultures, different families. It is a world of bewildering difference but with a common purpose to improve the quality and richness of education in all its glory. They are not easy places to handle, to teach in and to be in. New entrants are invariably awestruck, not least the fledglings fresh out of the relative comforts of primary school. The issue that pervades everything else is transition. Transition into secondary school, transition from one class to another, transition into the senior layers of school life, transition out and beyond.

It can be no surprise that tensions of all kinds emerge and erupt along these transitional paths. Fears, furies, desires, hurts, losses and outrages abound, some fully vented, others covered over in various defensive disguises. There is so much in the living of adolescence that is both deeply troubling and powerfully invigorating. It is difficult to define what the course of a 'normal' adolescence is. Anna Freud (1958) once wrote that 'the adolescent manifestations come close to symptom formation of the neurotic, psychotic or dissocial order and merge almost imperceptibly into . . . forms of all the mental illnesses' (p. 267).

It takes a rare combination of skill, thoughtfulness and imagination to work well psychotherapeutically with adolescents. None of us get it all right, almost by definition. But with perseverance, we can get close to being very helpful at least for the time being. It is difficult, too, to conduct counselling and psychotherapy in a school setting in the midst of the hurly-burly of its everyday business – it is not straightforward for a therapist to find his or her place in such large institutions as schools. But it is well worth the effort, if for no other reason than that many of the adolescents who are referred for help would probably not seek therapy outside of school.

What the authors of the various chapters in this book show in their fascinating accounts of their work is their therapeutic preparedness to work flexibly and adaptively in the school setting and to carefully find and hold time and attentiveness in the sessions they arrange with their adolescents. Within these sessions, they convey so clearly the essential ingredients of psychoanalytically influenced therapy – starting where the adolescent presents himself or herself, being open-minded without preconceptions, listening both to the adolescent's feelings and those brought up in themselves, providing opportunity for expression and understanding, and opening up the possibilities of different ways of looking at things.

There is more than enough in this book to be of interest to anybody interested in young people. It is primarily intended, however, as a clinical workbook for counsellors, psychotherapists and arts therapists. At the end of each chapter, there are a variety of study questions, vignettes for discussion, resources and references. All of this is about developing the good practice – counsellors and therapists learning to be lively practitioners in lively schools in the interest of adolescents learning to be lively grown-ups.

Peter Wilson

Reference

Freud, A. (1958). 'Adolescence'. In *The Psychoanalytic Study of the Child* (Vol. 13, pp. 255–278). New York: International Universities Press.

Acknowledgements

We are indebted to A Space for Creative Learning and Support, a project set up in 1997 by Alex Sainsbury in partnership with the Social Science Research Unit at the Institute of Education, University of London and Hackney Education, for providing the context for this book. A Space has expanded significantly since then, offering therapeutic services and specialist projects to primary and secondary schools across Hackney.

As we have done in Volume 1 (*Therapeutic Practice in Schools: Working with the Child Within*), we would also like to thank all the trainee therapists from postgraduate courses at Birkbeck College (University of London), Roehampton Institute (University of Surrey) and the University of Hertfordshire, who have taken up placements at A Space with enthusiasm, dedication and a wish to learn more. In addition, we would like to acknowledge the many teachers and school staff who have welcomed and supported therapists working with their pupils, and of course we are grateful to the children and young people who have had the courage, willingness and motivation to use school-based therapy services.

Numerous individuals have made publishing this book possible. In particular, we would like to acknowledge the significant contributions of Alex and Elinor Sainsbury of the Glass-House Trust (a Sainsbury Family Charitable Trust) and Nicola Baboneau, the chair of A Space.

Introduction

Lyn French and Reva Klein

One of the most iconic teenagers in literature is the angst-ridden Holden Caulfield, the narrator of J.D. Salinger's *Catcher in the Rye*. Although the book was written in 1951, the content of Holden's thoughts and the emotional rollercoaster he rides capture timeless adolescent experiences as well as providing a salutary reminder of how dizzyingly agonising, ecstatic and confusing these years can be. We've all been there in our different ways, and while not (hopefully) in the extreme forms that Salinger's protagonist takes, we bring to our work as therapists some understanding of what it means to be in the grip of the often destabilising adolescent years.

The Contemporary Adolescent is the second volume of *Therapeutic Practice in Schools: Working with the Child Within*, which was published in 2012 by Routledge. *The Contemporary Adolescent* introduces key features of adolescence before going on to explore some of the main challenges which therapists face working with this age group. In common with *Therapeutic Practice in Schools: Working with the Child Within*, the book serves more as a practical handbook than a theoretical text for school-based counsellors, psychotherapists, arts therapists and play therapists. It is written in accessible language and is eminently applicable to the practice of both qualified and trainee therapists.

It is widely acknowledged that engaging troubled or troublesome adolescents in therapy can make an enormous difference to their lives. However, encouraging them to make a commitment to an introductory block of sessions and then supporting them sensitively and effectively enough to enable a therapeutic alliance to be formed can be challenging for the school therapist. This reflects a number of factors. Adolescents are in a transitional phase, moving away from childhood, a period marked by reliance on adults, and into a time when they test out their autonomy sometimes thoughtfully, at other times recklessly. Willingly meeting with a therapist to explore deeply personal feelings, thoughts, wishes and fears is often counter-intuitive at this time of life, suggesting as it does a return to dependence on a parental figure. In addition, peer perceptions are becoming increasingly important to adolescents; how one is seen by others can generate enormous anxiety, and most will try to avoid situations, relationships and ways of presenting themselves which could carry the risk of social criticism or rejection. Seeing a school therapist is unlikely to be perceived as an attractive option by many adolescents. It is often further complicated by issues relating to gender, culture or class. The teenager who has no real experience of talking about the emotional content of everyday life or who has not known the value of reflection in general may find it at best puzzling or confusing and at worst embarrassing, alienating or invasive to see a school therapist.

Although the purpose of this book is to provide a practical approach to working as a counsellor or therapist in secondary schools, therapeutic practice cannot be reduced to formulaic responses. Through providing practical suggestions of what to say and do as well as study questions and vignettes, we aim to demonstrate the basic grammar and vocabulary necessary for each counsellor or therapist to build her or his own unique language for use in sessions with adolescents, a language which is flexible and fluid enough to be shaped within the collaborative working relationship with the client.

Therapeutic Practice in Schools: The Contemporary Adolescent begins with an inside look at the adolescent experience and some of the key developmental tasks young people face (Chapter 1). This is put into a theoretical context in Chapter 2, which highlights how early attachment patterns impact in adolescence, emphasising that brain plasticity means that there is still real hope for these patterns to be modified and for more secure attachments to be made. Chapter 3 transports us straight into the school setting through the presentation of a case study by a senior practitioner who is able to contribute to the whole-school agenda of supporting young people. Applying psychoanalytically informed ideas and practices, the chapter offers us a view of a working school and the very real differences a therapist can make.

One of the most significant changes in recent years is the widespread use of social media by young people. In the increasingly complex contemporary world we live in, the impact of the internet and social media is inestimable, transforming the way we access information, knowledge and each other. A potent tool for connecting us with the world, its potency has a less positive nature. Early exposure to sexualised material can be confusing for young people on the cusp of exploring their own sexuality and grappling with how to express it. The risk of bullying and the sometimes destructive impact of peer rivalry, always present in adolescence, are amplified in the world of instant messaging and online groups which include or exclude at the hit of a button. Chapter 4 explores these complexities and looks at how the therapist might think about these subjects in sessions with adolescents.

The many challenges implicit in engaging secondary school students in therapy in the first instance, and the ways the therapist can sustain the relationship in the face of ambivalence or defiant resistance, are the focus of Chapter 5. The advantages and limitations of working with adolescents in the educational setting, where school staff will have their own reasons for referring students for therapy while the young people themselves might come with a very different agenda, are explored. Also discussed is how the therapist might manage the tensions between meeting the school's aims while simultaneously addressing the pupil's concerns to avoid splitting. Adolescents can tend towards black-and-white thinking, and there is always a risk that, in the client's mind, the therapist will be perceived as being aligned with the school (the 'voice of authority') or, conversely, as being on the pupil's side, in rebellion against the status quo. Chapter 6 takes on the much-debated subject of 'measuring outcomes' in school-based therapy, thinking about whether or not to introduce such practices and, if so, what form they might take and what kind of information could usefully be passed on to school staff.

Moving on from investigating the particular nature of working in the school setting, the book turns its focus on some of the key reasons why staff recommend their students make use of the therapy service. The common reasons adolescents are referred and the issues they bring cover themes which will be familiar to any school therapist. Chapter 7 traces the roots of anger from a psychoanalytically informed perspective before discussing how it might present in the therapy room and how it can be worked with. Adolescents can stir up a great deal of anxiety in adults, especially when they are drawn to self-destructive behaviour, as Chapter 8 illustrates. There are no easy answers as to whether or not client confidentiality should be broken if the therapist senses that the adolescent is at risk of self-harming. This chapter lays out various scenarios and possible ways in which the therapist can think about the unconscious communications embedded in the behaviour as well as how one might work with it in the room.

Significant life events such as those which bring loss, including bereavement, family changes or parental separation, are universal and will always feature in this work, as Chapter 9 highlights. Unprocessed or undigested feelings linked with losses, perceived rejection and insecure attachments in general often lead to more florid acting out, which can result in exclusion. Chapter 10 looks at this problem before unpacking what it means for the adolescent as well as for the therapist working in the school. Relationships with adults can be fraught territory for all teenagers, some more so than others, as Chapter 11 reminds us. We all have a transference to authority figures, and for a significant number of young people, this will hinder rather than help them. Offering them a way of thinking about relationships and reducing their tendency to see adults only in terms of power dynamics is an important aspect of working with adolescents.

Another dimension of work with adolescents which gives us much to reflect on, and can be, at times, highly anxiety provoking, is that of their relationships with peers, including experimentation with sex and sexuality. As Chapter 12 illustrates, every young person will have their own conscious and unconscious assumptions, attitudes, anxieties and hopes about this side of life as well as degrees of confusion about what kind of person they would like to become. Issues of class, race, gender and social or political understanding are all bound to percolate to the surface when thinking about this domain of adolescent life. Chapter 13 builds on this, giving us a close-up picture of the nuances of difference, widening the angle to include how it might be expressed in the therapeutic relationship itself.

Any discussion of work in secondary schools must include an exploration of bullying, both the virtual and the real. Chapter 14 takes us down this path, describing in detail the unconscious motivations driving adolescents to inhabit the position of 'bully' or that of 'victim', including how this kind of behaviour can impact on school staff as well as on the therapist. Bullying often has at its core a desire to push 'the other' into the role of the outsider or the rejected. The theme of needing to belong gives a particular shape to Chapter 15, which takes as its subject the often thin line between gang and group. Looking at this from a psychoanalytic perspective helps us to better understand the draw gangs may have for vulnerable young people. The experience of difference and the myriad ways in which it manifests in adolescence are woven into most of the chapters. Those whose way of being in the world makes relating to others difficult terrain to navigate feature in Chapter 16, which sensitively explores working with teenagers on the autistic spectrum.

Change and transition are yet another dominant trait of adolescence, one that is powerfully experienced in particular during the first year of secondary school. Chapter 17 reminds us of how important it is to look out for vulnerable Year 7 pupils and to include in our school therapist's 'toolbox' non-stigmatising ways of providing low-key interventions for them, an example of which is offered in this chapter. Other techniques and approaches that school therapists may like to add to their 'kit' are covered in Chapters 18, 19 and 20, all of which offer practical suggestions and ways of thinking about adolescents from the perspective of applied dramatherapy (Chapter 18), art therapy (Chapter 19) and systemic family therapy (Chapter 20).

As will be immediately apparent, this book is written from the perspective of the secondary school therapist, who is often grappling with significant challenges in his or her day-to-day work. In contrast to those working in clinic-based settings, we function without the benefit of a team of like-minded practitioners to draw on or senior mental health specialists to help hold the client during anxiety-provoking phases. Adolescents frequently present school therapists with the kinds of challenges which can stir up deeply felt anxieties triggered by concern about young people's ability to look after themselves and an urgent pressure to take some form of action, which usually has to be resisted in favour of thinking.

The book looks headlong at and offers practical solutions for the tensions we face in our day-to-day work: those between working in a focused and accessible way with the adolescent client, aiming to gain their trust and respect, and holding in mind a duty of care while all the time thinking psychodynamically: a tall order to be sure. Vignettes, study questions and suggested resources are included along the way to ensure that discussion is grounded in practice and that ways of working developed by school-based therapists and supervisors can be shared.

In contemporary society, there appears to be a crisis of confidence in parenting adolescents, with the result that many young people may be losing their way. Offering therapeutic services in schools is a vital provision but one which is yet to be embedded in many of our educational establishments. Ensuring that trainees and qualified therapists new to the secondary school context have access to the experience and the thinking of more established therapists is a key aim of this book. Although this book focuses on complexities and challenges, we know from our own experience as well as from our work that adolescence is also a time of curiosity, stimulation, intensity, experimentation and potential, providing many opportunities to re-shape core identities, make positive changes and plan for the future.

Part I

The context

Chapter 1

Working with adolescents

Sue Kegerreis

A book about working therapeutically with adolescents in schools will, almost by definition, include an exploration of the particular dynamics generated by the educational and social aims of the organisation. It will also examine the particular tasks, challenges and characteristics of adolescence itself that practitioners need to engage with in order to be closely attuned to what their clients are grappling with. We can listen more perceptively if we are primed with an understanding of the preoccupations and dilemmas – conscious and unconscious – that they are likely to be bringing.

However, if we make assumptions about the preoccupations and worries of our clients, we run the risk of not being open to something very different being on their minds or in their way. There is nothing more likely to put a client off (whatever their age, although this may be particularly acute in adolescents) than a therapist whose preconceptions about them pre-empt the desire to find out what their problems are. So we need to achieve a balance: being wary of jumping to conclusions while also having a good working map of the territory they are in, so that we can help them find a viable route through their difficulties present and future.

We need to be realistic about what can – or even should – be achieved. As Phillips (2011) says, 'Resistance to being helped is to be expected rather than lamented, having developmental value as well as being a difficulty.' We need to bear in mind that 'once we start thinking of adolescent symptoms as self-cures – as the best way the adolescent has come up with so far not to solve a developmental problem, but to keep an essential conflict alive – we won't be quite so keen to try and rid them of their symptoms' (p. 192). On the other hand, this period, to state the obvious, is where their choices can make a monumental difference to the shape of their future, so when we can help we may have a life-changing effect.

The adolescent experience

We are bound to be selective in the memories we have of our own adolescence and are unlikely to remember what we actually experienced at the time. Not only that, but while there are some universals in the process of growing up, the emotional and practical landscapes have changed a great deal over the last decades and are changing further and faster all the time. In the back of our minds we need an understanding of what the constants are, together with an appreciation of the particular context of today's adolescent, while giving our full attention to the individual in front of us.

The constants have been very well described elsewhere (see, for example, Noonan 1983; Phillips 2011; Waddell 1998, 2006; Wise 2000; Youell 2006), eloquently evoking the universal struggles of becoming an adult individual: of beginning the process of separating from family and establishing one's own identity, negotiating friendships, becoming acquainted with and beginning to explore one's sexuality, testing out early partnerships, and thinking about the future through taking suitable steps in school or training. In adolescence we have to start to take responsibility for our own choices, taking risks but keeping this side of disaster. We work at getting to know ourselves both inside and in relation to others, developing a capacity to look after ourselves once parents are no longer doing so much for us, and finding ways of caring both for ourselves and for the wider world in some kind of balance. All this goes on while the young person is prey to sometimes violent and uncontrollable feelings – with the newly acquired power to act upon them with genuine and serious effect.

The powerful and rapid physiological changes that take place in adolescence are well documented (see, for example, Coleman and Hendry 1999). But more recently we have also acquired greater knowledge of the neurological processes at work, with increased insights into the plasticity and particular vulnerabilities of the adolescent brain. As a consequence, we have a new and deeper understanding as well as a more scientifically supportable language with which to describe the upheavals and volatility of the adolescent state of mind (Music 2011). Being able to see inside the brain allows us to map the structural changes which occur in neural networks associated with both cognition and social connectedness (Blakemore 2008). In early adolescence there is 'another intense moment of brain reorganisation' (Gerhardt 2004, p. 195) in which different areas of the brain mature at different rates; those areas that are linked to the capacity to plan ahead and to restrain impulsivity come later than others.

While these ways of looking at the adolescent mind illuminate and expand our ways of thinking about why young people manifest certain traits and behaviours, as therapists we have to be wary of this new window into the brain leading to scientific determinism. While neuroscience can support our understanding of certain aspects of human psychology, it does not cancel out a psychodynamic way of understanding the mind. If anything, rather than showing that all is predetermined, the neurological evidence strongly indicates how much the young mind is still growing and changing and is available to be influenced by experience.

One key experiential outcome of the physiological and psychological processes occurring in adolescence is the rapid development in the capacity to understand themselves and others. This brings with it a new sense of responsibility for how they conduct themselves, creating, in turn, a great deal of internal conflict as they become much more aware of their capacity to affect what happens and, crucially, how others feel. Paradoxically, even as young people take more fully on board the way they are emphatically not the centre of the universe, they also have to recognise their agency: that they affect everyone around them and have great power to create or destroy. They might be able to manage this reasonably well if they have hitherto had good, solid relationships and have established emotional resilience. But if their early experiences have made them vulnerable and less able to tolerate psychic pain, they might be knocked off course by it and/or find unhelpful ways to avoid and evade the pain.

Issues of belonging and of sexuality

Friendships at this time of life are intense arenas for both loyalty and ferocious rivalry, with the power of feelings about belonging or being an outsider that were first felt in the context of family relationships now transferred to the social sphere. While in infancy this was indeed a life-or-death issue, in adolescence the feelings of inclusion and exclusion from the group feel almost as crucial. The need to belong can be so powerful that it can drive us into behaviour (delinquency, cruelty to those more vulnerable, extreme risk-taking) which would otherwise be anathema to us and propel us into unhelpful decisions. Genuine and intense anguish can be felt in reaction to slights or the ebbs and flows of alliances. However, pain and anxiety can be avoided in a number of ways: by passing such feelings on to others in the form of bullying and exclusion, by opting for outsider-ship or by choosing relationships which offer some degree of safety even if they are unsatisfactory in other ways. As Waddell (1998) stresses, projective mechanisms are very much in use in this period. In adolescence we use other people to carry aspects of ourselves, to test out different parts of our identity, to have a relationship with denied elements and to work out how to consolidate a coherent core. We use our friends to establish who we are, and to see them and the reflection of ourselves in their eyes in order to choose and/or reject elements of our personalities.

In this period of development we are also learning for the first time the unique power of sexual attraction and desire, as well as the intense self-consciousness, risk of humiliation, longing and fear of rejection that go with entering the sexual arena. These concerns may not overtly be what brings clients to our door – especially in school settings – but they may underlie some seemingly unconnected symptom, and our capacity to realise how powerful these elements are can be pivotal in helping us understand the deeper levels of what our clients are struggling with.

Separation and moving on

There is always going to be difficulty in coping with the inherent ambivalence of separation from family, characterised as it is by the longing to remain in the comparatively safe position of the young child set against the drive to establish a separate identity. It can lead to exaggerated aggression and disillusionment in reaction against the tug of family. It is perhaps necessary, if painful for all concerned, to respond to the inevitable imperfections of one's parents by becoming judgmental, partly in order to create the impetus to forge something different for oneself (Dartington 1994). It is also a key task of adolescence to forgive our parents sufficiently and let go of our grievances (whether justified or not), thereby avoiding wrecking our own lives in order to punish them (Dyke 1985; Kegerreis 2010). To move on into a healthy future is a hugely generous act (Williams et al. 2003), especially, but not only, if we have been badly let down. Leaving childhood behind also means relinquishing the possibility that this part of our lives will ever be redeemed and accepting that we will never get the parenting that we may have missed out on. This is something that has to be mourned and let go of; it is not easy and can be used to justify internally a great deal of self-destructive behaviour which punishes ourselves as much as our parents.

The heavy use of projective mechanisms means that the internal conflicts that are part of growing up are played out in arguments between the rebellious adolescent and the worried/outraged parent or teacher rather than being encountered internally. Furious rows over control and risk are commonplace, with anxiety being hived off into the parent and a fantasised invulnerability leaving the adolescent feeling in no need of being taken care of. However, for those who find the conflict with parents too painful to face, the opposite mechanism can prevail, with the young person turning on themselves. As Rustin says (2009, p. 216), 'The depressed individual is burdened by hopelessness because of the tendency to turn aggression against the self in order to protect the object.' Adolescents' necessary, healthy anger and disillusionment with their parents are then experienced as despair, fierce self-deprecation and even self-destructiveness. It is so hard to try to fight the negative and destructive in oneself – and to have faith that the good and loving will win out. Often the result is to exaggerate one's badness and to write oneself off as wholly horrible, rather than to grapple with the need to manage oneself (Kegerreis 1991). Self-destructive self-criticism is often easier, however agonising, than attempts to challenge and modify the things we do that are unhelpful. It can feel so daunting to look squarely and specifically at what is wrong that the impulse is to see *everything* as useless and hopeless.

Particular challenges for adolescents today

These universal struggles are now being played out in an arena that is different from the one parents, and we ourselves, were familiar with. Today's young people are growing up amid the significant generalised anxiety about the world having been ruined for them and the absence of clearly available ways of reversing this. Climate change and environmental degradation are the backdrop for them, and it is a battle for any of us to stay hopeful that we can make changes sufficient to alter the future. In psychoanalytic terms, the overload of depressive anxiety – the sense that damage has been done and repair is needed – bears down particularly heavily on adolescents; they are deprived of the heady promise that is part of the positive delusional qualities of youth. A certain omnipotence – believing, however fleetingly, that one can achieve anything – is perhaps vital on the way to working out what is more realistically achievable later on. But today's adolescents are more likely to be brought to the realisation of the extreme limits of what can be achieved and how much less reason they have to be hopeful.

This chapter is being written amid the economic fallout from the 2008 crash and ensuing recession. Even before this, employment prospects in the UK had become less secure; patterns that had been taken for granted in the late 20th century were no longer on offer (Stokes 1994). Short-term contracts and career flexibility are much more the norm, with the expectation of stability and a higher income in the future rendered far less realisable. Consequently, the economic pessimism that has permeated public and private discourse is having a powerful effect on adolescents today. They live with the realisation that the previous assurances of a hopeful future if they worked hard and achieved well are no longer valid.

All of us working with today's adolescents would do well to hold in mind the extent to which the inevitable swings between idealistic omnipotence and self-doubting despair are affected by the real world into which the young person is trying to move. If our clients are struggling with internal difficulties when it comes to applying themselves in order to invest in their own future, how much harder is this if the real world looks as if it is reluctant to welcome them and offer them something positive? Despondency and the lure of giving up are always a danger in adolescence. The question of what they are going to make of their lives is completely open. Refusing to achieve what they can is one way to protest against the hand they have been dealt, and the worse this deal is, the more it will feed into any tendency towards self-destructiveness.

With so much uncertainty, we are asking a lot of our young people to keep hopeful, to put in the work needed to get good grades and to develop a stake in a society that offers them less. Not only that, but what is offered is more contingent and precarious than anything previous generations have faced.

Furthermore, the infrastructure within which adolescents conduct their lives has changed very rapidly. There are now ultra-loud, wide-reaching and ineradicable broadcasting media in which anything they do, think and say may be exposed to an audience. It is hard enough to manage one's reputation at the best of times, but with social media being ubiquitous and woven into the way young people relate it has become a major preoccupation (Balick 2013). Living one's life online as well as in ordinary reality has immensely liberating features but is also deeply problematic and full of dangers. One of the features of adolescence is a struggle to relate to the consequences of one's actions and to live with one's mistakes. We all have memories of moments in our lives which can still fill us with shame and embarrassment, but the pain is constrained by the fact that the only remaining witnesses are ourselves and maybe one or two others. The internet amplifies consequences and immortalises our mistakes in a way that brings intense humiliation, sometimes just when we are most vulnerable to exposure.

There is of course so much more about online life that impinges on adolescents; for example the still unknown effects of exposure to pornography on early sexuality, the relationship with anxiety that develops when we are never properly alone and the capacity to measure and monitor concretely those key concerns of adolescence: popularity and attractiveness. However, these are way beyond the scope of this chapter. We need, in our work, to be able both to be aware of these issues and to make sure we hear from the young person in front of us how they are actually experienced. Such rapid social change always brings with it the likelihood of our being so embedded in our own preconceptions about the new ways of doing things that we lose some of our capacity to hear how it feels to our clients. (See Chapter 4 for further discussion on the impact of social media on young people.)

Adolescents and time

A crucial feature of adolescence is that young people have to build a viable relationship with time. In childhood, time is mostly managed for us, with our awareness of it very patchy and lacking in reflexivity. Young children are, of course, aware of years passing and of there being a future and a past. However, when you see a little boy walking in the street looking over his shoulder, at his feet or up into the sky, one cannot but be aware that he is *not* thinking of what is to come. He is immersed in the *now* and depends on others to do the looking around and ahead. In later childhood we gradually become more aware of and increasingly able to reflect on time and look both forward and back with more coherence and clarity. However, it is usually in adolescence that the dimension of time truly comes into one's awareness. The march of school-term times and particularly the impact of public examinations brings time into the frame with increasing insistence and urgency.

There is much said about the way in which adolescents act as if they are immortal: that 'it won't happen to me'. What is less clearly stated is that this is perhaps an understandable flight from the first awareness of what adults also struggle with: the idea that time is unstoppable and mortality inevitable. Jaques (1965) concentrates on the idea that it is in mid-life that we begin to take seriously our own mortality, but it is in adolescence that the first steps are taken in this direction, when we have to start getting our heads around the whole notion of time and what it means to us.

This awareness gives us another way of making sense of some typical adolescent symptomatology. For example the pursuit of mindlessness, whether through obsessive gaming, drink, drugs or other high-octane risk-taking, is often usefully understood as demonstrating how, when anxieties and internal conflicts are too painful, blotting them out is pleasurable – at least in the short term. However, a related but different way to understand these activities is that they put a temporary hold on time. Mindlessness is a way of protesting against the onward march of life, a way of putting two fingers up to the relentless pressure of the constant move into the future.

Another way to protest is refusing to complete required schoolwork. This of course has many features, often explored as deriving from fear of failure, fear of success and the young person's relationship with authority, including a working through of transference dynamics via school (Barwick 2000). The element I want to emphasise here is that complying with the school's timetable and agreeing to get work done also implies acquiescence in the same onward march: agreeing that it's okay for the world to go on turning, even when you may desperately want it to stop (Kegerreis 2013b). No one has control over the passing of time, and our struggle with this fact is a life-long one, but one which we truly grapple with initially in adolescence.

It is not surprising that so many adolescent symptoms involve some kind of slamming on of the brakes in a desire to make things stand still when each forward step can feel as if they are complying with the demand that things must keep moving. Anorexic symptoms are at one extreme of this, when the body shrinks through lack of food. Especially for girls, the minimising of breasts and curves demonstrates that the clock *can* be turned back after all. Surely if one protests strongly enough that you don't want to grow up it can be made to stop. The transition between who one is now and who one will eventually be is felt to be so full of uncertainties and painful relinquishments that perhaps it feels best to refuse to grow, to move on. It is an omnipotent fantasy, but one with very real consequences.

One effect of thinking this way is that it can help us, whether as parents, therapists or teachers, to understand the excruciating and exasperatingly self-destructive nature of adolescent acting-out. What we as adults often do is stress the consequences of their actions, trying to get them to act differently in the service of their future. This is very often self-defeating because it is precisely the demand that they invest in the future that is causing the problem in the first place. Truly encountering time creates so much anxiety that the very idea of the future is contaminated, and many adolescents try to abolish awareness of time's flow in one way or another.

At the other end of the spectrum, some adolescents will respond by wanting to grow up more quickly rather than put it off, rushing to become instant adults as if there is no process to go through. At a conscious level they want to escape what they see as the restrictions of childhood and launch themselves into an idealised version of what the 'freedom' of adulthood will hold. As Marvell said in his poem 'To His Coy Mistress': 'though we cannot make our sun stand still yet we will make him run!' (in Gardner 1957, p. 250). Desperate accelerations such as rushing into partnerships, leaving home precipitately or becoming pregnant are often manic attempts to brush away the terrors involved in accepting the reality of time and with it the need to take over the care of ourselves. We might want to cut through and avoid the mourning of childhood that adolescence necessarily involves (Noonan 1983) and demolish the travel through time that growing up demands.

Adolescents and the superego – our dialogue with ourselves

Related to these dynamics, it is in adolescence that we develop more consciously articulated internal conversations. We are brought into fuller awareness of our internal conflicts, particularly our relationship with, and the nature of, our super-ego. In younger children superego difficulties can be manifested in a wide range of symptoms, from conduct disorders to obsessionality. But adolescents become more conscious of having a complex relationship with themselves, whether this takes the form of hating and berating, or of elevating themselves narcissistically in elaborate wish-fulfilling scenarios. Taking up the responsibility of running their own lives brings with it many things, including an increasing awareness that if they say no, or choose something others disagree with, no-one can actually exert absolute power over them anymore: a huge difference to the position of a smaller child. With this awareness comes a need to encounter and work with the figures they have built up in their inner worlds. Often this is both partly avoided and partly worked through by provoking extreme superego responses from the adults around them. Doing this allows the superego to be repressive, so that the young person can fight and kick and scream against it rather than get into serious negotiations with themselves about the choices they need to make.

Alternatively, young people can become obsessively dominated by a horrific caricature of a conscience, buried in excruciating self-hatred, viciously critical self-consciousness and a particular kind of despair about themselves. It is during this period, as they take on board the need to assume their part in the wider world, that the destructive superego can become a ghastly, sometimes deadly, internal antagonist (Freud 1923; Lawrence 2011). It is no help to know that this may in part be a reaction to the gathering realisation that they are the centre of their own universe but not of anyone else's. There is an element of grandiosity in the depths of the despair of the self-attacking adolescent, but this does not make it any less dangerous. Quite the opposite: while the grandiosity may share some of its roots with the grand fantasy of being the next shining light who will change the world and can actually lead to young people doing good, creative, adventurous things, the destructive version can drive them to starve or cut themselves, to crush their hopes of academic achievement, to lose all sense of enjoyment of life and in some cases to kill themselves.

Recognising the vicissitudes of this developing internal dialogue will inform the way we help young people identify and develop the capacity to manage it, which is a major task of therapy. What we hope to do is help them move from being either crushed by a cruel superego, projecting it onto others to be fought there, or defying it with omnipotent behaviour. Ultimately, the aim is to move them towards establishing something kinder and more supportive within as a resource, both for comfort and for guidance (Kegerreis 2013a).

The past and the present

Of course, all the processes mentioned above will be heavily influenced, if not driven, by the early relationships that, in the adolescent, are becoming fully inter-nalised. When one is working with a young person, especially in a school rather than a clinic setting, the scope for delving very deeply into the past may be limited.

Even more important, the job of the adolescent is to find a way of moving beyond what has happened in the past. Understanding an adolescent's current dilemmas requires deep and subtle thinking about what has led to the establishment of relatively benign or, alternatively, destructive internal figures. An appreciation of how and why they are acting in ways that are not helpful to them involves insights into the internal drama they are playing out with internalised parents, siblings and others. Developing a coherent narrative for this may be crucial in helping them move on.

However, the urgent task is to try to help adolescents act on their own behalf, to find ways to get free of the dominating need to please or attack their actual and internalised parents, and to develop an internal dialogue which is more benign, so that they can be on their own side. This sometimes means that the focus has to be on the current internal dynamics far more than on where these came from, however much the understanding of their roots informs the therapist's thinking.

Conclusion

Working with adolescents is both uniquely rewarding and uniquely disturbing. As is described later in this book, offering this help in the school setting has its own particular challenges but is also hugely valuable. Not only does it provide young people with easily accessible support, but it also conveys a symbolic message to the whole school community that the terrors and excitements of adolescence can be contained, thought about and worked with. The therapist is ideally placed to raise awareness of key features of adolescence and to help school staff to understand the powerful feelings they often carry on behalf of young people. Adolescence is bound to be rocky for most; as therapists we have the capacity to listen closely to what they bring, to take on board and process both their own 'felt experience' and that of being alone in the room with them. We have the space to think without being compelled to act. The young people bring their upheavals and internal chaos for us to share, and at times this can feel overwhelming to the therapist. However, the rewards of helping a young person to (re)discover that their life is worth living and their future is worth investing in cannot be equalled.

Study Questions

- Looking back, what strikes you most about your own adolescence?
- What was your family's understanding of adolescence? What influenced their views? To what extent did you conform or rebel?
- In what ways did then-current perspectives on adolescence help or hinder you when you were growing up?
- What experiences have you had of other people's adolescence (e.g. family members, relatives, friends, your own children)?
- What are your hopes and anxieties about today's adolescents?
- What influenced your decision to work with this age group?

References

Balick, A. (2013) *The Psychodynamics of Social Networking: Connected-Up Instantaneous Culture and the Self*. London: Karnac.

Barwick, N. (2000) *Clinical Counselling in Schools*. London: Routledge.

Blakemore, S. (2008) The social brain in adolescence. *Nature* 9, 267–277.

Coleman, J., and Hendry, I. (1999) *The Nature of Adolescence*. London: Routledge.

Dartington, A. (1994) The significance of the outsider in families and other social groups. In Box, S., Copley, B. and Magagna, J. (Eds.) *Crisis at Adolescence*, pp. 91–110. New York and London: Aronson.

Dyke, S. (1985) Getting better makes it worse – obstacles to improvement in children with emotional and behavioural difficulties. In *Maladjustment and Therapeutic Education* (Winter), repr. in Trowell, J., and Bower, M. (Eds.) *The Emotional Needs of Young Children and Their Families*, pp. 101–109. London: Routledge.

Freud, S. (1923) The ego and the id. In Strachey, J. (Ed.) *Standard Edition* 19, pp. 3–68. London: Hogarth.

Gerhardt, S. (2004) *Why Love Matters*. London: Routledge.

Jaques, E. (1965) Death and the mid-life crisis. *Journal of Psychoanalysis* 46, 502–514.

Kegerreis, S. (1991) Using the positive: is the truth always the awful truth? *Journal of Child Psychotherapy* 17 (1), 41–59.

Kegerreis, S. (2010) *Psychodynamic Counselling with Children and Adolescents – An Introduction*. Basingstoke: Palgrave Macmillan.

Kegerreis, S. (2013a) Freud and Klein in *The Lion King*. *Journal of Child Psychotherapy* 39 (3), 334–345.

Kegerreis, S. (2013b) When I can come on time I will be ready to finish: meanings of lateness in psychoanalytic psychotherapy. *British Journal of Psychotherapy* 29 (4), 449–465.

Lawrence, M. (2011) *The Anorexic Mind*. London: Karnac.

Marvell, A. (1957) To his coy mistress. In Gardner, H. (Ed.) *The Metaphysical Poets*, pp. 250–252. Harmondsworth: Penguin.

Music, G. (2011) *Nurturing Natures*. Hove: Psychology Press.

Noonan, E. (1983) *Counselling Young People*. London: Methuen.

Phillips, A. (2011) The pleasures of working with adolescents. *Psychodynamic Practice* 17 (2), 187–197.

Rustin, M. (2009) The psychology of depression in young adolescents: a psychoanalytic view of origins, inner workings and implications. *Psychoanalytic Psychotherapy* 23 (3), 213–224.

Stokes, J. (1994) Institutional chaos and personal stress. In Obholzer, A. and Roberts, V.Z. (Eds) *The Unconscious at Work*, pp. 121–128. London: Routledge.

Waddell, M. (1998) *Understanding 12–14 Year Olds*. London: Jessica Kingsley.

Waddell, M. (2006) *Inside Lives*. London: Duckworth.

Williams, G., Williams, P., Ravenscroft, K. and Desmarais, J. H. (Eds) (2003) *The Generosity of Acceptance: Exploring Feeding Difficulties in Children*. London: Karnac.

Wise, I. (2000) *Adolescence*. London: Institute of Analysis.

Youell, B. (2006) *The Learning Relationship*. London: Karnac.

Chapter 2

The impact of early attachment patterns on adolescent development

Jenny Dover

Keith had suffered early abuse and neglect and had been taken into care. At secondary school he was constantly on the move, roaming the halls, responding to provocation with considerable violence and highly controlling of teachers and peers. Eventually he was excluded and sent to a Pupil Referral Unit (PRU).

In this more containing setting with attentive adults and a proactive keyworker, he began to settle and his behaviour improved. But during weekends and holidays, he would break into the PRU and spend time in the empty building. He was unable to say why he did this – but it seems likely that he had begun to build a significant relationship with the adults in the unit. He had not yet been able to internalise these safe, reliable figures and, like a small child, sought their concrete physical presence. Keith appeared to be on the brink of a journey that might lead to more secure attachments.

Bowlby (1988) maintained that we are all happiest, "from the cradle to the grave", when life is organised as a series of excursions, long or short, from the secure base provided by our attachment figures. He said that the child's fearful response to experiences and situations is really a fear of the absence of someone the child needs. It seems likely that Keith's out-of-control behaviour in secondary school was underpinned by severe anxiety.

The major upheavals, stresses and emotional chaos characterising the teenage stage of development are described in detail in other chapters of this book. When a student is also struggling with longstanding difficulties around relationships, the impact on his or her development is profound. Providing a good therapeutic experience can be a challenge.

However, in working with this age group we have a great deal on our side. The teenage years are characterised by a desire to find new attachment figures outside the family, and young people can respond to a non-intrusive, interested adult who is sensitive to their need to be emotionally 'held'. In addition, the adolescent brain undergoes significant development and pruning based on current experience. This builds on that period of rapid growth in the first three years of life and is the second most prolific episode of brain growth and reorganisation. It can therefore be a real window of opportunity for change.

In this chapter I would like to explore attachment theory as a useful way of making sense of a young person's response to us in the therapy room and to consider how attachment style informs our work.

The history of attachment theory

John Bowlby is considered the 'father of attachment theory'. In the 1950s he developed the theoretical basis for the development and meaning of relationships using biological and ethological research. He was influenced by psychoanalytic ideas and incorporated interpersonal and intra-psychic approaches. He challenged the prevailing view that attachment was a drive secondary to feeding or sex and claimed that it existed in its own right. He maintained that human babies actively seek a relationship to provide protection, initially with a particular adult – often the mother.

Fear, illness, anxiety and threatened separation all intensify attachment-seeking behaviour. Separation can lead to protest from an infant and, if prolonged, to despair and finally detachment. The Robertson films in 1952 movingly illustrated the devastating effect on a child in hospital when her parent became unavailable (Robertson 1952). It is interesting to note that two risk factors for exclusion from school are early separation from parents and parental illness.

Bowlby considered that the quality of a child's early attachment experience with his carer and the negotiation of separation and, inevitably, loss are at the heart of social and emotional development. The baby develops a mind of its own by being in close touch with a reliable adult. He said that a child who experiences sensitive and responsive parenting is securely attached and tends to "approach the world with confidence and, when faced with potentially alarming situations, is likely to tackle them effectively or to seek help in doing so" (Bowlby 1973, 280).

Adverse early experiences of care, however, lead to insecure attachment, with profound consequences. Hopkins (1990) said, "In homes where the baby finds no mutuality, where the parent's face does not reflect the baby's experience and where the child's spontaneous gesture is not recognised or appreciated, neither trust in others nor confidence in the self develop."

Research suggests that the quality of the attachment experience directly affects the developing brain. Early interpersonal experiences inform the selective development of neural pathways within the brain and nervous system (Balbernie 2001). Healthy attachment relationships foster learning, and repeated good experiences with an attuned and reflective carer lead to the formation of a well-organised and well-regulated 'baby mind' (Schore 1994). The outcome is an individual with a strong sense of self and agency.

Conversely, as with Keith, adverse early experiences with adults who have not been able to regulate his emotional states can result in brain structure that is oversensitised to threat at the expense of the development of the part of the brain which is concerned with emotional regulation and reflection. So when Keith later found himself in contexts that unconsciously reminded him of an earlier traumatic situation, his responses tended to be reactive rather than thoughtful. Such early experiences powerfully affect the ease with which the adolescent relates to others and negotiates separation from his or her family.

Working with the insecure young person

We learn who we are through the eyes of our parent. Our clients, like Keith, may have had a parent who had a distorted view of them – or was simply incurious about their minds. The therapist's capacity to look beneath the surface – beyond defensive responses – and to reflect back the client's 'real' self is at the heart of our work. We aim to give our clients a different and coherent story about themselves in relation to a significant other.

The therapist strives to foster a significant working partnership with the clients, providing a 'secure base' from which they can explore aspects of their own personalities and the outside world of ideas and relationships. Getting alongside them to do this is a major challenge. Erikson (1963) pointed out how adolescents consider perfectly well-meaning adults as their adversaries.

Lyn Murray's (1980) still-face/video experiment with 6- to 8-week-old infants vividly demonstrates how a sensitively responsive 'other' is vital for an infant to develop a sense of agency. Infants, when faced with a live responding mother on a video link, actively engaged with her. But when shown a pre-recorded videotape of the mother's face from the previous happy interaction with her in which the responses were out of sync, the infants did not initiate behaviours to engage her.

In a similar way the adolescent needs a reciprocal and contingent response. According to Hughes (2009, 137), "unless the (adolescent) experiences himself as able to have a positive impact on the adult, he is not likely to be receptive to having the adult have a positive impact on him." Hughes felt that this means responding to the adolescent's affective tone. He said that replying in a level, reasonable tone to an incensed adolescent does not give the latter the sense that the adult 'gets' him or her.

'Getting him or her' means being open to the powerful impact of projections from a young person who may be confused, anxious and in emotional turmoil. In our attempt to attune to him there is a danger of mirroring anger or hostility: it can be hard to stay in role as a thoughtful adult. (Support from colleagues in school can help in managing this. De-briefing can be important for an inexperienced practitioner, who needs to move on to her next client in an emotionally intact state.)

We cannot assume we are on the same wavelength as our adolescent clients. In fact, we know that the teen brain differs from ours and may not match what we are trying to communicate. Interestingly, in facial recognition tests only 50% of teenagers read fear correctly. Body language has a greater impact than we think. In social interaction, it carries about 50% of the message, vocal characteristics 40% and verbal content a mere 10%.

Of course, giving adolescents words for experiences is hugely helpful. Labelling feelings activates the pre-frontal region of the brain associated with thinking in words about emotional experiences and reduces the response in the amygdala. "In the same way when you are driving and see a yellow light, you hit the brake. Putting feelings into words seems to put the brakes on our emotional responses" (Liebermann et al. 2006).

The adolescent brain is a work in progress, and some areas do not fully develop until the early 20s, so reasoning with or lecturing a teenager may reap no benefits. Goal-setting, prioritising and organisation are difficult at this stage. "His pre-frontal cortex, where judgements are formed, is practically asleep at the wheel. At the same time, his limbic system, where raw emotions such as anger are generated, is entering a stage of development in which it goes into hyper-drive" (Brownlee 1999).

Worries about a client's risk-taking and awareness of the potential for 'hard-wiring' can push us into being too proactive in terms of our own agenda. Demonstrating an interest in the client's enthusiasms and preoccupations is vital. Focusing entirely on presenting problems is counter-productive. Fonagy (2001, 167) reminds us of the importance of parental figures who are able to permit and support autonomous development of a separate self without contamination by their own unresolved issues.

Winnicott (1971) cautioned therapists about being too active and suggested the need to tolerate the moment of hesitation, allowing the patient to use him as someone who is there to be found, not shoved down the patient's throat (Abram 1996). He felt playfulness and humour were helpful – distancing and non-threatening. Later analysts using Winnicott's concept of 'squiggles' built upon the idea of incomplete 'shapes' in work with clients, a half-way step to interpretation for the clients to do something with, rather than having the adult monopolise insights in a session.

In the therapy room our client may require or elicit a different 'other' at various times. A major challenge of the work is getting the distance between us right and giving the client control over this so we experience each other in manageable doses. We cannot always get it right. It is the coming back together after being out of synchrony that is critical. The idea that things can be managed and made positive again – repairing the rupture – leads to resilience.

Of course, being very alert to what the transference and counter-transference tell us about early attachment patterns is germane to our work: we can observe a young person's preferred way of relating to us and use our understanding of infantile and adolescent development to create the 'facilitating environment' (Winnicott 1990) that may not have been available in his or her early years. This requires a subtle blend of meeting the young person where he or she is psychologically but also giving him or her a different experience with a significant adult. An adult provides a novel response but one that is within a young person's comfort zone.

Attachment patterns

Ainsworth and Wittig (1969) devised an experimental procedure for studying the interplay between attachment behaviour in infants and their exploratory behaviour in conditions of low and high stress. This was the Strange Situation Test and was based on the way a toddler responded to the reunion with a parent after a separation. This enabled the researchers to categorize the children's habitual attachment pattern. Later, Main and Solomon (1986) added a fourth category.

The majority of behaviour patterns identified reflected a secure attachment and were related to sensitive parental responses. However, babies who didn't believe that a reliable parent would return were identified as insecurely attached and demonstrated their uncertainty in diverse ways, organising their behaviour to provoke more care.

The patterns identified were the following:

Secure attachment

The carer is attuned and responsive to the child's needs. The child is able to use the parent as a safe base from which to explore.

Insecure

Avoidant Attachment: The carer is consistently rejecting. The child minimises attachment behaviour in an attempt to keep the carer close. These children appear passive and withdrawn with little emotional response.

Resistant/Ambivalent Attachment: The carer is inconsistently available. The child maximises attachment behaviour to elicit care. His behaviour is clingy and yet hostile, extremely distressed on separation and resistant to being comforted.

Disorganised Attachment: The carer may have severe mental health difficulties, may abuse drugs, or has suffered trauma or unresolved grief – and may be experienced as frightening or frightened. The child uses a mixture of approaches in an attempt to manage an intolerable situation where the carer is both the source of fear and the potential for safety. Later, some of these children solve the dilemma through self-reliance and highly organised, controlling ways of interacting with the carer.

The attachment patterns were consistent over time, and a further research procedure, known as the Adult Attachment Interview, showed how a mother's attachment style tended to be transmitted to the child. Parents who were rated secure on the Adult Attachment Interview (George et al. 1996) were most likely to foster a secure attachment in their children. Interestingly, an insecure parent with a high reflective function and the capacity to give a coherent account of her or his experiences was also able to promote a secure attachment in her or his infant.

The internal working model

Bowlby posited that the infant internalises the characteristics of the early attachment relationship in procedural memory and later brings expectations based on this to other significant relationships – such as with teachers and therapists. He called this the child's internal working model. The nature of this model influences the adolescent's capacity to separate from parents and to seek new attachments to partners or groups. Internal working models are thought to be continually updated as a result of interactions throughout childhood and into adulthood and can be modified positively or negatively. Keith, in the PRU, benefited from having his negative representations of adults consistently and proactively challenged.

Every dyad is unique, and children can hold different attachment patterns with other significant adults, such as a father; their relationship to a particular therapist or teacher may be distinct from that with another. It is possible, too, that a child or young person may hold multiple models with the same person. Therapists must consider what they themselves bring to the interaction, what they represent to a young person at the time and what kind of attachment response is being elicited. It seems, however, that habitual early defences developed with the primary carer can be a 'default' behaviour and come to resemble a character trait.

> Experiencing secure attachment in groups that are moderated by adults, and dyadic attachments with sensitive adults and/or adolescent intimates, may be sufficient to begin to steer the inner working model of attachment of an adolescent with attachment difficulties onto a new, more secure track – perhaps for the first time.
>
> (Brisch 2009, 27)

Case examples

A securely attached adolescent

Samira, 13 years old, and her family fled from her country of origin when civil war broke out. Her mother had become depressed, and her father searched desperately for work after arriving in this country. Samira was referred when her grades dropped and she became withdrawn and irritable.

In the therapy room she was able to express and explore her feelings of loss – of her homeland and relatives – and also her sense of being bereft of the support of her parents. Her therapist helped her to create a narrative of her experience and, importantly, to acknowledge angry feelings towards her unavailable mother. Samira made excellent use of the therapeutic space, and her mood and performance improved relatively quickly. It was clear that her resilience, founded on a secure attachment in her early years, enabled her to be supported through the lapse she was experiencing.

Like many securely attached teenagers Samira was popular in her class and increasingly turned to a small group of good friends for support and containment, which enabled her to loosen her strong ties to her family, though she was comfortable moving between her parents and her peer group. Her friends provided a supportive bridge during the turbulent time before she was ready for a sexual pairing later on.

At the stage when a search for a new identity is powerful the group plays a vital role. Different aspects of the self can be located and explored in individuals in the group until such time as the feelings can be owned. So groups can be safe places in which to experiment with versions of oneself.

Avoidant anxious attachment

> Avoidant or dismissing attachment can be conceptualised as involving restrictions in the flow of energy and information through the mind. Acquired from emotionally distant communication patterns, this pattern of attachment organises the mind to reduce access to emotional experience and information in memory.
>
> (Siegel 1999, 99)

Ben was born with dyspraxia. His mother was faced with a baby she experienced as flat and unresponsive. It is likely that her efforts to elicit a livelier response made it hard for her to modulate their interactions. After a while she concluded that he disliked her, and she mirrored his supposed rejection.

Ben was referred for therapy because he was 'a loner' in school. His teacher found him distant and aloof, leaving her feeling impotent. He appeared to prefer independent study and never asked for help. While he incited peers to misbehave, he rarely challenged her directly. His reluctance to attend individual sessions with his therapist was clear, but he agreed to 'have a go' for a trial period.

Following is an extract from his case notes:

Ben held his head averted from me, his coat zipped to the chin and was largely inexpressive. He made no response to my suggestion he might be worried about being here – or that it might be hard to feel this was a safe place to try things out. Like an infant with a rejecting parent, Ben seemed to believe I couldn't bear him to make any demands on me. Whilst he engaged in some expression work, his responses were minimalist and bleak. His drawings lacked imagination and human figures. He was competent in learning tasks, preferring concrete closed-ended ones although sometimes he 'rubbished' the task. I resisted a strong desire to inject more life and fun into the proceedings and found myself feeling irritable with his passivity.

As sessions progressed it became clear that Ben needed to regulate our interaction by keeping me at the right distance and pacing the activities. His expectation seemed to be that I might foist my agenda on him. He was able to communicate this in the metaphor when he insisted that there would be nothing in the speech bubble of the boy in our shared picture.

Ben's capacity to tolerate the one-to-one sessions seemed linked to the use of activities and tasks that I introduced. These created a buffer between us that helped to maintain the comfortable distance he needed. Whilst open exploration of real issues in his life was not welcomed, Ben was able to explore and express experiences and feelings through metaphor. In particular, a book by Michael Morpurgo,

Kensuke's Kingdom, about a boy becoming marooned on an island, seemed to reflect the difficulties of his struggle to be self-sufficient. Avoidant young people are often very inarticulate, and it seemed important to help Ben to learn words for thoughts and feelings. I noticed aloud his need for independence and praised him when he did allow me to help.

Unsurprisingly, Ben's need to feel self-reliant meant he failed to use a peer or group for emotional support or for a gradual separation from the family. Avoidant young people often jump before they are pushed, leaving the family prematurely to embrace a pseudo-independence. The struggle to relate to group members expecting intimacy – such as securely attached peers – has led to conflict when Ben felt his space was being violated and his response to this was aggressive. Research indicates a link between avoidant attachment and later conduct or depressive disorders.

Ben's responses were clearly linked to the experience of early rejection. Sometimes, however, apparently avoidant behaviour can be related to preoccupations in a child's inner world. One very distant girl did a series of drawings on the theme of stillbirth. Once this issue was explored she came out of her shell.

Resistant ambivalent attachment

> The ambivalently attached child has learned that his own mental state may be intruded upon and disrupted by the parent in unpredictable ways. Nevertheless, the developing child needs to have the attachment figure psychologically accessible in order to feel secure. Ironically, the ambivalent child is left with an internal sense of uncertainty, which gives him an even more urgent and continuing need for comfort from external interactions.
>
> (Siegel 1999, 103)

Aysha, 14 years old, sits at the table with me in the therapy room. She has decided to make something out of balsa wood and says it will be a double bed. After some discussion we agree we need to join two pieces of wood together to make a strong base. I wonder aloud how we might do this. Aysha fixes me with her large dark eyes and says, "Dunno . . .!" I suggest she look in the toolbox for ideas. She does so and says, "There's glue in there. That won't work. Not strong enough. Not sticky enough . . ." I say I wonder if she can think of anything else in the toolbox that may hold two pieces of wood together. She sits passively chewing her gum and then says sneeringly, "What are you going on about? What do you mean?" I feel disconcerted and silly. I say she seems to want me to do all the thinking here. I ask her what she thinks might happen if she lets me know she can manage this task on her own. Will I stop thinking about her or noticing her? Will I leave her to manage everything on her own while my mind goes to other things? Aysha shakes her head, saying, "You are stupid!" But she picks out the hammer and nails, and we get started. Aysha's teacher tells me, "She is constantly in my face – very verbally abusive. She demands my sole attention all the time – and doesn't let me help her to do anything on her own."

It would be interesting to think about the meaning the double bed may have for this girl, but I want to focus on our interaction. Aysha expresses hostility towards me, but at the same time her behaviour is designed to keep me totally focused on her; she mainly uses the balsa wood activity in the service of managing my response. She appears to believe that unless she actively engages me – in this case by assuming a helpless stance – she will simply fall out of my mind. The distinction between positive and negative attention loses its significance when being held in mind is paramount.

It seems likely that Aysha's expectation of adults is modelled on her early experience with an inconsistent carer who was only sometimes emotionally available. The unpredictability causes her such anxiety that she cannot use her teacher or me as a secure base from which to explore independently or lose herself in the activity. All her energy goes into monitoring our response and staying connected to us. The dependency on emotional support often leads to academic underachievement.

A young person like Aysha has conflicting desires – to cling to the family and to be part of a group. So she is caught in a dilemma: being angry with a family on whom she feels so dependent and at the same time not being able to whole-heartedly connect to the group. This means that using the group for self-exploration and help in loosening family ties is impossible. Close friendships with individuals can be hard too. Peers can experience her as emotionally overwhelming or as distancing herself in favour of her family.

In working therapeutically with Aysha I needed to be very clear about my availability outside the sessions, putting clear boundaries down at the same time as noting her need to keep close and be constantly supported. It was important to convey the belief that I did not need her physical presence to hold her in mind. I also had to avoid enmeshed thinking and to resist her invitation to 'triangulation', where she pressured me to join her in her critical view of other adults who failed to meet her needs. I encouraged her to express her hostility and anger towards me and to link this with fears about my unavailability.

Disorganised anxious attachment

The most troubled young people

> Children with disorganised/disoriented attachment have been found to have the most difficulty in later life with emotional, social, and cognitive impairments. These children also have the highest likelihood of having clinical difficulties in the future, including affect regulation problems, social difficulties, attention problems, and dissociative symptomatology. Unlike the other forms of insecure attachment, which are 'organised' approaches to the pattern of parental communication, this form of insecure attachment appears to involve significant problems in the development of a coherent mind.
>
> Siegel (1999, 109)

It is possible that Keith belongs in this category, which represents the smallest number of young people in our schools, although they are over-represented in PRUs. Individual work is not always indicated for such young people, who may find one-to-one therapy intolerably tantalising and their neediness and vulnerability too challenging.

In Keith's case, he needed a preliminary period where he engaged with the institution as a secure base before individual therapy could be considered. During this time his keyworker drew on all her personal resources and the support of others to provide the necessary experience for him in the unit. Pre-organised and consistent plans were agreed to help Keith to cope. His behaviour was understood to be defensive, an expression of anxiety, and so he was carefully prepared for changes, and his life in the unit was designed to be highly structured and predictable.

Theoretical frameworks helped his worker to make sense of his behaviour and to keep thinking in the face of his projections and provocation. She knew that such youngsters were likely to be highly controlling of adults, in either a caring or a punitive way, and could demonstrate extreme behaviour of either a withdrawn or hyperactive nature.

Keith was highly vigilant with regard to her vulnerabilities and masterful at pressing her buttons. She understood that he needed to feel in control of their emotional and physical proximity; she needed to be 'found when needed' and to be extremely reliable and resilient. She took every opportunity to notice triggers to outbursts and to find words for his experience. Keith was functioning at a very immature level emotionally because he had missed out on important early experiences of playful relationships, and so she provided opportunities for these.

The following is an extract from one of their interactions:

> Keith and his worker were playing a game of throwing soft teddy bears at each other. She would say, "I'm getting ready to THROW the teddy at you." Keith squealed with laughter, thrilled at the anticipated attack. It was then his turn and he would enjoy her playful pretence of alarm. This was reminiscent of playing with a toddler. At that moment the scary teenager was nowhere to be seen.

Once Keith embarked on individual work his difficulties became very manifest. In the therapy room he was tantalised by the regular one-to-one session and desperately sought ways of being close to his therapist. He had no idea how to do this and tried a range of strategies – including physically threatening behaviour and inappropriate touching. Once he sat in front of her and chewed and swallowed tissues. Like many hyper-vigilant and distrustful young people he needed to keep his therapist's mind where he could 'see' it.

> For children and young people who have suffered abuse or trauma over a period of time, the memories of that abuse do not remain in the past but become actions in the here and now. Such memories may be triggered by a number of things around them, including the experience of a close relationship

and at the point where they become threatened by the intimacy they act out in defence and for their own survival.

(Rose 2010, 26)

For Keith's therapist the challenge was to manage the intimidation and anxiety he engendered. The level of distress underlying his behaviour was so high that it was hard to accept his projected feelings and help him to make sense of them. She relied on the support of colleagues and supervisors to keep reflecting, rather than reacting. She found it helpful to hold on to realistic goals and to believe that giving him an experience of being with a resilient adult might help him to be in touch with less destructive parts of himself.

She tried to keep him calm by introducing structure and ordinary activities that would appeal to the 'thinking part of his brain' and was aware that situations where he lost control or could not manage something pitched him back into feeling overwhelming shame. She noticed his difficulty with symbolic, creative thought and reflection and the way in which he quickly became overwhelmed by anxiety when he had a go at imaginative thinking. Whenever possible she put his feelings into words and spoke of his desire to be close to her but how hard it was for him to know how to do it.

It was clear that Keith's peers regarded him with extreme wariness. The young people in the PRU needed support from adults in managing his provocation. Provoking peers to react gave him a feeling of control over others, but rejection by the group activated his attachment needs further. He seemed to feel overwhelmed both by relationships and also by a desire for closeness, though he was unable to appropriately manage closeness with others.

Research has indicated that violation of personal space is the most damaging social gaffe in peer culture. When group members failed to respond supportively, Keith quickly became angry and physically violent. He needed constant reassurance that peers were 'on his side' and sometimes caused splits in the group according to who was sympathetic at any given time.

We saw how Samira was able to use the peer group to appropriately distance herself from her family and explore a different identity. But groups are not always healthy. When several insecure and troubled young people band together, they may form gangs that serve the function of protection against anxiety for individual members, all of which is directed outwards. The group then becomes a vehicle for the expression of destructive feelings that may be hard for an individual to express alone. The fear and attachment needs underlying this are denied and defended against.

Conclusion

In this chapter I have outlined attachment research and described some common attachment patterns and their implications for understanding both why young people may respond to us in particular ways and how this impacts on our work. I have also touched upon the challenges for adolescents in separating from their families.

References

Abram, J. (1996) *The Language of Winnicott*. London: Karnac.

Ainsworth, M.D.S. and Wittig, B. A. (1969) Attachment and exploratory behaviour in one-year-olds in strange situation. In B. M. Foss (Ed) *Determinants of Infant Behaviour*, Vol 4, pp. 111–136. London: Methuen.

Balbernie, R. (2001) Circuits and circumstance: the neurological consequences of early relationships and how they shape later behaviour. *Journal of Child Psychotherapy* 27(3), 237–255.

Bowlby, J. (1973) *Attachment and Loss*. Vol 2, *Separation Anxiety and Anger*. London: Karnac.

Bowlby, J. (1988) *A Secure Base: Clinical Applications of Attachment Theory*. London: Routledge.

Brisch, K. H. (2009) Attachment and adolescence – the influence of attachment patterns on teenage behaviour. In A. Perry (Ed.) *Teenagers and Attachment*, pp. 9–31. London: Worth Publishing.

Brownlee, S. (1999) Inside the teen brain. *US News and World Report,* August 1.

Erikson, E. (1963) *Childhood and Society*. New York: Norton.

Fonagy, P. (2001) *Attachment Theory and Psychoanalysis*. New York: Other Press.

Geddes, H. (2006) *Attachment in the Classroom*. London: Worth Publishing.

George, C., Kaplan, N. and Main, M. (1996) *The Adult Attachment Interview Protocol*, 3rd ed. Department of Psychology, University of California, Berkeley. Unpublished manuscript.

Hopkins, J. (1990) The observed infant of attachment. *Journal of the Institute of Self Analysis* 4(1), 460–470.

Hughes, D. (2009) Principles of attachment and intersubjectivity – still relevant to relating with adolescents. In A. Perry (Ed.) *Teenagers and Attachment*, pp. 123–141. London: Worth Publishing.

Liebermann, M., Eisenberger, N., Crocket, M. J., Tom, S. M., Pfeifer, J. H. and Way, B. M. (2006) *Putting Feelings into Words: Affect Labelling Disrupts Amygdala Activity in Response to Affective Stimuli*. Los Angeles: University of California Press.

Main, M. and Solomon, J. (1986) Discovery of an insecure-disorganised/disorientated attachment pattern. In T. B. Brazelton and M. W. Yogman (Eds) *Affective Development in Infancy*, pp. 95–124. Norwood, NJ: Ablex.

Murray, L. (1980) The sensitivities and expressive capacities of young infants in communication with their mothers. PhD thesis, University of Edinburgh.

Robertson, J. (1952) *A Two-Year Old Goes to Hospital* [Film]. London: Tavistock Child Development Research Unit.

Rose, J. (2010) The nature of nurture. *Caspari Foundation Journal* 17, 23–33.

Schore, A. (1994) *Affect Regulation and the Origin of Self*. Hillsdale, NJ: Lawrence Erlbaum.

Siegel, D. J. (1999) *The Developing Mind*. New York: Guilford Press.

Winnicott, D. W. (1971) *Playing and Reality*. London: Penguin.

Winnicott, D. W. (1990) *The Maturational Process and the Facilitating Environment*. London: Hogarth.

Chapter 3

Keeping the school in mind

An example of a therapy service contributing to the emotional wellbeing of the whole school

Norma Gould

The core task of all schools is teaching and learning; staff aim to ensure that students leave with the knowledge, skills and understanding needed to forge a meaningful and fulfilling work life. In tandem, the school supports the emotional and psychological growth of its students so that they develop into healthy, considerate and responsible young people who can form and maintain honest and open relationships with others and, internally, with their own self. Schools strive to achieve these aims within a climate of scrutiny and seemingly ever-shifting policy changes. Office for Standards in Education reports are published online, and examination results are often felt to be the only indicator used to judge whether a school is successful or failing. Education can be a 'vote winner'; all political parties will have views on what – and how – it is delivered, how grading systems are structured and what the school's priorities should be. Radical changes to the curriculum, changes to marking criteria, alterations in grading boundaries and re-shaping of schools' strategic aims in general are frequent features in contemporary society especially when there is a change in government or an election is looming. These external demands make the task of attending to the internal and emotional developmental needs of young people very challenging.

We know that adolescence is a hugely turbulent time marked by powerful emotions which young people tend to communicate through acting out. It is important to have a framework which enables us to think about and make some sense of these emotions and accompanying behaviours. In this chapter I will be drawing on Bion's theory of 'Container-Contained' (1962, p. 86). From the beginning of life, the infant needs an adult mind that can take in extremes of emotion, which are accepted, digested and then returned to the infant in a moderated way. As a result the infant can take back the feelings and not be overwhelmed by fear of them. The regular repetition of this process allows infants to learn to do this for themselves, thereby internalising a function in the mind that can bear anxiety and engage creatively with learning and life experience. Out of this experience, patterns of relating are set up but are not fixed; they remain flexible enough to adapt to the new. This process is fundamental to managing all new experience. Adolescents face many unknowns as they move towards young adulthood. They need to navigate a significant shift from dependence to independence, often fluctuating between the two. At the same time, adolescence provides a unique opportunity to revisit early trauma and losses and understand them in the light of present experience and knowledge gained. As a result, development can move on.

While the core task for the therapist is therapeutic, providing a containing mind for her or his clients, it is important that the service offered is not a 'stand-alone' one that has moved too far from the primary task of the school. Consideration needs to be given to how therapeutic understanding can dovetail with the educative. It is essential that the therapeutic voice is heard, and the therapeutic conceptual framework understood, if the school is to fulfil its task of supporting young people as they grow into responsible adults. To do this effectively, it is most useful if the therapy service can be embedded across the organisation, with the therapist, or a small team of therapists, meaningfully contributing to the development of a psychological culture within the whole school.

What is suggested here is a model of working which sees the whole school as 'the client' in an attempt to create an environment that actively facilitates learning and personal growth and development for all the young people, staff and parents within the school community, akin to what Winnicott described as the facilitating environment (1963, p. 223). In order to create such an environment, the therapist is required to step literally and symbolically out of the clinical room and into the emotional life of the school. It involves listening not just to the anxieties of the young people who come for therapy but also to the concerns of senior managers, teaching and support staff, parents and all students. Schools are fast-moving, pressurised and emotionally charged places. The school therapist can make a significant impact on the emotional culture if she or he looks to create systems and to make space where conversations can be initiated about the conscious and unconscious emotional experience of teaching and learning and the particular challenges and anxieties that adolescents experience when faced with this task.

Context

The model described in this chapter is based on a therapeutic service established eight years ago in a large inner-city academy in London which takes a whole-school approach to emotional wellbeing. Students aged 11–18 arrive at the Academy as children and leave as young adults. The Academy has a Christian foundation, but students do not have to be Christian nor come from any faith tradition to attend. It holds predominantly to Christian values while being inclusive of students from other faith backgrounds and those from none. The Academy is situated in an area of economic deprivation with high levels of unemployment and low levels of educational achievement.

Setting up the therapy service began when I was first taken on in a fulltime senior counsellor's role and started the slow and careful process of building up the provision. As I hold a teaching qualification it was, perhaps, easier for the post to be embedded in the organisational structure from the start, and my past professional experience working in schools will have gone some way towards winning the confidence of the leadership team. This meant that from the beginning, I had access to senior staff and was able to take a pivotal role in developing emotional wellbeing across the Academy.

As my work evolved, there was a growing recognition of the needs of students who were never going to access one-to-one therapy and an understanding that they too needed a safe place in which to explore personal and developmental issues. Within a few years of my appointment, another therapist was employed. Soon after, the work of emotional wellbeing was expanded through employing an Emotional Wellbeing Co-ordinator. Currently, the team at the Academy includes three therapists, one of whom is a family therapist, whom I oversee in my current role as Assistant Headteacher with key responsibility for the school's wellbeing and inclusion agenda. This in-school therapy service is supplemented by other interventions offered to students within Student Support Services; these interventions include a team of three Learning Mentors, a Peer Mediation Service, a Parent Support worker, and a number of peripatetic staff who deliver additional wellbeing programmes for students within the College.

Raising awareness of the service

It is important for the school therapist to explain to and explore with young people the meaning of therapy in order to challenge the myths and fantasies around mental health. The process of encouraging young people to take care of their emotional and relational needs in the same way as they would their physical health is crucial. When I was setting up the therapy provision at the Academy, a first task was to visit every teaching group to explain the service, explore the issues young people might seek therapy for, and outline the contract and limitations around confidentiality and child protection. This also provided an opportunity to educate the staff about the service, as they remained in the classroom during these sessions. In discussing why students might want to access the counselling provision, the key tasks of adolescence were highlighted and the challenges that can arise during the teenage years were normalised. It was felt that this process was essential both to raise awareness of the service and to convey fundamental ideas of how therapy works, including what it can and cannot offer. In addition, staff and students were introduced to the psychological and emotional tasks which define adolescence.

Establishing the role of the PSHE emotional wellbeing co-ordinator

Once the counselling service was up and running, I was asked to help with a review of the Personal, Social and Health Education (PSHE) curriculum, which traditionally puts more emphasis on our social responsibly within society; it was clear that this was an opportunity to match the curriculum much more closely with the inner emotional needs of the students. An emotional wellbeing co-ordinator – an experienced teacher with a keen interest in psychoanalytic therapy – was employed by the Academy, and a model of delivery was developed which made time during lessons for the expression and exploration of students' worries, concerns and interests with regard to their experience of school and society. The emotional well-being co-ordinator was supported through regular supervision and management meetings with me. He was also supported in completing a Master's Degree in the emotional aspects of teaching and learning at the Tavistock Clinic. Both the observational and theoretical components of this course helped the co-ordinator to embed key psychological concepts in the PSHE programme and in all his work with the young people he teaches across the whole school.

Meeting diverse needs: therapy through sport

Those boys who regularly challenged Academy staff and disrupted lessons were often referred for individual therapy. Some of them found being in the therapy room too difficult to manage and were unable to engage in a meaningful way. While there might have been a number of unconscious reasons why these particular students couldn't use the therapeutic space, their resistance is not unusual at this stage of development. Many adolescents use action to replace thinking as a way of defending against the pain of helplessness and confusion which is often experienced during this phase of life. The fear of needing the therapist and facing their desire for dependence can be at odds with the developmental need to separate from parental objects. These boys, although able, were not achieving their potential academically. It was clear that they were struggling emotionally but unable to use the one-to-one therapeutic relationship.

In response to this, the Academy employed a therapist one afternoon a week to run a therapeutic programme using football as a forum for learning about the self, building relationships and thinking about group and relational processes. A school-based learning mentor was identified to work alongside this therapist providing regular one-to-one mentoring support for the boys. Through their experience of being both an individual player and, simultaneously, a member of the team, the students were helped to think about their behaviour and link this to how they presented and behaved within lessons and around the Academy in general. Because of the non-threatening way in which new ideas were introduced to them to help them in understanding themselves and the impact of their behaviour, the boys were able to form a positive attachment to the therapist, the learning mentor and the group. This allowed a working through of some of the more aggressive responses within the group, creating more space for reflection and thought. The group experience stimulated their aggressive experiences while also allowing an opportunity to think about and moderate this aggression. A more positive attachment to the Academy was evidenced through the significant decline in the number of behaviour incidents logged against the boys and an increase in the number of positive points rewarded to them for increased effort in class and improved behaviour across the Academy.

Setting up a Peer Mediation Service

The experience of making friends and finding a place in a peer group is a very important and often painful aspect of teenage life; many young people will adapt themselves and change their behaviour in order to fit in. They can, at times, be very hard on each other and may come across as unforgiving, making or dropping friends according to fixed ideas of what is acceptable or not. While claiming that they want to be allowed to be different, very often they have strict 'rules' for themselves and others to adhere to. As adolescents struggle to find their own identity, they fear any signs of weakness or neediness, which if spotted may be picked on mercilessly. In order not to be seen as vulnerable, they will play out different roles, one of which is to be hard, tough and critical, which can quickly evolve into being a bully.

The forms bullying takes and their unconscious roots are explored in detail in Chapter 14. However, understanding bullying behaviour is not enough. Strategies need to be developed which deal with bullying behaviour. It is a serious issue for schools. However, staff often feel powerless and disheartened about the lack of impact they feel they can have on the thoughtless and careless way that students can treat each other. Bullying entails splitting off hated and weaker disowned aspects of the self and projecting them onto others so that these self-parts can be kept out of conscious awareness and attacked. These kinds of attacks can be enacted over and over again within the school through teasing, low-level bullying, scuffles in the corridor and even vicious fighting.

Helping young people to manage conflict and supporting them in developing more empathic relationships with each other were identified as a priority for the Academy in order to decrease bullying. As the senior therapist, I approached a local organisation with the aim of co-establishing a Peer Mediation Service within the school. The aim of mediation is to provide a non-punitive space to bring together young people in conflict so that they can listen to each other, face the hurt they caused, own the damage they have done and grow in understanding of themselves and others. Psychologically the mediation process represents an attempt to enable students to take back into their own minds' disowned aspects of themselves, which up to this point they have continued to project outside into the 'enemy'. It confronts students with their part in causing conflict, and if denial can be broken down, it allows the mind to let in differing aspects of the self.

A group of sixth form students from the Academy were trained to deliver the service. These older students act as role models for the young ones, demonstrating that conflict can be resolved by talking and working it through. I continue to meet regularly with the mediation staff, who in turn provide weekly supervision meetings for the sixth form students on the peer mediation team. While these young people are not providing therapy, a key aim of the supervision provided is to hold in mind the psychoanalytic framework for understanding emotional and mental conflict, thereby offering containment to the team. The Peer Mediation Service at the Academy has now been in existence for a number of years. Its impact has been significant; while conflict and bullying continue, young people now regularly refer themselves, requesting help with resolving issues with their peers. Students who experience bullying, especially cyber bullying, are provided with a vehicle which gives them a voice and challenges some of the fantasies and fears about bullying, giving them back a sense of control and improving self-confidence as a result.

Managing transition

Young people have to negotiate three significant points of transition during their time at secondary school: the moves from primary to secondary school (which is covered in Chapter 17), from Year 11 to Sixth Form and from Sixth Form out of school to university, apprenticeships or work. These moments of transition are fraught with anxiety for students and provide ample opportunity for them to act out instead of engaging creatively with their experience. The challenges that face adolescents during these points of transition come from moving on and taking a step into the unknown, which can reactivate earlier losses and separations. Providing support to these students during these transitions is crucial if they are to feel contained enough to face the unknown and develop the inner structures and resilience to carry out the tasks required of them.

Within the therapy service at the Academy, a range of interventions are provided to help the students respond to these developmental challenges; one of the school therapists runs a transition nurture group for the most vulnerable new Year 7 students, and all Year 11 students take part in a 'past, present and future' workshop during which the students are encouraged to reflect on their experience to date, think about present choices and behaviours and explore their feelings about going forward including their hopes, fears, values and aspirations. At the beginning of Year 13 all sixth form students engage in a two-day conference titled 'Entering Adulthood'. This involves students attending a range of workshops which address both the emotional and more practical issues around leaving school and moving into the world of adults.

Developing the emotional intelligence of staff

Staff at the Academy often seek out one of the school therapists for guidance about the young people in their teaching or pastoral groups, especially those whose behaviours are challenging and confusing. Sometimes advice is sought about students who appear troubled, live in challenging circumstances or have had a traumatic experience. More often school staff want to discuss those who present as troublesome and who struggle to comply with the rules and procedures of the school. These conversations provide an opportunity to introduce staff to new ways of thinking about the meaning of behaviour and to the idea that behaviour is the means by which young people convey their distress and anxiety.

Our role as adults working with these students is to try to understand what is being communicated and provide consistent support for these young people so they feel contained and begin to manage. This is no easy task as often their behaviour is disarming and infuriating and may touch on our experience in a way that can blind us to what is going on for them. Adolescents can be provocative and frightening as well as vulnerable and helpless. Through unconscious processes, young people project onto us disowned aspects of their emotional experience, and we can get caught up in their feelings, either acting them out or colluding with the roles adolescents assume we will take up, such as the angry or ineffectual or rejecting parent. Helping staff to understand the process of projection and introjection enables them to feel more contained and helps them to create thinking space, especially in those emotionally charged moments when they feel under intense pressure to react in the moment.

While individual consultations with staff can offer insight into, and understanding of, the complexity of individual students, it is my view that an intrinsic part of the school therapist's role is to create forums in which to develop the emotional resilience and intelligence of staff. To follow are two examples of how the Academy's therapy service has worked to achieve this aim.

Workshops for staff on defusing difficult situations

The Academy's leadership team was keen to help staff to deal positively, calmly and effectively with disruptive behaviour and to avoid exclusions or the use of punitive sanctions as much as possible. A significant amount of staff time and energy was being taken up dealing with this behaviour, which was having a notable impact on the quality of relationships in lessons and students' ability to learn. While some staff were very experienced at calming and refocusing disruptive young people, other staff felt paralysed and powerless to manage them and ended up feeling angry and humiliated. As a result, the situation often escalated rather than being resolved. During a whole-school staff training day, two school therapists and the emotional wellbeing co-ordinator ran a training workshop for all staff on the psychological function of behaviour, including an understanding of projection and transference, and provided guidance on how to manage when staff found themselves caught up in difficult encounters with students.

Integrated services panel

In 2000 in London, England, an eight-year-old Ivorian girl, Victoria Climbié, was tortured and murdered by her guardians. Her death led to Lord Laming's appointment by the Department of Health to chair a public inquiry into the case. His final report, published in February 2003, led to many child protection reforms, including the formation of the Every Child Matters programme, a framework to improve the lives of children, and the introduction of the Children Act 2004, an Act of Parliament that provides the legislative base for many of the reforms recommended.

At the heart of the Laming Report is an emphasis on the importance of professionals working together and sharing information if we are to keep our most at-risk children safe. Schools are very busy and fast-moving places; working with troubled and troublesome young people can be extremely anxiety provoking. It is often the adults around them who carry the worry about the consequences of their risky behaviour. Too often decisions are made swiftly and in reaction to a stressful situation that occurred in the day. Little time is made to think or to link up with other professionals to reflect on the needs of the most vulnerable.

In an effort to counter this, a weekly panel is convened at the Academy by me as the senior therapist (now the Assistant Headteacher) that is attended by key academic leaders and pastoral staff, including members of the therapy team. The panel dedicates time to thinking about such students and their needs. Decisions are made in a more thoughtful and contained way. While the panel plans intervention for the most needy, its very presence significantly lessens anxiety in the staff and offers them a sense of a 'team around the child'. Because the needs of such students are complex and multilayered, the panel also decides when to refer to outside agencies, recognising that sometimes the needs of these young people are beyond the resources of the school.

Working with parents

Parenting a teenage son or daughter can be daunting. During the primary years, it is not unusual for the teacher to have regular contact with parents in which advice and support are given when the parent is concerned about some aspect of the child's development. Generally it is unrealistic for parents to expect to have the same level of contact with secondary school staff. Their child will have a number of teachers. While the student does have a form tutor who oversees their wellbeing while in school, there is no equivalent to a primary school class teacher whom parents can regularly meet with. Discussions about their teenage child are often confined to the annual parents' evening, where the emphasis is on academic progress and achievement or discussions about disciplinary action being put in place by the school. In addition, some parents have a very negative transference to the school, and contact can stimulate their own early experience of learning and school and of their own adolescence. So at a time when parents need more support to manage the shifts and dramatic changes occurring within their adolescent children, they are often most alone.

The extremes of emotion experienced by adolescents are both witnessed and experienced by their parents; often this is hugely painful and confusing for the parents as they try to bear and understand how their once placid, good-humoured and interested child has transformed into someone they don't recognise or know. Providing parents with a way of understanding these changes and their emotional meaning has proved to be a very fruitful role for the school therapist and can enhance the quality of communication between school and home. At the Academy, individual consultations are regularly offered to parents. Also a programme called 'Walking with Adolescents' has been developed specifically for parents.

Regular evening discussion groups feature a guest speaker such as a child or family psychotherapist talking about an aspect of adolescent development with a particular emphasis on the experience and role of parenting a teenage child followed by an open discussion and question-and-answer session.

The Academy model: complexities and limitations

If the school therapist is to take up the role I suggest in this chapter, then it inevitably means that she or he will be more visible within the school. This can cause some difficulty, especially for those young people who are engaging in individual therapy. Each client will have their own transference to the therapist. This is an 'as if' relationship, shaped by fantasy and based on the young person's earliest experiences of parental objects. An essential part of the therapeutic task is to understand and work with these fantasies. Their experience of the therapist engaging in a classroom setting or speaking at an assembly or meeting parents can be very unsettling, causing the client degrees of anxiety and in some cases threatening the therapeutic relationship. Some clients can feel extremes of jealousy, sibling rivalry and rage that they have to 'share' the therapist with others. In addition, they might become more concerned about confidentiality and how real it is especially when they witness the therapist engaging in conversation with other staff or going into meetings. It is important that the therapist explains to clients during the assessment session or the initial phase of the work that she or he has additional roles within the school other than the one-to-one therapeutic role, informs them about occasions where they might 'meet' outside the therapy room and, if possible, explores during the course of therapy the impact and meaning of this for them.

In my experience, young people are able to manage the school therapist taking up other, more active roles outside the clinical room once it is acknowledged and worked with in the 'here and now' of therapy. It can also provide a fruitful way of exploring clients' inner states of mind. Exploring their transference to the therapist provides a very useful insight into their transference to the school and to the process of learning. Whether this transferential relationship is persecutory and inhibits learning or more benign, where something good can be taken in and learning made possible, provides rich ground for the exploration of the psychic reality of the adolescent client.

There are a number of points that need to be made about the model more generally. It is not one that can be easily imported into any school context. A key factor is having a Head Teacher or Principal and a Senior Leadership team that place as much value on the personal development of students as on the quality of teaching and examination results. In addition, coherent systems need to be in place such as a clear and robust behaviour policy, interesting and engaging lessons, comprehensive Special Educational Needs (SEN) provision, and so forth – this model then becomes part of a network of systems that work together to create the emotional culture of the school.

The model described in this chapter evolved over time. It involved – and continues to take account of – shifts between inner and outer realities. For example, school staff will have conscious and unconscious responses to the provision of therapy during curriculum time for students, opinions on whether attending sessions justifies missing lessons and so on. These perceptions will come and go and will need to be openly addressed from time to time.

Before embarking on developing a whole-school model such as this one, it is essential that the school therapist has had enough time to solidly establish her or his identity as a psychodynamic practitioner within the school setting. Because of the external pressures of school, developing the capacity to reflect rather than react and to help staff and students alike to explore internal meanings is core to this. It is only when the school therapist is firmly rooted in her or his psychodynamic identity that developing this model in close partnership with the school should be considered.

As has been implied, building the trust of senior staff and the leadership team is crucial, whatever kind of provision is offered by the therapist. The fact that I held a teaching qualification and had school leadership experience as a previous Department Head prior to my training in counselling and psychotherapy with children and adolescents probably supported this, but it is not an essential feature of my role. More important is how the school therapist is experienced on a day-to-day basis and the quality of relationships formed with students and staff.

Finally, this model involves the development of a team of staff who are committed to working therapeutically with students and who bring a range of expertise and complementary skills to bear on the work. The school therapist's role throughout is to hold in mind the psychoanalytic framework for understanding adolescent emotional states, thereby offering containment to the team and, in turn, enabling them to better manage their relationships with students, especially those who are troubled and troublesome. An extremely valuable aspect of this model is the involvement of students. Through the work of the mediation service, young people show that they have enough self-agency and inner authority to be able to face, work through and resolve conflict themselves.

Conclusion

In this chapter I have attempted to show how the school therapist can have a positive impact on the emotional life and psychological landscape of the school. I have explored how the therapist can significantly contribute to the school's primary role of teaching and learning through holding in the mind the need to attend to the inner emotional development of students. The school therapist is well positioned to provide a framework which enables the insights and understanding gained from a psychodynamic perspective to be brought to bear on the professional development of staff and the emotional containment of parents. By listening carefully to the emotional needs of the whole school as expressed by students, parents and staff, the school therapist can have a pivotal role in creating a school which is psychologically more mature, emotionally more resilient and more able to respond thoughtfully to the educational and developmental needs of the young people within the school.

References

Bion, W. R. (1962) *Learning from Experience*. London: Heinemann.

Winnicott, D. W. (1963) 'The mentally ill in your caseload'. In *The Maturational Processes and the Facilitating Environment*, pp. 217–229. London: Karnac (repr. 1990).

Chapter 4

The impact of social media on young people

Reva Klein

Adolescence is, among many other things, a time during which young people explore questions around who they are and who they want to be; it is a time, too, for experimenting with projecting different images and aspects of themselves onto others. The desire for intense relationships with peers runs parallel to these processes. Attachments to others can indeed seem to supersede everything else in the teenage years, and the need to be in contact with peers, to touch base and share experiences, can often have a sense of urgency to it. In such a tumultuous and disorienting period in their development, young people have a need for reassurance from others that they're heard and seen, understood and valued. They yearn to belong, despite and because of often feeling alone, misunderstood, alienated.

Secondary school students in the 21st century are in a unique position compared to their adolescent predecessors in a number of ways. Technology has taken centre stage in the way they spend their time, whether it's used for doing schoolwork or for amusing themselves and communicating with others. There has been no other time in history when young people have had the freedom to make connections – with both close friends and total strangers – instantaneously, privately and en masse. Along with offering users of social media networks previously undreamed-of opportunities to be in touch around the clock and around the world with whomever they choose, technology has opened the door for anyone to reinvent themselves into whatever they desire to be. Like an endless hall of funfair mirrors, Facebook, Twitter, My Space, YouTube and other sites have the potential to enhance, distort and exaggerate users, even beyond recognition. And because the gratification the media offer is immediate, the sometimes negative consequences of these quick and effortless online communications are often overlooked or downplayed by users until things go wrong and someone gets hurt. Reflectiveness is not, to put it mildly, something that is engendered by tweets, texts, instant messaging and Facebook.

The way social media are used is consonant with Freud's idea of pairs of opposites: those seemingly contradictory drives that are mirror versions of each other. In the context under discussion, they can be categorised as scopophilia and exhibitionism – the desire to look and the desire to be seen (Freud 1905/1953). It is a dualism that belongs not only to the 'perversions', as Freud conceptualised it, but one which exists in ordinary neurotic psychic structures: 'active and passive forms of the same component instinct' (Laplanche and Pontalis 1973, p. 295). Put another way, engagement with social media and the virtual world is 'fundamentally tied to both our motivation to relate and our desire to discover and be discovered' (Balick 2012, p. 122). Whether they are the ones who gaze or the ones who expose themselves to the gaze – or, as is usually the case, both – adolescents' use of social networks can be instrumental in helping them explore questions around identity, self-image and identifications with others, whether the portals they employ usher them into the world of reality or fantasy (or both). And it is also true that while social media can facilitate connections with others, they can also block them, leaving individuals feeling more alone and unseen than if they had never used these sites and technologies.

This chapter will briefly explore some of the internal and external effects of the social media world that the contemporary adolescent inhabits and will suggest some of the insights into our clients we can gain from their online behaviour.

Working with our ambivalence

Any discussion of this subject has to start with the acknowledgement that we as therapists don't come to it with a blank slate. Those of us who use Facebook and Twitter or have other online profiles will be all too aware of the pitfalls inherent in exposure, self-generated or otherwise, over which we have no actual control. We take a risk every time we press the send key, a reality that we more often than not turn a blind eye to for the sake of expedience. The contrast between the instant online or text communiqués that we fire off many times in a working day and our considered, thoughtful reflections in the consulting room is nothing short of glaring.

Whether we use social media ourselves or not, we are as susceptible as everyone to the waves of moral panic that engulf the public in the wake of children and young people whose suicides are attributed to cyberbullying, sexting, Facebook, instant messaging and the like. The reporting of these incidents, which often includes heart-rending descriptions of the desperation caused by vicious public betrayals by supposed friends, is deeply unsettling. Young people's vulnerability, often in part a product of their desire for connectedness, acceptance and social status, is palpable in its own right as well as stirring up our transference to situations in which we have experienced – or perhaps even perpetrated – acts of cruelty, betrayal and humiliation (see Chapter 14).

For those of us working with young people whose use of social media appears compulsive and impulsive, we may struggle to maintain our professional role and contain our anxieties about these clients finding themselves in painful or dangerous situations. The ease of use and ubiquity of these media enable young people to send out messages without thinking, sometimes while drunk, high or only partially awake. It can be the most benign and fun of interactions, but when it goes wrong, it can go very wrong. When that happens, the knowledge that our clients have no place to run and nowhere to hide can be a heavy burden for them and for us.

The illusion of omnipotence

Our clients exist in two parallel and in many ways mutually exclusive realms. One is highly boundaried, circumscribed by the laws, rules, conventions and schedules of school, home and civil society; transgression of many of these parameters carries the risk of punishment. These rules provide and represent structures and frameworks within which we all go about our lives. When they are perceived to be benign, we feel contained by them and protected from chaos.

When they are not, they can feel oppressive, claustrophobic, persecutory. In adolescence, these frameworks can take on meanings that they may have lacked earlier in the individual's development. 'Fairness' and the absence of it becomes acutely felt at a time when adolescents' internal and external loci have shifted radically. Often they feel torn between two positions: that of the dependent child, which equates with a lack of agency, and that of the myth of the independent teenager, who has ever more privileges and freedoms. Young people may feel that they continue to be treated as a child when their bodies are telling them that childhood is now in the past – but where they fit into the present, let alone the future, is far from clear.

Social media and cyberspace in general offer the illusion of potency and agency to the young individuals who feel the gaping lack of both in their lives. Where the real external world is made coherent by rules and laws, the virtual world is bound by nothing but an aura of boundlessness. It's an endless expanse where there's no one looking over their shoulder. They can reinvent themselves into whatever guise(s) they choose, 'engag[ing] in the art of the self' (McGowan 2012, p. 65) without the looming threat of obvious constraints or repercussions. This escape into assumed freedom can function as a psychic retreat from the internal slings and arrows beleaguering them with feelings of alienation, exclusion or inferiority. Adolescents who feel out of synch with their peers, whose sense of their differentness silences them and leads them to self-effacement for fear of being seen and ridiculed, become empowered through the anonymity of technology. They can undergo transformation, rendering themselves unrecognisable from what they perceive to be their sad, unlovable self. With the press of a button they are able to project an image of social confidence out into the virtual world, drawing on influences from sources real and imagined, admired schoolmates and celebrities. Opinions, jokes, shared hero worship of pop stars or hobbies or other interests are all there to be expressed in ways that can be learned from others, seemingly without risk. Having 700 'friends' on an Xbox site, as Shane, an eight-year-old boy with Asperger's once boasted to his school therapist, softens the blow of having few or no friends in the real world. Similarly, self-harmers can easily find kindred spirits from whom they can learn all there is to know about cutting techniques and ways to evade detection when they're committed to anorexia or bulimia. Through whatever part of the looking glass the young social media user chooses to enter, there is an unlimited expanse of people waiting to be connected – for good or ill. And the effect of those consummated acts of connection, one after the other or many all at once, can lead effortlessly to a return to a sense of omnipotence: the psychic state of ultimate power that we experience and then lose as we move through infancy.

Immediate gratifications, instant attachments

For the adolescent, connectedness with peers is a strong, almost magnetic emotional pull as well as an anchoring. Cruelly, this stage of development also brings with it painful self-doubts, self-consciousness and confusion around identity. Given the instabilities that are often present at this time, the instantaneousness of online networking can feel irresistible and compelling. Indeed, it can become precisely those things for some adolescents, who find it hard to switch off.

The young person who hungers for affirmation can get it through the ether from others who have similar problems or ways of looking at themselves. There are also those who are driven not necessarily by acute hunger but by a need of reassurance from friends real and virtual and who will impulsively seek it through social media.

The immediacy of the connections is particularly compelling for those whose need for gratification takes an urgent form. As therapists, we work with the vulnerabilities of clients who lack internalised good-enough objects. These young people tend to be particularly susceptible to the blandishments of instant attachments which offer the promise of unconditional and everlasting love. Their often insecure attachment patterns have left them, in the real world, with a valency for strongly defensive behaviour. As a consequence they may all too easily suspend their disbelief in others once there is no here-and-now-ness to negotiate. So in the world of virtual reality, they may rush into disclosing intimate details or photographs of themselves or even arrange a rendezvous in the belief that the person they think they're connecting with is different from all the others and, as such, worthy of their trust. How much easier it is to make friends with someone with whom the ordinary obstacles to social intercourse and attraction don't exist. Out of context, out of sight, the semiotics of how people of whatever age read each other in face-to-face interactions no longer exist.

Working with the virtually connected adolescent

Where does this leave us as therapists working with young people, sitting face to face for a set time once a week, in a room devoid of everything except ourselves? As uncomfortable as the awareness is, we must accept that what we represent and offer is a huge disjuncture with the way our clients communicate their thoughts and feelings in their day-to-day lives. The 'evenly suspended attention' we present to them may be a rare and discomfiting form of interaction in their experience (Freud 1912, p. 111). The extent to which the therapeutic setting and process will be felt by some clients as the antithesis of the rapid responses that characterise their online interactions is entirely understandable. They enjoy and crave the adrenalin sport of being one of many people at one time bouncing gossip and quips off each other. In a social world that is constructed around performance and audience, excitement, action and reaction, the quiet therapeutic space in which there is no technology, no distraction, no contact with the outside world can feel threatening, exposing, alien and 'downright anachronistic' (Balick 2012, p. 124). While in the psychodynamic world these boundaried parameters exist for a purpose, for our adolescent clients they may seem meaningless and sometimes persecutory.

Our clients' differentness to those they are in contact with online or through texting and instant messaging is obscured by the media they use for their communications. But in therapy it's different. They experience us in an intimate situation. We're not peers, not teachers, not potential friends. In fact, we're probably not like anyone they have known before. And they are sitting face to face with us, these unknown quantities in uncharted territory, not knowing who we are or where we want to take them.

To work with clients whose lives are split between the real and virtual worlds requires an understanding on our part of the magnitude of that split. While many use social media to enlarge their social contacts, get involved in projects or just stay in touch with friends and acquaintances, for some young people the virtual world will be experienced as a far more compelling and comfortable place to inhabit than the actual world. Contrary to the therapist's desire for the individual to 'be themselves', online networking offers everybody the heady opportunity to be anyone they want to be – and that can mean being anyone *but* themselves. Winnicott's (1965) concept of the false self goes some way to helping one understand this, but the parameters of cyberspace take it much further, beyond any specific relationship that the young person is engaged in. It enables them to construct and enact a fantasy of the self.

If and when clients disclose the nature of their online identity and relationships, they will be saying different things to the therapist including: 'I'm a much more attractive and desirable person than you may think I am.' They may want you to know that their profile in school, perhaps defined by their difficulties with teachers and peers, is not the *real* them. Outside the straitjacket of school, away from the authority figures and competition that bring out the worst in them, they may be projecting an image of someone very different, someone deserving of positive attention.

Alternatively, clients who talk about their vivid relationships through Facebook and so on may be telling you that while they feel good when they're online, they may be worried about where it may lead. The young people we work with in schools are very much of this world and will be aware of the high-profile cases where children and teenagers have gotten into dangerous situations – and worse – as a result of being too trusting, too naïve, too desperate for positive attention. While they may desire to turn a blind eye to the possible risks when they're on their own, they may not be as successful when it comes to denying their vulnerability to us, who are hopefully perceived as trustworthy objects in the real world.

As mentioned in the Introduction, it can be a challenge to keep our maternal transference in check when confronted with clients who tell us about situations that may be putting them at risk. We need to try to use our judgement and our analytic skills to assess, first of all, what is real and what is not. Are we being presented with fantasies that the client hopes will elevate them in our eyes? Is the client challenging us to see whether we are trustworthy or 'just like the rest of them'? Or is the client looking to us to help disentangle them from a situation they no longer feel right about?

If the risk appears to be real, it will become a child protection (CP) concern that needs to be shared with the school after explaining to the client why, because of the school's duty of care, you are going to do so and why it's a good idea for that to happen. Whether it is a CP issue or not, the therapeutic work is likely to focus on the hopes and expectations that the young person has of online relationships and why they feel these connections can't be easily hoped for or realised in the day-to-day real world. Exploring their internal objects is likely to be a key to opening up their thoughts and feelings about how they are perceived by themselves as well as by others. With gentle direction, such an exploration can lead to the young person acknowledging that they may be stuck in a way of thinking about who they are and that their projections may be further entrenching them in this position. Subtly challenging old ways of thinking and looking at patterns of behaviour that repeatedly get them into unhappy positions can then become the focus of the work.

Conclusion

As therapists we need to be aware of how complicated and split young people's lives are thanks in large part to the technology at their disposal 24/7. The virtual world can become an idealised one, where attachments are quickly formed and have an intensity that adolescents may crave and value above less dramatic but more real relationships.

While we may have strong reservations about them engaging in potentially risky practices such as exchanging personal/intimate details and photographs with others, we need to beware of jumping to conclusions too and to ask ourselves and our clients what the aim is of these communications, what they believe might result and whether the situations they find themselves in are compensating for deeper connections that they desire.

Social networks are a fait accompli in our world, probably for many generations to come. By understanding the drive for more and more connections online and the nature of the relationships that our clients get involved in, we can better help them to look at their desires from a more thoughtful, analytic and hopefully constructive perspective.

Study questions

Vignette 1

Mary, 12 years old, is secretive, avoidant and volatile in sessions generally. In one session she talks about having 'met' a nice person she's excited about linking up with in a public place after school today. She says this person really understands her and makes her feel good about herself. It soon becomes clear that Mary has 'met' this person online and believes him to be a 12-year-old boy. *How do you manage this?*

Vignette 2

Ahmed is a withdrawn 14-year-old boy who doesn't seem to have any friends. He talks in sessions about spending most of his time on the computer and reveals that he's seen a lot of disgusting things that he wishes he hadn't. It's made him feel depressed and hopeless, but he can't stop looking at them. *How do you manage this?*

Vignette 3

Shanice, 15, regularly complains of being too tired to do anything and not being interested in school anyway. She goes to sleep at around 3 a.m. every night after instant messaging for hours. She says it's the only thing she enjoys doing. *How do you manage this?*

Sample responses

Vignette 1

Mary needs to be told that you are concerned about her meeting someone she doesn't know and that after your session you'll be having a word with the special needs coordinator about what she's told you. You can say that while you can understand that she's excited about making a new friend, we need to make sure we know who people are before we make any kind of arrangements to meet them because they may be different from who they say they are. You can acknowledge that she may be angry and frustrated with you, but your main concern and the school's is to make sure that children are safe. Once the safeguarding has been put in place, you will want to explore with Mary her desire to find someone who will understand and value her and how she feels that she can achieve this only with people outside her real life.

Vignette 2

You can say to Ahmed that it can be deeply upsetting to see some of the disturbing images that are online. These pictures can distort things in our minds, making us feel like there's something wrong with us and making the world seem like a harsher, uglier place. You can talk to him about sexual feelings and how these images are not about being intimate and close with somebody but about using their bodies. You might ask him about his ideas on what it means to be with someone and explore his attitude towards his own sexuality. You could also suggest that he move his computer out of his room and into the living room to prevent him from looking at these sites.

Vignette 3

You might try to ask Shanice what they talk about online all night and whether it's become a way of avoiding doing things in the real world that need to be done. Does she feel fidgety if she isn't in touch? Does she worry that if she turns her phone off she'll be marginalised or excluded? Is it possible that she could have a better time with her friends seeing them face to face?

References

Balick, A. (2012) TMI in the transference LOL: Psychoanalytic reflections on Google, social networking and 'virtual impingement'. *Psychoanalysis, Culture and Society* Vol 17, 2, 120–136.

Freud, S. (1905/1953) Three essays on the theory of sexuality. In J. Strachey (Ed.) *Standard Edition* 7. London: Hogarth, 135–163.

Freud, S. (1912/1953–74) Recommendations to physicians practising psychoanalysis. In J. Strachey (Ed.) *Standard Edition* 12. London: Hogarth, 109–120.

Laplanche, J., and Pontalis, J.-B. (1973) *The Language of Psychoanalysis.* London: Karnac.

McGowan, T. (2012) Virtual freedom: The obfuscation and elucidation of the subject in cyberspace. *Psychoanalysis, Culture and Society* Vol 17, 2, 63–71.

Winnicott, D. W. (1965) Ego distortion in terms of true and false self. In *The Maturational Process and the Facilitating Environment: Studies in the Theory of Emotional Development*, pp. 140–152. New York: International University Press.

Chapter 5

Engaging adolescents in the secondary school setting

Lyn French and Sue Lund

Engaging adolescents in therapy is bound to present challenges specific to their stage of life. We know that many teenagers may find it counter-intuitive to share personal information with an adult. For some, becoming more at ease with how we work can take longer if their class, culture, family values or religious beliefs mean they arrive at our consulting room door with scepticism, confusion or uncertainty about what we can offer them. As this chapter illustrates, in order to reach them in the first instance and then to sustain our relationship with them, we may need to re-think aspects of our practice and be prepared to adapt our ways of working, even quite considerably. Building the skills and the confidence to do so without feeling we are leaving behind important aspects of our psychoanalytically informed training is a learning curve we all go through.

There is much to think about when starting work with adolescents, ranging from our own transferences to school life to the conscious and unconscious views school staff hold about our work through to our clients' presenting issues. This chapter cannot cover all aspects of engaging adolescents in therapy, but we hope that we have focused on some of the most important ones. *Therapeutic Practice in Schools: Working with the Child Within* (French and Klein 2012) can also be used as a resource. It provides a detailed guide to the general practice of working with both children and adolescents.

Our work as school-based therapists is complex but ever stimulating and usually very rewarding. Not only do we have the chance to address young people's difficulties before they become too entrenched or their defences too rigid, we also have the opportunity to revisit our own adolescence, in the process gaining a better understanding of the ways in which personalities are shaped, relationships formed and collective identities developed.

The school context

The primary task of schools is to educate their pupils. Therapy services offered in curriculum time are usually viewed by staff as being in support of this; managing staff expectations and raising their awareness of the kinds of gains that can be achieved are usually seen as core tasks for the therapist. To this end, a shared understanding between the therapist and school staff is essential so that the therapist is identified with the school setting, and splitting is avoided.

It is useful if the client knows from the beginning that the therapist works collaboratively with school staff and that there could be times when the therapist needs to bring something to the session which has been passed on by the school, if it is in the young person's best interest to do so and the school would like the therapist to do so. When these instances arise, it can be helpful to link it, if possible, with material already being explored, saying, for example, *You've just been talking about being treated unfairly. This brings to mind something your teacher mentioned to me. As we discussed when we first started to meet, the school gives me information from time to time if they feel it will help our work together. I've been told that you had a detention last week, which I understand you were upset about. I'm curious about this as you haven't yet told me about it. I'm wondering why you haven't brought it up here.* Once the client's resistance has been explored, you can go on to say, *Tell me what happened in your own words. Let's think about it together.* If there is no link to make, you may want to bring it up in the last 10 or 15 minutes, saying, for example, *I need to make some time to share something with you* before reminding the client that the school passes information to us when warranted; we can then continue as outlined above.

Another possible modification of the therapy frame concerns the limits of confidentiality. Clients need to feel that the private nature of their thoughts and feelings and of how they use the time are (and will be) respected. However, if a fully collaborative relationship is to be fostered with school staff, the therapist may feel it is necessary and helpful to pass observations and low-level concerns on to relevant staff members. For instance, a therapist may tell a form tutor that the client is currently in a 'very low mood' that might need to be monitored by the school, or that the young person would really benefit from some encouragement from school; both these short examples illustrate how the therapist can share impressions with the school without breaching personal confidentiality.

If feedback like this is to be given on a fairly regular basis, the bounds of confidentiality will need to be discussed with the client and its parameters explained. The therapist might confirm that intimate information of a highly personal nature will not be shared; however, general observations about on-going difficulties or progress made may be passed on. Most therapists agree that reviewing confidentiality now and again is a useful way into exploring related themes such as how difficult it is to be between childhood and adulthood; adolescents want their privacy and independence, but until they are 18, adults have a duty of care for them.

Thinking about referrals

In many schools, the majority of pupils are referred by teaching staff or their head of year. Referrals are made for a host of reasons, ranging from concerns about lack of academic progress and its causes through to difficulties at home or with peers both in and out of school. Young people arrive at the school therapist's door with a seemingly endless variety of concerns, anxieties and preoccupations. Many are referred by the school following some kind of crisis, which may relate to what could be viewed as common life circumstances such as family illness, bereavement, parental separation, becoming part of a reconstituted family or facing frequent losses and changes that are difficult for them to think about and assimilate. There are also those who are referred as a result of their behaviour, which is often a reflection of home circumstances that the school is unaware of.

As therapists, we have an internalised set of theories to draw upon and an understanding of how emotionally potent experiences impact on adolescents. We also have an awareness of the defences which they might erect to avoid the pain triggered by these difficulties. The knowledge and insight gained from our training support us and help guide us in our thinking about the young person's situation. However, encouraging our client to think *with us* may be a protracted process, taking considerable time, care and sensitivity.

Every client referred to us will have a view about attending sessions offered in school, which will be influenced consciously or unconsciously by several factors. These include how they feel about the reason for the referral, their impressions or experience of the school staff member handling the referral and the way the lead-in process itself is managed. An adolescent who is referred because of a family bereavement, for example, may find it potentially less stigmatising to attend as there is an obvious rationale for seeing a therapist and a clear-cut explanation that can be given to others. But the reaction of a pupil who is referred because of a complex home life may fall anywhere on a spectrum of responses from relief through to panic about the possible consequences, including fear of a referral on to social services. Loyalty to family and scepticism about the therapist's role, which could be perceived as that of the 'meddling professional', may result in an initial or intractable negative transference to the therapy and the therapist.

Some clients hold the firm conviction that their referral to therapy is just another form of punishment or a sign that 'something is wrong'. Others may feel acute embarrassment, as if a referral suggests that their vulnerabilities – which they may have thought they had successfully covered up – are visible. They could feel anxious about being perceived by staff and peers alike as 'needy' or being associated with students who are frequently referred to a therapy service, such as those who have obvious problems or who are known to be from a troubled family. It is useful to explore sensitively what each client feels about meeting with you, perhaps saying, *I wonder what you feel about coming to talk to someone like me.* If the young person finds it hard to respond, you might carry on, saying, *Some students are relieved, others embarrassed; some are confused or even angry about being asked to see me, or maybe they have a mix of feelings. What is it like for you? You can be honest and say what you really feel.*

Adolescents are often highly – and painfully – conscious of how they are seen by their peers. Some may be ambivalent about attending sessions in school in case the curiosity of their friends or classmates is aroused and uncomfortable questions are asked. Transference issues and anxieties are unavoidable in any setting, whether a student self-refers or the referral is made by somebody else. In the school setting this can be exacerbated because students attend sessions during class time so that their absences are likely to be noted or commented on. Exploring their response to their allocated time with you can be a useful way into related conversations around what therapy can and cannot offer as well as addressing some common misconceptions about it.

Managing a diverse caseload

It is common for school therapists to see a wider range of students than might be the case in the community or clinic setting. Along with those who will be referred because of obvious distress or known difficulties will be students who come for a limited time, for support when settling into secondary school, for example, or to help with exam anxieties. A mixed range of referrals has its advantages, conveying to the school population that the service is not just for pupils who have a high level of need.

However, such diverse referrals can lead the therapist to feel s/he is being called upon to be all things for all people. The caseload might be so wide in scope that it can initially be difficult to hold a model in mind. Experienced school therapists will usually have built their skills and their confidence so that they can more easily 'shift gears', moving between sessions which sit more comfortably within a traditional child psychotherapy model and those which are one-off consultations or are primarily task-focused. When first working across the spectrum like this, some therapists can feel they are being pulled further and further away from the very kind of approach that drew them to the profession in the first instance. It is useful to remember that what we all internalise is a way of thinking psychoanalytically and that it is the thinking that is core to our work, however we deal with the 'here and now' of the session itself.

Forming a therapeutic alliance

Many young people find it hard to know where to turn for support and understanding. There can be an almost palpable sense of relief when they experience the therapist as someone who can take in and reflect upon their feelings and preoccupations without censure. Such students can find it a wrench to relinquish the sessions when therapy comes time to end. Just as common are those clients who might not have had experiences in infancy and early childhood that enable them to believe in the possibility of forming a good enough relationship. Some of the young people who come to us will have had an early life marked by poverty, parental illness, distressing family changes or a combination of adverse circumstances which remain unnamed and undigested. Often inadequately equipped to deal with the turmoil of their teenage years, they may be difficult to reach. Moreover, even those who do want to engage may lack the ability to describe their experiences or put their feelings and thoughts into words, never mind have the capacity to see things from different perspectives. They may get through life acting and reacting without pause for reflection.

One of the first challenges for the therapist will be to help the young person to experience therapy as meaningful. Engaging an adolescent in therapeutic work depends on the therapist and the client gradually co-creating the kind of reflective space which allows for the young person's past and present experiences to gradually take shape so that, over time, they can be slotted into a narrative whole. Establishing the therapeutic relationship is the first step in this process and is rarely easy. To be too accommodating is to invite contempt; to be too distant can be very frightening for an anxious adolescent. As a starting point, it may be helpful to spend some time reviewing why the young person thinks the school made the referral whether or not this reason matches what the client would like support with. This naturally leads into collaborating on formulating a focus for the sessions which can be revisited throughout the course of the work. A sense of shared confidence and therapeutic intimacy can be built through discussing together what may be most useful to work on from the young person's perspective. Clients may even begin to feel that there might be 'something in this for them', and their curiosity could be aroused about how their problems or difficulties have arisen.

A 'lead-in' period like this goes some way towards helping clients to acclimatise to what may, after all, be a very new and somewhat unnerving, threatening or even frightening experience. Once a focus is agreed, it can be written down or held in mind and referred back to in later sessions, enabling the therapist to comment on the progress made and to involve clients in reflection on how far they've come as well as refining what they still might wish to work on. Checking in on progress on a fairly regular basis provides 'evidence' to clients that the venture is worthwhile and helps them to begin to internalise a more positive image of themselves and of the therapy. Authentic feedback identifying incremental gains can generate a sense of possibility, counteracting feelings of hopelessness and despair.

Some of our clients may use 'stepping stones' on the way to revealing their most personal concerns. For example, a young person might hint at difficulties a 'friend' is having as a useful way to introduce and discuss a potentially embarrassing subject and see how the therapist responds. Others might need to distance themselves from material that makes them feel too vulnerable, exposed or self-conscious and so will talk about a film or a book that features a character or a theme that resonates for them.

In making creative use of the material our clients are willing to bring, we can usually find ways of linking it to the agreed focus of the work while also weaving in important new strands. However, some clients might be less able to sustain a focus and will jump around, skimming over a wide number of subjects. In such instances, we need to try to identify and address the most emotionally potent themes. While time pressures may not allow us to cover as many of their concerns as we might like, we trust that a 'good enough' experience can give young people the hopefulness and confidence to seek therapy again at a later stage in their school career or in adult life.

How difference and diversity can impact on the first phase of work

Differences in culture, educational background, economic status, perceived social status, gender and sexuality will often make themselves felt before the first session even takes place. Every young person referred to us will have conscious and unconscious reactions to, and fantasies about, what is being offered and why, regardless of the reasons given to them by the school. These reactions will be based partially on their assumptions about the therapist's gender and social positioning or, if they do not know who the therapist is, on more general assumptions about the profession as a whole. The media have a powerful role in shaping perceptions; for some, reality television or popular journalism will have provided their only exposure to what therapy may be, who provides it, the kinds of people who may see a therapist and what it is ostensibly for.

There will always be differences to take into consideration even if in some cases they are very nuanced or outweighed by similarities. We'll need to ask ourselves what the implications of these differences might be and how they could potentially affect our feelings about our client and vice versa. We may have to work on managing our responses to those aspects of our client's life that contrast with our own circumstances, choices, religious beliefs or values. Although working cross-culturally is discussed in more depth in Chapter 13, it is important to reflect on the impact of differences within the context of engaging adolescents in the first phase of the work.

Obvious differences can intensify the scepticism of our most anxious young clients and may be best addressed from the beginning. A simple comment to acknowledge difference can be very helpful, such as *You may be wondering how an older, white British woman might have something helpful to say and how we might be able to work together. It's natural to be curious about this.*

When we find that we do have experiences of race, culture or family circumstances in common, we may assume that we understand our client. However, the therapeutic venture is all about being sensitive to difference, catching ourselves when we're making assumptions and enabling the client to develop the capacity to recognise the 'separateness of the other' without feeling too threatened by it. In those instances when we believe we have some knowledge of our client's culture, it is still important to avoid generalisations. If we recall the families we know best in our everyday lives, however similar they may seem to be, each will express values and attitudes in individual ways, conveying a unique version of their cultural or familial heritage. Within all families, every member will enact its 'cultural norms' in different ways. With time, we learn more about our client's family culture, or what might be thought about as 'how things are done' in their family, and we may need to tread carefully so that we are not perceived to be in any way judging them or taking a critical or 'superior' stance. The tone of our conversation and even the language we use may need to be modified if we want to be 'heard'.

Our age is an obvious difference and will influence the transference relationship that evolves. If we are relatively young ourselves, we may trigger an 'older sibling' or even 'peer' transference. In such instances, we need to ensure we are not seen as trying too hard to be on their 'wavelength'. Those of us who are older may find that a parental or 'grandparent' transference evolves, which can have both advantages and drawbacks. For example, we may be experienced as a benevolent figure but at the same time as someone who is out of touch with teenage culture. Others may see us more as teachers or learning mentors or social workers; in such instances, the transference that unfolds will be primarily negative or predominantly positive depending on the young person's previous experiences. Either way it will need to be worked with.

The 'culture' of therapy itself may be the most significant difference our clients face. In the course of school life, young people become used to meeting a range of adults whose role it is to support them (although they may not always be experienced as such). Most are there to teach them or to give advice or guidance in some form. This can make it difficult for our clients to acclimatise to the open-ended, non-directive experience that we may be offering if our training has been psychoanalytically informed. To avoid the discomfort of encountering something unfamiliar, adolescents may try to position us in a role such as the older 'best friend' in whom they can confide. Or they may try to set up a 'doctor-patient' dynamic, attempting to coerce us into offering 'expert' advice. Needing to place us in a familiar role can be the young person's defence against feeling humiliated or judged. We may need to fall in with this dynamic for a short spell, but in a measured way which doesn't take it too far. Transference roles of this type can have a positive spin-off: they may facilitate some difficult discussions of what could otherwise be even more painfully embarrassing personal subjects related to family, friendships, 'crushes', body image, sexuality, sexual identity and so on. In these instances, the therapist may need to inch towards involving the client in a more equal alliance. A gradual shift towards shared thinking can be worked towards over time, making possible a more collaborative relationship with a less pronounced division of power. As we might expect, every client-therapist relationship is different, and each evolves in its own way with a unique pace and rhythm. The presenting problem and initial transference relationship formed is usually only a small part of the story. As the work unfolds and trust builds, more is gradually revealed.

Reflecting on the role of silence in the initial phase of work

Silence denotes a wide range of communications. It might signify anxiety, withdrawal, anger, rebellion, regression to infancy or rejection of the therapist or whatever s/he stands for in that particular moment. It can also convey uncertainty, sadness, embarrassment, confusion, a sense of feeling lost or persecuted, a defence against fear of intrusion or even paranoid feelings. Alternatively, silence might be used to digest an experience or make space for reflection, or perhaps may be experienced as a 'resting place'. Sometimes it can point towards the struggles some young people have to gather their thoughts, or towards their inability (for whatever reason) to put very painful and subtle feelings and experiences into mere words. With more settled clients, the silence might be understood as a shared pause for thought, with perhaps an understanding that this is 'how therapy works'.

Teenagers in general and boys in particular can find silences awkward and anxiety provoking. They may also feel annoyed about what they perceive as the pressure to fill it, not knowing what they are 'supposed to say'. In the early stages of therapy, it can be helpful to acknowledge the feelings and not prolong the young person's discomfort.

While our training might suggest that silence should be respected and thought about rather than broken, the nature and quality of the client's feelings in the room can be a sign that if it is extended, it could deter the client from engaging and thinking with us, or stop the young person from coming to therapy at all. It can be helpful to think in advance of ways in which we might respond to silence, including formulating what we could say to invite reflection on the different meanings and functions of silence such as *You've gone very quiet. I'm wondering what this silence is telling us. Maybe it's difficult to know what to talk about.* Depending on the client's response, the therapist may need to be prepared to help the client get going, saying, for example, *Last week, we were touching on family. I wonder how things have been since we met.* Sometimes we have to keep gently putting ideas out there, perhaps even presenting something to look at together such as a cognitive behavior therapy (CBT)-style worksheet we've downloaded from the internet beforehand or a list of different feeling states that can be explored together.

Managing 'failure' and when things go well

There will always be adolescents who are not ready to engage, no matter how sensitive, compassionate, warm, friendly or insightful the therapist is. If we have a resistant client who feels 'forced' to attend the first session but adamantly refuses to come again, it can be unnerving for us, especially when we are new to the role. We can feel under the spotlight ourselves, as if we've been unsuccessful in our role, and imagine that our perceived 'failure' is visible to all staff and students. Even if we accept that there is nothing more we could do or say to make the relationship with the young person 'take', it is difficult to ever feel at ease with such experiences. When there are several clients who do not wish to work with us, it can amplify our feelings of 'failure' or reinforce the idea that somehow it is our fault. There will, of course, be times when we *have* had a part to play. For example, the client may have unconsciously sensed that we were too close to or too distant from his/her life experience or current circumstances. Perhaps we are carrying unresolved material of our own that got in the way. Or, for one reason or another, our anxieties were perceptible, making it impossible for the client to connect. We all respond to each other in and out of the consulting room on conscious and unconscious levels. Just as in real life, sometimes a 'match' isn't a good one, or there is dissonance that cannot easily be worked with. However, in the secondary school setting the more common reason for lack of engagement is either the adolescent's understandable resistance to thinking or feeling too much or else unfamiliarity with personal encounters of the kind we are offering.

This underlines how reparative and fulfilling the experience can be for both therapist and client when the young person is able to make use of what's on offer. In such instances, it can be truly touching and life affirming to witness at close hand an adolescent discovering previously unknown parts of their identity and naming feelings, gaining some relief from our interpretations or links and making sense of what was previously perplexing or too overwhelming to think about.

Conclusion

Students are commonly referred for therapy when school staff have significant concerns about their home life, their relationships in school or their poor academic achievement – and often for all of these reasons. Teachers want to be able to deliver their lessons effectively and to create a mutually respectful culture in their classroom. Having a disruptive, disengaged, anxious or depressed teenager in a lesson can be at best frustrating and at worst demoralising for the whole class. The pupil who is asked to see the school therapist may initially resent the intervention and can be prickly, hostile or uncooperative. All of us working in the field, no matter how experienced we are, have had times – and, inevitably, will continue to – when we've felt hopelessly deskilled, wondering what on earth we can possibly do to help our young clients. Talking to trusted peers and to a supervisor can help sustain us in these moments. As well, we usually have at least a few students coming to us who are receptive to what we have to offer and are appreciative of the support.

Regardless of the level of engagement, the school will want the therapist to try to address the concerns which prompted the referral in the first place and will be keen for sessions to be on-going. As we have illustrated, the therapist working in this context will need to develop the skills required to hold in mind the school's reasons for the referral alongside what the client would like support with, sometimes being called upon to balance very different expectations. Therapists often need to be much more flexible than they might initially anticipate; however, we do not lose sight of our main skills, which include our capacity to manage tensions, hold anxiety and carry on thinking.

Working with adolescents is at one and the same time hugely stimulating, anxiety provoking, frustrating, confusing, deskilling, enlivening and never without challenges. From our personal experience we all know how complex negotiating this phase of the life cycle can be and how important it is to have someone who can help us navigate unknown terrain. Some of us hope to offer young people the kind of support we never had ourselves or provide them with something akin to what we found most useful in our teenage years. If we build the resilience and skills to tolerate and work with the negative transference which often makes itself powerfully felt in one way or another when working with adolescents, we will have much to offer. All of us based in schools are inspired by adolescents who show great courage and take what can feel like a significant risk in stepping into something completely new by coming to see us and engaging in the process of fostering a therapeutic relationship.

Study questions

Dealing with 'worst case' first sessions

Vignette 1

As Sade (aged 14) sat down across from her school therapist for her first session, she said, 'I didn't ask to come here – I want to go back to my lesson. This is rubbish!' *What would you say?*

Vignette 2

In the autumn term, the school therapist was told that Marta (aged 15) had learned over the summer of her mother's cancer diagnosis and it was thought she would not live beyond the spring term. This was all the information given to the therapist. In the first session, the therapist explained to Marta why the school had suggested they meet. Marta said she hardly saw her mother. She'd lived with her paternal grandmother since she was a baby and hated her mother. Marta said her mother was a drug user and no good and that no one in the family wanted anything to do with her. *What would you say?*

Vignette 3

Krishnan (aged 16) had to be collected by his therapist for his first session. He sat down and stared mutely at her as she gave a short introduction as to why they were meeting. Krishnan looked blankly at her and seemed not to take in what she was saying. A simple question about whether or not he'd been told about their session met with no response. *How would you deal with this?*

Sample responses

Vignette 1

One way of responding would be to reply, *It is hard to be expected to talk about yourself with someone like me who's a complete stranger. It can feel like 'rubbish' to start with because it takes time to develop trust and to discover how our time together can be used. Why do you think the school recommended that we meet?* If she responds only by turning away or ignoring you, you can go on to describe in positive and helpful terms the reason the school gave you, for example: *Let me tell you what I understand. The school thinks you may be unhappy here some of the time, and they'd like you to have a better experience. They know you get annoyed in class now and again and can feel treated unfairly by some of your teachers. Does this sound like an accurate description to you?* Depending on the reply you can open this conversation up further, or you may need to take a different angle, going on to say something like, *It may feel like coming here is a form of punishment. Perhaps it's hard to believe that I'm here to help. I want to get to know you better and to find out about what's going well in your life, too. I'd be interested to hear if you have a favourite subject or a favourite time of the school day?*

Vignette 2

You may want to say, *I was given very little information by the school and only know your mother is seriously ill. The school prefers pupils to have the chance to tell me what's most important to them. From what you've said, it seems that you're closer to your grandmother than to your mother. When someone in our family has an addiction, it's very disappointing and hurtful. It's as if they haven't cared enough about us to stop. Maybe if they get ill, we feel they've brought it on themselves and that they even deserve it. It's hard to be sympathetic and to remember that people usually use drugs or alcohol to get rid of painful feelings. Does any of this make sense to you?* You might add at some point, *This is a place where you can say whatever you want. We can focus on what you choose to talk about. We'll make time to think about good things in your life as well as some of the challenges. I recommend students come for a couple of sessions so that they can see what this is like before they make a final decision about whether or not it will be helpful.*

Vignette 3

A way forward could be to describe out loud how it can feel coming to a first session. For example, you might say, *Often people just don't know what to expect or what's expected of them when it's suggested they come and see me. They can feel self-conscious, embarrassed, bored or secretly angry about it. Most students are used to teachers or other adults telling them what to do. Coming here and being asked to talk can feel quite unfamiliar and uncomfortable. I'd like to get to know you a little. Maybe you could start by telling me about your time in this school. Did you come here in Year 7? . . . What was the move from primary to secondary school like for you? . . . Do you still have some of the same friends from primary school? . . . What do you miss most from your childhood years? What's it like for you to be 16 years old?* and so on. Safe, open questions like this could help your client feel more at ease and less under the spotlight.

Reference

French, Lyn and Klein, Reva (eds) (2012) *Therapeutic Practice in Schools: Working with the Child Within*. London: Routledge.

Chapter 6

Shaping the beginning and ending phases of school-based therapy

Reflecting on assessment and evaluation processes

Angie Doran and Lyn French

Understanding when, why and how therapy sessions are helpful not only ensures that clients are best supported but can also serve to build an evidence base which may strengthen the case for continuing funding for such services in the future. It is also important to give careful thought to why some adolescents are not able to make use of the sessions offered to them. A Space for Support, based in the London borough of Hackney, conducted a piece of research over a three-year period in partnership with the Centre for Psychoanalytic Studies at Essex University, which contributes to our knowledge of these areas of therapeutic practice (Doran, 2013). The study looked at how therapists in training, experienced therapists and senior practitioners shape the beginning and ending phases of their work with adolescents in the school context, including whether or not they identify a focus with their clients, as well as working with the school's reasons for the referral, and how any goals that are formulated might be reviewed at the end of the work. The findings from this study confirmed much of what might have been expected: there is no 'one-size-fits-all' way of working with young people, but there are good reasons for the therapist to actively frame and guide the adolescent client's entry into and exit from therapy. This framework for starting and concluding therapy may include using beginning and ending questionnaires that either are developed by the therapist or are in the public domain.

While the vast majority of school-based therapists are stimulated by the challenges implicit in our work and are committed both personally and ethically to providing a service that is meaningful, valued, effective and reality based, most of us have had to process the losses inherent in letting go of an idealised picture of what we thought our therapeutic relationships would be like. Of course, therapy with adolescents can be everything that it originally set out to be. We may find ourselves in the privileged position of working with clients who are emotionally receptive and psychologically minded. They may be able to bear uncertainty, have the capacity to make links and feel motivated enough to keep coming back as well as being willing to try to make changes in and outside of the consulting room. However, when working in inner-city secondary schools, such clients are usually the exception rather than the norm. Our chances of making connections with the young people we see are often limited, especially as the majority are sent to us and self-referrals are less common. We need to be able to find a way through to clients within a couple of sessions at the most; otherwise, our opportunity to engage them can be lost.

Most school therapists work very hard in the initial phase, using the first few sessions to sensitively gather background information while also trying to build a good enough therapeutic relationship to better ensure that the client will continue coming. The majority of therapists, especially those who are psychodynamically trained, know that beginnings and endings are particularly resonant, and many of us have felt – or even still feel – varying degrees of discomfort about the idea of bringing in questionnaires at the start and finish of the work, many of which include grading responses on a scale of 1 to 10.

However, using questionnaires or frameworks needn't be intrusive or obstructive. The therapist can draw on her or his psychoanalytic skills in the process, closely observing clients and, when relevant, commenting on their unspoken responses to this approach as well as making low-key transference interpretations. A main objective of our practice is to sensitively co-construct a therapeutic alliance that is rooted in the relational experience; using a printed questionnaire to scaffold this process does not have to be detrimental to this task. In fact, many therapists working with adolescents have found the opposite to be the case. In inner-city schools in particular, many adolescents come from a home culture where thinking and talking about personal issues or feelings are not valued. If plunged straight into client-led therapy, some young people can feel out of their depth and may even refuse to come back. A printed questionnaire that is gone through with the therapist may feel less alienating and can seem to have more in common with the school conventions teenagers are used to. It can ease their way into the culture of therapy, providing a safe and known place from which to start.

Referring back to the questionnaire at various points in the course of the work can aid the task of identifying insights gained and the resulting changes. During the last phase of therapy, the initial aims as well as progress made can be reviewed. Using the beginning therapy questionnaire alongside an ending questionnaire can support this. Tracking incremental progress and being able to observe small yet highly significant changes will have a deeper significance than simply positively affirming the client; the therapist creates a more authentic and 'whole' portrait of the client comprising both strengths and vulnerabilities, which are conveyed over time both verbally and through 'felt communication'. The picture the therapist carefully composes and holds in mind is unconsciously registered and internalised by the young person, providing something of inestimable value to take away at the end of the therapy.

Conveying the value of a therapy service

Every school therapist will need to work out for themselves how they feel about assessment and evaluation structures, including their own transference to paper forms or to the very concept of measuring outcomes. There are those who place a high value on the experience of the therapeutic relationship in its own right and see it as the primary agent of change. For such therapists, the idea of introducing frameworks for the beginning and ending stages of the work is viewed not only as unnecessary but as hindering rather than helping the relational and unconscious processes. They believe that school staff will intuitively and experientially know if the therapist's input is making a difference. To jump on the 'evaluation band-wagon' may be seen as misdirected and something to be avoided at all costs. At the other end of the spectrum are the school therapists who feel quite strongly that our profession needs to be able to prove its worth and that its value must be evidence based rather than anecdotal. Many therapists will fall somewhere in between these two positions, taking into consideration what might best sit within their school environment as well as what they feel comfortable with.

There are a number of factors that will need to be thought about when planning how to structure a service or how to add an evaluation process to an existing provision. These are likely to include:

- how long the therapist has worked in the school;
- whether or not they are employed directly by the school or by a therapy or counselling organisation working in the school;
- the quality and nature of their relationships with school staff;
- whether or not the school has a strict culture of setting and measuring targets for other support services;
- how the leadership team views the purpose and function of the therapy input.

In addition to how we promote the efficacy of our service to school staff, we must consider how we convey its value to the pupils with whom we work. Using some kind of beginning therapy form which can be referred back to at the end of the work can signify to the adolescent that we have faith in our practice and in the capacity for change.

The initial phase of therapy

Most school therapists carry out some form of assessment, including:

- gathering background information, which may be minimal or non-existent at the referral stage;
- forming an initial impression of the young person and their underlying issues;
- gauging the degree of the client's distress or disturbance;
- assessing motivation;
- getting a sense of the client's capacity for psychological mindedness and potential for mentalisation;
- assessing the possibility of risk.

All of this information can help to establish a baseline to return to at the end for evaluation purposes. Embedded in this process will be attempts to spark the young person's curiosity and set the scene for a collaborative working relationship. It is common for therapists to build the assessment process into the first few sessions, which is often described as an induction phase, rather than conduct an assessment as a stand-alone exercise or as a block of appointments. More experienced therapists may weave sensitive exploration seamlessly into the first phase of the work, while still allowing the therapeutic relationship to unfold at the client's own pace. If information is not naturally forthcoming, it is likely that carefully worded observations will be used to elicit background information at the same time as making space available for the client to take the lead. An example of this would be saying to the client, 'You haven't mentioned your father yet. I wonder what this is telling us about his place in your life.'

Often the young person, who more often than not has been referred to counselling by the school, arrives feeling they come with a negative label given to them by the school. It is important for therapists to take note of the school's reasons for the referral and to hold those concerns in mind. But it is of equal value both for the formation of the therapeutic alliance and for the purposes of tracking changes to give time and consideration to the client's own perception of what they need help with or how they feel sessions might be of benefit to them. They may be preoccupied with very different issues from those highlighted by the school. Helping the young person see that you are there to understand their experiences from their point of view is the first step to building trust and developing a therapeutic alliance.

Research tells us (Cooper, 2008: 65–68) that well-considered induction procedures contribute to reduced dropout and less anxiety about therapy, increasing both overall attendance and positive outcomes. Engaging adolescent clients in therapy can sometimes be difficult and needs to be thought about with professional peers as well as in supervision. For example, all therapists – even established ones – need to consider what best suits their service, the school it is based in and the clients being seen.

Psychodynamically informed school therapists have traditionally used free-flowing, responsive conversation that takes place within the unfolding therapist-client relationship as the basis for their assessment process, with the underlying aim of creating a fertile ground for unconscious material to emerge. For many, the use of a written assessment and outcome evaluation procedure *within* the session itself is thought to obstruct or distort the transference and divert attention from the relational dimension of the work. These are valid concerns and need to be carefully thought about by each practitioner. Increasingly, however, therapists are choosing (or being required by their organisation or school) to incorporate written assessment processes into their practice.

Standardised questionnaires

There are a number of report forms in use and available online that elicit information directly from clients as a way of building a picture of their current circumstances and establishing a context for the work. The most commonly referred to are the Achenbach Youth Self-Report, the Goodman Strength and Difficulties Questionnaire (SDQ), the Young Person's Clinical Outcomes in Routine Evaluation (YP-CORE), the Adolescent Well-being Scale, the Health of the Nation Outcome Scales for Children and Adolescents (HoNOSCA), and the Goal Based Outcomes Measure (GBOM) developed by the Child and Mental Health Service (CAMHS) Outcome Research Consortium (CORC).

Including report forms, such as the ones listed above, in the first phase of psychodynamically informed work with a new client requires professional skill and confidence. In addition, the commonly used forms raise a number of points that are worth noting:

- Outdated or inappropriate language may be inhibiting for the client.
- Forms can be dense and lengthy but at the same time may omit important areas that need to be thought about at the start, such as whether or not there are risk factors as well as the client's personal strengths and what they want to get from the experience.
- The opportunity for the client and therapist to set goals and identify a focus for the work together is often missing, which makes it more difficult to reinforce the collaborative nature of therapy.
- As the more standard forms are not usually completed with the therapist, there is no opportunity to give the client the chance to provide a fuller picture or to explore in more depth the answers provided.
- Short forms may be experienced by young people as simply 'box-ticking exercises' and could miss deeper difficulties as well as convey an unhelpful message about what therapy might offer.
- The standardised forms offer no opportunity to gather the client's life history, and the therapist may have only patchy or incorrect information provided by the school at the time of the referral.
- One key developmental task for all teenagers includes working out 'who they are'; often their identity is in flux, and being asked to give what can come across as a snapshot account of themselves may be counter-intuitive or even confusing.

Using a framework for the beginning and ending phases of school-based therapy with adolescents

School therapists know that adolescent clients referred to them may not be at all motivated. Quite the contrary – they can be suspicious and distrusting of what is on offer. On arrival at the first session, the young person may be unclear about why they were asked to attend in the first instance and what the therapist can and cannot provide. They may not even be certain they want or need emotional support at this time.

Many young people may not be ready to take the lead at the start of therapy and can benefit from being gently eased into the process. Using a questionnaire or some kind of prepared framework in the first few sessions can helpfully function as a containing structure for those clients unfamiliar with talking about themselves, giving the sessions a format to which they can more easily relate. At A Space for Support we have developed questionnaires that guide the therapist and client more fully than many standard forms, so that they become a frame on which to begin building the therapeutic alliance. Using age-appropriate language, the questionnaires contain a mix of scaling and open-ended questions, which offer opportunities for the therapist to contextualise the therapy; open up discussion around the client's concerns; explore sensitive issues, including risk factors; identify a focus for the work with the young person; uncover the client's strengths; and gather the client's life history information (French, 2013). Even those who are more receptive to the process can gain from going through a paper questionnaire with the therapist in the first few sessions. The process of providing background information in a guided conversation supports clients by helping them to find words to describe their experiences and to start to identify some of their feelings. Through this exchange, they can begin to give a more coherent shape to their life story.

Filling out a questionnaire or, alternatively, being asked guided questions planned by the therapist beforehand can also convey an important message about the nature and culture of therapy. Throughout the initial phase, the therapist will have opportunities to clarify how the sessions work by making observations along the way, such as 'This is something we'll want to return to and think about in more detail'; 'Maybe what you feel about this will become clearer over time'; and so on. The therapist can also acknowledge that talking about one's personal life and intimate feelings is never easy, such as 'Sometimes talking about family can feel disloyal – it's important to remember that we want to understand feelings and relationships, not assign blame'; 'It can feel awkward or embarrassing to reveal feelings here with me – it takes time to feel more comfortable with this aspect of our work'; 'I'm not trying to pry or be intrusive. I simply want to understand your situation better. If you can be honest and open with me, it will help us make more sense of what's going on for you'; and so forth.

Use of a beginning therapy questionnaire can be stretched over a number of sessions as asking simple questions about family and relationships can open up important conversations. The therapist has the choice of how far or how deep to take the exploration in that moment in time. It might be most helpful to continue or, alternatively, to remind the client that there will be more opportunities to return to the topic under discussion in future, saying, for example, 'This sounds like an important relationship – I'm sure there will be opportunities to come back to it.'

Some therapists introduce questionnaires later on, perhaps at the end of the first term of work, as a way of summing up and recording what is now known, filling in any gaps and agreeing a focus or setting goals for the next phase of work. There is no 'right' or 'wrong' way to use a questionnaire. Hopefully this initial work will set the scene for the on-going therapy, and over time the young person will relax into the relationship, feeling increasingly comfortable about bringing material to explore and gradually taking over the lead in the sessions.

The ending phase of therapy

Although psychoanalytic theory highlights the importance of mourning past losses through working through endings, research into short-term psychodynamic therapy (Fortune, 1987; Marx and Gelso, 1987; Quintana and Holahan, 1992) reveals that more often than not client and therapist do not experience the ending of therapy as dominated by loss. Marx and Gelso (1987) found that the majority of clients use descriptions such as 'calm', 'alive', 'good' and 'healthy' when describing the concluding phase of their therapy. Similarly, in his study Fortune (1987) found that positive reactions in clients (for example, a sense of pride and self-accomplishment) were more common than negative reactions (such as anger at having to end, discomfort around re-experiencing previous losses or feeling more intense moments of separation anxiety in general). Interestingly, research has identified that difficulties associated with endings seem to be closely related to the quality of the therapeutic relationship rather than to loss *per se*. Research by Quintana and Holahan (1992) suggests that therapists find it more challenging to end with clients who have not experienced positive change during the work. This research found that the final phase evoked positive feelings when therapists made preparations for finishing with clients, such as thinking about the course of the work in supervision and identifying changes that could be fed back to the client; using the ending phase to review with the client the course the therapy had taken; and processing the client's emotional reactions to the ending, both in the sessions and outside in writing process notes and in supervision. It seems quite likely, then, that the therapist's careful preparations for and management of the final phase can have as much impact on the client's experience of the ending as any past losses may have.

When it comes time to end, the original questionnaire can be brought out or simply referred back to verbally. Both the therapist and client can note the progress each has observed relating to the aims they jointly formulated at the start as well as any other gains made. An ending therapy questionnaire can be used to support this process, and a balance struck between exploring emotionally potent themes and making space to reflect on positive outcomes.

While school therapists usually aim to have thought about and prepared for endings with their clients there will be unplanned-for endings to manage as well. For instance, the impulsivity of adolescents means that they can suddenly stop of their own accord and refuse to return. Or the school may withdraw them because of exam preparation or important course work. Some students move home or school or are excluded. In such instances, it may be possible for the school to pass on a note from the therapist to the student that acknowledges the ending and goes some way towards bringing the work to a close. There will also be those times when the ending will need to be processed in supervision as the therapist is likely to be left with quite powerful feelings when there is no opportunity for a last face-to-face meeting.

When we do have the opportunity to work through an ending, specific acknowledgement of the client's move towards more mature functioning, along with the therapist's affirmation of even incremental progress made, will contribute to the young person's positive regard for the therapy and leave them with a sense of developmental gains. For some clients, engagement with therapy may be the single most important achievement of any kind that they have had, or are able to have, in the school environment. Knowing that they have had a part to play in sustaining a relationship over time might leave the adolescent with a deep and abiding sense of accomplishment. Endings can offer an experience of letting something go and moving on, a vote of confidence in the future and the recognition of the beginning of the next new phase of life.

One of the most important transformative experiences for clients during the last phase of therapy is the 'de-idealisation' of the process. We know that many clients admire and even exaggerate what they perceive as the therapist's 'expert' knowledge and higher-level personal skills. They may have idealised what therapy can achieve, which could reflect unrealistic expectations in more general terms of what life can offer. It is increasingly thought to be important that clients end therapy with a reality-based view of themselves, the therapist and the work they have been doing together. 'De-idealisation' is a step that clients need to take so that they can come to understand and value their own role in the process and have a belief in their capacity to continue the work of therapy after the ending. Research suggests that some therapists may intuitively 'de-idealise' in a number of ways such as by pointing out specific examples of the client's contribution to the therapy, selectively disclosing more of their personal reactions to clients when appropriate, transforming the structure of the client–therapist relationship so that it is more egalitarian and responding to clients' inquiries with less interpretation (Quintana and Holahan, 1992). Quintana (1993) draws useful parallels between 'de-idealisation' in therapy and the process of 'de-idealisation' that takes place in healthy adolescent development. All adolescents need to achieve a more realistic view of themselves and of their parents as people with shortcomings as well as strengths. Young people have a better capacity to rely on their own resources when they can accurately appraise their own abilities and self-agency while also coming to appreciate the limits of parental control on their lives. Therapists can help them with this developmental task by noting in specific terms how they have improved in, for example, their capacity to stay with difficult feelings (e.g. by tolerating anxiety and uncertainty); thinking creatively; taking on board constructive feedback; making links by being reflective; and finding the words to describe what they are trying to convey. Using an end-of-therapy questionnaire or protocol can help to emphasise the development of relational skills and reflective capacities in a meaningful way, further reinforcing the internalisation process.

The fact that the therapist remains in the school following the last session and is seen in passing by ex-clients is sometimes thought to confuse and compromise the symbolically significant finality of ending in psychotherapy. But perhaps it can be viewed as a positive contribution to working with teenage clients. The developmental tasks of adolescent years bring to mind Margaret Mahler's work on separation and individuation. Mahler (1972: 337) describes the infant's early experience of the mother as a base to which he or she can repeatedly return. Similarly, the adolescent may need the reassurance that there is a safe and familiar 'mother/therapist' to whom they can return in future if need be. According to a report published in 2011 on counselling in schools, and in support of this view, flexibility and accessibility are noted by both staff and students as positive attributes of school-based services (Cooper, 2011: 10–11). Bearing this in mind, many therapists offer adolescents review appointments, especially if the school lets them know that renewed support might be viewed favourably by the student.

The completion process may include feeding information back to the school. Views on this vary; each therapist will need to work out in supervision and with key staff in the school what, if any, reporting back he or she will do. Some therapists feel that sessions with their clients should be completely confidential, running in parallel to their life in school, functioning very much as a 'stand-alone' service. Others hold the view that feeding back via a written report on each client builds a strong evidence base for their work and raises awareness across the school staff team of what therapy can and cannot achieve. A detailed example of an end of therapy report is provided in *Therapeutic Practice in Schools: Working with the Child Within* (French and Klein, 2012). In brief, therapists who do write reports often include the following information:

- the reason for the referral
- the number of sessions attended
- basic or more detailed information on the client's family
- general therapeutic aims
- the therapist's impressions of the client
- aims and goals which were met
- aims and goals originally identified which were not met and why
- contextualisation for a premature or unexpected ending
- if applicable, recommendations for future support or intervention.

Conclusion

Providing a therapy service in a secondary school is always a creative undertaking. No two schools are exactly alike, and therapists will need to develop their provision in line with their school's culture and ethos. Whether or not a structure such as a questionnaire is used to shape the beginning and ending phases of the work, the majority of therapists give time and space to planning and reflecting on how best to manage the entry into therapy and how to scaffold the completion process. This thinking takes place in supervision, in personal therapy where feelings about beginnings and endings and therapeutic processes in general can be explored, in conversation with professional peers and in collaboration with school staff. Although we may choose to adapt our practice when working with adolescents, psychoanalytic theory provides us with a way of thinking which stands us in good stead. However we structure the actual sessions, we try to take into account the impact of emotionally potent past and present experiences and continue to look for signs of unconscious expression, making best use of whatever material our client brings to us.

Study Questions

- What are your initial reactions to using beginning and ending questionnaires in sessions with adolescents?
- What are your own experiences of 'form-filling' or completing questionnaires? In what ways do these experiences colour your response to using questionnaires in the therapy setting?
- If you don't use a questionnaire to structure the beginning and ending phases of your work with clients, how might you shape these stages of your work?
- What anxieties come up for you around providing school staff with evidence that your work with most adolescents makes a difference?
- If you were to give your school written reports on your clients, what would you include?

References

Cooper, M. (2008) *Essential Research Findings in Counselling and Psychotherapy: The Facts are Friendly*. London: Sage.

Cooper, M. (2011) *Evaluation of the Welsh school-based counselling strategy—executive summary*, Welsh Government Social Research.

Doran, A. (2013) 'Beginnings and endings: a study of how UK secondary school-based psychodynamic therapists at different stages of their careers approach initial and final phase practice', unpublished doctoral thesis, Centre for Psychoanalytic Studies, University of Essex.

Fortune, A. E. (1987) 'Grief only? Client and social worker reactions to termination', *Clinical Social Work Journal*, 15: 159–171.

French, L. (2013) 'Adapting our psychodynamic practice: using protocols and questionnaires developed by A Space in the secondary school setting', unpublished paper available online at www.inivacreativelearning.org.

French, L. and Klein, R. (2012) *Therapeutic Practice in Schools: Working with the Child Within*. London: Routledge.

Mahler, M. S. (1972) 'On the first three phases of the separation-individuation process', *International Journal of Psychoanalysis*, 53: 333–338.

Marx, J. A. and Gelso, C. J. (1987) 'Termination of individual counseling in a university counseling center', *Journal of Counseling Psychology*, 34: 3–9.

Quintana, S. M. (1993) 'Towards an expanded and updated conceptualization of termination: implications for short-term, individual psychotherapy', *Professional Psychology: Research and Practice*, 24(4): 426–432.

Quintana, S. M. and Holahan, W. (1992) 'Termination in short-term counseling: comparison of successful and unsuccessful cases', *Journal of Counseling Psychology*, 39: 299–305.

Part II

Common themes

Chapter 7

Understanding anger

Stefania Putzu-Williams

Much has been written about the sources of anger and its conscious and unconscious forms of expression. Anger often covers up feelings which are more vulnerable-making and therefore may be harder to acknowledge, such as fear of rejection or of loss in all its aspects (including loss of face and the attendant humiliation), sadness, depression, envy or jealousy. Anger directed inwards may be used as a means of protecting others from what is, in fantasy, murderous rage. The feelings and mental states associated with anger are many; however, the term is often used colloquially as a catch-all description, and its deeper roots, often dating back to infancy, may be overlooked.

School staff frequently refer young people for what they describe as 'anger issues', and there are valid reasons for this. Such pupils can be difficult to contain in class as their feelings might be easily triggered, or they may use provocative behaviour to make others feel and act out their anger on their behalf. An angry adolescent can stir up unconscious fears of latent hostility being unleashed resulting in destructive mayhem. School staff may hold out the hope, unspoken yet conveyed, that the therapist can step in and help the young person by offering what is now commonly called 'anger management', a descriptive label which has become popular, perhaps because it reduces the unconscious threat that uncontained anger poses. Part of our role in school includes raising awareness of the challenges and complexities of adolescence in general and of the source and nature of anger in particular. In doing so, we both manage the expectations of staff and help them to understand their students from a different, more psychoanalytically informed perspective. This chapter aims to deepen the therapist's understanding of the unconscious feelings and mental states underlying anger and to aid thinking about what to do and say in sessions with adolescents.

The roots of anger

Students are often referred to the school therapist when their anger is acted out against others or directed towards themselves; either way, their negative behaviour captures the attention of others. Some adolescents behave as if they were intent on keeping their teachers interested or simply ensuring that the adults around them notice them. Acting-out behaviour as described by Winnicott (1956/1984) alerts adults to the need to intervene and will frequently mask the adolescent's yearning for connection. Winnicott understood the child's antisocial act as an expression of hope and object-seeking; such a child still believes in the possibility of being seen, understood and related to. 'Attention seeking' often has a negative connotation in schools, but it is not unusual to find that, even in the first encounter with the therapist, such an adolescent shows a desire to be understood by someone and seeks relief from feeling unnoticed, invisible and rejected.

Acting out of anger can have different origins, including unacknowledged and unprocessed anxiety and rage dating back to infancy or early childhood. Trauma has been recognised as playing "a significant role in the psychogenesis of violence" (Fonagy 2001). With regard to emotionally and sexually abused children, Fonagy (2004, p. 40) cites research showing that their sense of shame "is replaced by intense rage that is apparently generated to restore the vulnerable sense of self". Adolescents who are maltreated in childhood, have witnessed domestic violence or have suffered physical abuse in an environment where control and safety are usually absent, often present in school as hyper-vigilant and sometimes become overactive and act out in lessons. Their need to be watched or witnessed by others can be seen as an attempt to master an earlier or current trauma through repetition. They have not learned how to deal with conflict and negative feelings without over-reacting and seeking immediate discharge through 'fight-or-flight' responses. Mental health issues or addictions in parents are inevitably significant, possibly resulting in love and care being only intermittently on offer and often linked to insecure attachments, impulsivity and difficulty in regulating emotions.

Those adolescents who tend to externalise and act out their feelings come to counselling highly defended and struggle to think or talk about themselves. They may present in the room as monosyllabic, empty or sullen and angry, or look depressed. Sometimes it feels as if their story cannot be told because of internalised shame, which may be rooted in family secrets that feel almost impossible to reveal. They resist even the most sensitive attempts at engaging with the therapeutic process; it's as if they imagine that if they allow themselves to think, they risk having to acknowledge the damage they have both inflicted and experienced, expressed in the unspoken questions: *What have I done to myself and to others?* and *What has been done to me?* As well, they risk making contact with the loss and emotional pain associated with unbearable feelings and experiences. It is then difficult to allow good experiences to flourish, hope to be kindled, and good things in general to be taken in (Williams 2004). They also fear that the therapist will want to make them dependent and weak, and so they will often defend against this by telling us they don't see how 'just talking' can make things better.

Becoming angry is experienced by some young people as something happening outside of their control. As discussed by Shuttleworth (1991, p. 38), Bick (1968) describes how they seem to have learned early on to use their bodies and physical movement to hold themselves together, rather than seeking or depending on human contact and a loving mind to contain and hold them. This can lead to the development of what has been described as "a 'second skin' formation" (Bick 1968, p. 115). It is as if these young people literally have an outer skin which functions as a protective barrier, making it impossible for them to be 'touched' inside and thus guarding them against vulnerable-making and even good feelings (Shuttleworth 1991, p. 38). Such children and young people are characterised by pseudo-independence and rigidity in their ways of dealing with the emotional impact of everyday life and show little evidence of having internalised the experience of being 'held together' physically and emotionally. An increasingly common example is the large number of adolescents and younger children who literally grow up in their bedrooms with console games, often playing violent games meant for adults only, and with access to 'X-rated' television shows or the internet (including to pornography) without much parental supervision.

Bereavement and loss can have a part to play as well. If unprocessed, a form of agitated depression with outbursts of anger can dominate. Thus, underlying depression and/or raw grief in the adolescent or in a parent may be at the root of uncontained anger. A young person with an unresponsive mother, for example, can direct anger against her to try to 'revitalize' and shake her from her depression and numbness. Or a looked-after adolescent might use anger to cover up the trauma of having a birth mother who was unable to care for him or her.

If in the grip of manic defences, by contrast, the young person will insist that 'everything is fine', that nothing really matters and that the issues linked to their anger can be ignored. This kind of manic superiority serves to deny the qualities and importance of the other and to cut off awareness of any dependency needs. Instead, a sense of triumph is felt which, in fantasy, gives the young person what he or she sees as 'the right' to control others from an elevated position and to try to make them dependent on him or her.

Others (fortunately not many) may go a little further. Taking pleasure in their own aggressive actions with shameless excitement, they may boast about being part of a gang. They might talk of bullying, mugging or stealing and appear compassionless, triumphant and superior. The therapist is expected to witness and to be shocked by their stories. Or adolescents may try to coerce the therapist into doubting their accounts or minimising them even though the therapist may know unconsciously that there is an element of truth to what she or he is hearing. The therapist can be left feeling confused, hopeless, vulnerable, held in contempt, assaulted and rejected by the client and ultimately outraged. In such instances, we might ask ourselves if we are witnessing an adolescent's momentary loss of empathy or a more established state. Making sense of such a client takes patience. If the therapist can tolerate what can seem like a persistent negative transference and work with it, even the very angry client can be 'held' and progress made.

In the therapy room

Despite their reputation amongst peers for being tough and fearless, some angry adolescents come with very negative self-beliefs and an image of themselves as bad and useless. Even if they acknowledge that they are worried about their violent feelings and thoughts, they may say they don't need therapy because they have 'their mates', or they might want to be taught 'skills' to manage their outbursts. If asked why they think they become angry, their reply could well be offhand; for example, they may say, 'no reason', which might be intended to convey that they don't want to talk to you or anyone else about it. Or they may place the source of their anger outside themselves and claim it is usually triggered by someone else's 'random' and 'meaningless' provocation. When faced with such resistance and ambivalence, the therapist might choose to include in the introductory sessions attempts to normalise some of the adolescent's experiences and feelings by saying something like *Everyone, whatever their age, will experience at times strong feelings such as anger, jealousy, hatred, violent and even murderous urges in varying degrees, depending on personal experiences and circumstances. We all have feelings – it's what makes us human. What we do with those feelings is what counts. We are all responsible for how we act or speak.*

It can be helpful to introduce the idea of parts of the self so adolescents learn that none of us are defined solely by one aspect of our personality. We could say, for instance, *When we're angry, we might lose touch with that part of ourselves that wants to be liked or wishes to be closer to others. Or we may be out of touch with the part of ourselves that is actually frightened or sad.* We may also want to talk to them about the ways in which our experience of ourselves changes depending on whom we are with, and what the social circumstances are. We all have different ways of relating and different affective moods or patterns of thinking, depending on whom we're with, what our perceived status or identity is at that moment (for example, are we equals, or is there a power or class difference or a difference in position?), what our past and current history is with those we're engaging with and so on. A sense of self and one's own identity develops and evolves through relational exchanges and encounters. We learn about ourselves and develop new takes on our world through seeing how we are perceived by others and hearing about how they experience, and make sense of life.

When one is working with adolescents, it can be useful to combine psychoeducational observations that help young people to understand their internal states and begin to see how the personality develops along with challenging their assumptions and negative beliefs. This kind of approach can help adolescents to make sense of themselves and their behaviour and provide them with ways to think so that they are less likely to act out.

It is important to support young people in changing their view of themselves from being 'all bad' to seeing themselves as someone who has been through much in their short lives and is hurting inside. Adolescents who, as described by Bick (1968), have learned to project the social appearance of a personality without actually developing any sense of an inner mental space and internal resources can experience themselves more fully and meaningfully if they improve their self-esteem and self-image. We have a role to play in facilitating this by focusing on their inner strengths and competencies, their positive qualities and their skills as well as gently challenging their negative perceptions of themselves and their world.

Sometimes adolescents will find it difficult to express themselves in words and can struggle with the less structured approach of client-led therapy. Some school therapists make toys and even a doll's house available and encourage the use of free play, drawing or modelling with plasticine. Worksheets either created by the therapist or printed from the internet which facilitate emotional literacy can also be used. Emotional learning cards featuring culturally diverse contemporary artists and emotionally and psychologically resonant questions have, for example, been co-published by A Space and Iniva (Institute of International Visual Arts) and can be found at www.inivacreativelearning.org.

Other practices such as relaxation techniques, mindfulness and the Calm Place exercises can be introduced with some clients. Therapists can also give students useful websites on emotional health and mental health as well as other self-help sites for young people, with information on general services and on specific issues such as exam anxiety, controlling anger, sleep disturbances, self-harm and so on, that they can access themselves. As well, cognitive behavioural therapy (CBT) techniques may be used also by psychodynamically trained therapists as an extra tool to explore and challenge self-beliefs along with identifying the triggers for anger. CBT approaches can help to introduce the idea that we all interpret our feelings and invest them with meanings, which lead us to form core beliefs about ourselves. In addition, they can help illustrate how our thoughts influence our actions and other people's actions. One of the aims of therapy is to facilitate a shift away from acting out aggressively towards seeking meaning, tolerating vulnerabilities, accepting dependency needs and developing empathy and compassion, along with aspirations and hopes for the future.

Triggers

Themes which dominate in the social life of adolescents can best be summed up in questions such as *Will I be accepted for who I am? Which friendship group wants me – or does* anyone *want me? Do I want them? Where do I fit in? Am I admired or overlooked? How do I compare with others? What is my 'social currency'?*

An episode such as being teased in school or insulted via social media can arouse in the adolescent seemingly unbearable feelings of shame, self-loathing, confusion, insecurity, anger and anxiety about rejection from peers. Fears of inadequacy, helplessness and out-of-control feelings and unease about their changing bodies and their search for an identity commonly tip over into shame. Bravado and acting out can be understood as a defence against shame, which may originate from the feeling of not being good enough in the eyes of the mother and is the basis for acute self-consciousness, which leads to intense embarrassment, feelings of failure and what feels like a narcissistic wound which will not heal. Shame in-the-eyes-of-the-other arises when the expectation of a fulfilling connection with the other is disrupted and instead there is disapproval or no response at all from the other (Archer 2005).

Rejection from peers evokes strong feelings that may be expressed at home instead of at school. The young person may provoke an argument with their parent(s) (and/or siblings) in which they may eventually accuse the parent of not understanding them or even liking them. Such a scenario can also be enacted in the therapy room, which can give the therapist the opportunity to unpack and explore it with the client.

For some adolescents, acting out their anger will take the form of breaking boundaries, which leads to feeling powerful and even to gaining status amongst peers at school. The adolescent may be drawn deeper into this kind of 'bad' behaviour, aware of the seductive danger of crossing even more boundaries but not able to stop. When this happens, it often increases the risk of serious reactions from the school. Adolescents overwhelmed by their hostile and hurt feelings are terrified by these experiences and by their own, often impulsive reactions. They must project the terror into others to survive psychically and emotionally. The feeling of danger, and the attendant anxiety, comes also from the fear that they'll be left all alone with no parents or adults to take control and be depended on for safety.

By definition, adolescents have a valency for risk-taking. Fighting against authority, pushing against rules or the limits set by others, behaving impulsively and feeling omnipotent and unstoppable can make them do things that carry the frisson of danger. Where nothing is fixed and everything is in flux, as in adolescence, the therapist needs to consider the differences between pathological and healthy aggression while recognising how aggression is also a feature of the separation-individuation process. Separating from one's parents inevitably involves hostility. Parents or teachers sometimes feel they no longer recognise the lovely, affectionate younger child in the now brusque, offhand, bristly, rejecting adolescent, but it is essential for adults to continue trusting that they have not lost the love or affection of the young person.

The therapist's role

It is important for therapists working with angry and aggressive young people to explore the influence of clients' culture or subculture and social context. Therapists need to be sensitive to the diversity of values arising from social class, ethnicity and gender when trying to understand the meaning of the young person's behaviour in order to assess their vulnerability and establish an alliance with them. For example, in some adolescents' groups, masculinity seems to be equated with 'machismo': that is, an exaggerated bravery, a sense of pride in never showing vulnerability, valuing power and control and winning 'respect' through physical strength or displays of aggression, which young people of both genders may adopt to establish and re-establish their 'status' among their peers. This behaviour functions as a defence against a sense of inferiority and the fear of being perceived as vulnerable and weak. Some girls also glorify fighting and physical strength in themselves as well as in the boys they admire or select as boyfriends, who, in turn, may claim to be involved in gangs.

It takes time for the 'tough boys' in particular to trust the therapist and feel comfortable in revealing any vulnerability. These clients may perceive the therapist's interest in them, her or his gaze and curiosity, as intrusive, scrutinizing and critical, as if the therapist can see through their 'bad self' and arrive at their core belief – which is often that they are uninteresting and unlovable. Their worst fear is of being 'found out' and having their real, shameful self uncovered. At other times they will seem ready to use the thinking space offered by the school therapist and will welcome the interest and attentive listening. When the young person feels the referral was imposed on them, the therapist may be seen initially as malign or ineffectual and could feel pressured to take on this projection, thus fulfilling the young person's negative expectations. Disguised presentations of anger in the here and now of the session, such as being obstinate, disparaging the therapist or the work, assuming superiority and so on, may evoke a lack of empathy in response and arouse frustration and helplessness in the therapist. However, the therapist will know to look beyond the angry protest and become aware of the despair beneath, receiving it, bearing it and thinking about it, returning it in a more meaningful form, so that the feelings are transformed into a known and tolerated experience (Bion 1962b). Bion (1962a) made a distinction between 'memories' and 'undigested facts'. Therapy can facilitate the transformation of these undigested facts into memory through earlier experiences being given a new meaning.

By working in the 'here and now' and responding in a containing and reflective way to the adolescent's emotional experience, the therapist often functions as a new object of identification and attachment for them. When she or he is perceived as an empathic and receptive person who can tolerate ambivalence, aggressive feelings, love and hate and feelings of dependence and closeness, then the adolescent will be more able to tolerate their own vulnerability and share their feelings and experiences.

The therapist will be aware of the client's unconscious efforts to get her or him to conform to and re-enact the part of an important figure from their world by, for example, provoking the therapist's anger. When an adolescent is angry and becomes aggressive in the session, the therapist may say something along the lines of *You need me to feel concerned about (or afraid of or shocked by) your violence (or by your story) and about what you might do. This may be because you fear the power of your aggressive feelings, and you want me to help you manage and understand them.* The experience of the therapist's response as different from what they had imagined will make an impression. It represents the possibility of a new object of attachment who is benign and who has compassion as well as the ability to tolerate difficult feelings and projections. The therapist understands the adolescent's anger and contempt through the process of projective identification and responds by trying to explore and give meaning to the behaviour as a form of communication.

The pupil who angrily claims they don't need to come to therapy, saying that 'nobody understands anyway, and I don't need your sympathy!' can evoke in the therapist an image of the adolescent as a young child. The therapist may wonder who has been there for this young person and who has been able to respond to his or her angry protests. These thoughts can be shared with the young person and may even create a moment of connection. At other times, the therapist can introduce an outside perspective and share with the adolescent his or her own thinking processes rather than pointing out the destructiveness and the attacks, including those on the therapist. The therapist could say, *I find myself wondering what's happened to the part of you that feels sad.* When the young person lacks the capacity to think about the mind and how we use it, the therapy might instead focus on improving mentalisation skills, that is, recognising mental states in others and in oneself and seeing oneself as an 'agent' rather than just as a victim of others' behaviours and demands (including internal demands). The ability to develop insight into one's difficulties and to think about one's own contribution to conflicts and interactions with others becomes an important task of therapy.

One area of development that can be problematic for many is rooted in the physical. Adolescents experience a new sense of the power residing in their physical body, which, in contrast to the child's sense of the physical self, has the strength to cause real damage to others if anger gets out of hand, as well as the power symbolised by their sexual interests and capacities, which can also be experienced as dangerous. Often they feel they have lost control over their bodies and may even hold the conviction that they are being 'betrayed' by their new physical self, which is changing beyond recognition, together with the feeling of being 'ambushed' by sexual desires. They may react with anger to what they feel as the assault their body is waging on their sense of self, and on the attendant negative self-beliefs or critical thoughts that accompany it. This anger can be acted out by becoming involved in conflicts or fights in or out of school, or by engaging in self-harming. In addition, anger may cover up strongly felt envy and jealousy, easily aroused by comparing themselves to others and perceiving differences in themselves, which can be hard to manage especially when it springs up between close friends.

As therapists, we understand the value of moderating extremes of feeling and behaviour by gradually putting into words what has either been felt as a confusing mix of emotions or been acted out. Adolescents often experience their mental states and their feelings as larger than life. Seeing young people through the lens of compassion and understanding rather than from the position of passing judgement and assigning blame, which is what many expect, can give them a sense that their 'bad parts' have not fully obscured or even killed off their good internal objects and their 'good parts'.

Conclusion

This chapter has explored the forms anger may take as well as the underlying feelings that commonly fuel it. However, every adolescent will have a unique history and current life circumstances which will shape their sense of self and determine the source of their anger as well as how it is expressed or conveyed. The relationship between anger and early experiences of attachment is an important one to hold in mind and will colour the therapeutic relationship. The therapist, often through countertransference, recognises the more vulnerable feelings under-lying anger and finds a way to address them, sometimes by encouraging their expression indirectly through play or using other creative means. The challenge for the therapist is how to deal with openly expressed or disguised presentations of anger in the here and now of the session, which may include signs of disparag-ing the therapist or the work or homophobic, sexist or racist comments and so on. Every school therapist will have attempted to form therapeutic relationships with students who are referred for anger issues but who will not engage, leaving the therapist with the feelings that cannot be owned by the adolescent, such as those triggered by rejection, a sense of inadequacy and the experience of failure.

The work of the therapist is to contain and manage both his or her own feelings and those projected by adolescents while responding thoughtfully and meaning-fully to these young clients. In the case of the rejecting adolescent who refuses to return, the best we can do is to digest the feelings on their behalf using supervi-sion for this purpose and liaise with school staff. Such therapeutic tasks are easy to describe but much more difficult to fulfil. It is useful to remember that think-ing, exploring, processing and reflecting on their internal world may feel coun-tercultural to adolescents; in such instances our primary aim is to provide a good enough experience so that the young person is left with a seed of hope and may return to us in later years or seek therapy elsewhere.

Study questions

The first few sessions can be used to assess the young person's capacity for men-talisation and empathy. Questions at the core of such an assessment include the following:

- Can the client see any view other than their own?
- What is their capacity for insight into the impact of their aggressive behaviour on others?
- Do they show capacity for concern and remorse?
- Do they have any feelings for the target of their aggression?

Supervision and independent study can be used to speculate on the sources of the anger and ways one might explore this with clients.

- Is the aggression triggered by a perceived threat to the client's sense of self or physical safety? Or by the need to control and dominate, to achieve what they want without concern for the other?
- Do they think they know exactly what the other person is thinking and what that person's intentions are, or can they think around the situation, looking at it from different angles?
- Is there a tendency to interpret ambiguous situations as if the other person has hostile intent?

Some adolescents 'lose it' impulsively and lash out, in particular when their temper is triggered at the point of public humiliation.

- Can they reflect on what they have done and show some degree of regret?
- Do they have the capacity to use their mind to think about their own intentions or those of others?

Further questions which it can be useful to speculate on in preparation for work with adolescents referred for anger issues include:

- When the distress caused by internal and external conflicts is overwhelming for the adolescent, how might their thinking be impaired? How might the feelings be acted out and projected?
- How do we make sense of the adolescent girl who gives an account of being treated badly and hit by her violent and jealous boyfriend who demands sexual favours? How do we understand her unconscious use of her body in a destructive way, leading to her own exploitation? What kind of early history might result in a young girl subjecting herself to a relationship with a boy which is destructive rather than supportive and nurturing?

References

Archer, S. (2005) 'Shame, Doubt and the *Shameless Object*'. *Journal of the British Association of Psychotherapists*, 43, 1–107.

Bick, E. (1968) 'The Experience of the Skin in Early Object Relations'. In M. Harris and E. Bick, *Collected Papers of Martha Harris and Esther Bick* (ed. Harris Williams, M.), pp. 114–118. Perthshire: Clunie.

Bion, W. (1962a) *Learning from Experience*. London: Heinemann.

Bion, W. (1962b) 'A Theory of Thinking', *International Journal of Psychoanalysis*, 43, 4–5.

Fonagy, P. (2001) 'The Psychoanalysis of Violence'. Paper presented at the Dallas Society for Psychoanalytic Psychotherapy, 15 March.

Fonagy, P. (2004) 'The Developmental Roots of Violence in the Failure of Mentalisation'. In F. Pfafflin and G. Adshead (eds) *A Matter of Security: The Application of Attachment Theory to Forensic Psychiatry and Psychotherapy*, pp. 13–56. London: Jessica Kingsley.

Shuttleworth, J. (1991) 'Psychoanalytic Theory and Infant Development'. In L. Miller, M. Rustin and J. Shuttleworth (eds), *Closely Observed Infants*, pp. 22–51. Wiltshire, UK: Redwood Press.

Williams, G. (2004) 'The Fear of Hoping'. Paper presented at the conference 'Working with Difficult Adolescents', Tavistock Clinic, London, 19–24 July.

Winnicott, D. W. (1956/1984) 'The Antisocial Tendency'. In D. W. Winnicott, *Through Paediatrics to Psychoanalysis: Collected Papers*, pp. 306–315. London: Karnac.

Chapter 8

Working with clients drawn to self-harm

Lyn French

Along with the potential for change and development, there is mental pain to be borne when working with adolescents, particularly if they are drawn to self-destructive behaviour. The very term 'self-harm', highly emotive as it is, calls up associations for us all and can trigger an immediate and powerful reaction in school staff as well as in the therapist on the receiving end of a referral of this kind. If we are in our early years of working with adolescents, we might feel a rush of anxiety or even panic, wondering how we could possibly help. Our initial response may be that the young person needs to be passed directly on to Child and Adolescent Mental Health Services (CAMHS). While this could turn out to be the case, we do the young person a disservice if we act on our first impressions or get caught up in the reaction of school staff without meeting the adolescent, at least for an initial conversation or a few informal assessment appointments, to find out more.

This chapter will explore the theme of self-harming in adolescents from a number of perspectives, including what it evokes in the system and in the therapist, how to explore risk, how to work with the client in the room, and what dilemmas it presents around confidentiality. Self-harm is generally understood to take into its orbit all forms of self-destructive behaviour that are deliberate and non-life-threatening such as self-injury, substance misuse, promiscuity and eating disorders. In the school setting, students who self-injure, in particular by cutting themselves, are usually referred to school therapists more frequently than those with substance misuse issues or eating disorders. For this reason, the main focus of this chapter will be on self-injury. However, the ways in which it can be thought about, and the examples illustrating what the therapist might say, apply equally to all forms of self-destructive behaviour with some adaptations. The primary aim of this chapter is to provide an overview of the subject and to support school therapists in understanding their own reaction and that of staff to adolescents whose behaviour is self-destructive as well as to think about how to work with it in the therapy room.

Common reactions to the adolescent who self-injures

Self-injury is an increasing feature of adolescent behaviour, even, in some instances, sparking copycat behaviour through social media. We know that self-injury represents an attempt to shift the mind's focus onto physical pain and away from emotional distress or feelings that cannot yet be put into words. The very act of drawing blood, for example, can have a symbolic resonance, giving the adolescent the sense that unbearable tensions are draining out of the body along with the blood. However, what begins as an attempt to self-soothe, albeit a highly dysfunctional one, can become compulsive and may generate a confusing mix of feelings for the adolescent. It can provoke, for instance, a kind of excitement and triumph linked to having a 'secret life' which is in their control, as well as guilt and shame about what they are doing to their body and the unconscious attacks this may represent on internal figures. Of course, self-harming behaviour will have a different aim for all those who engage in it. Young people may act out in this way:

- to obtain relief from seemingly intolerable emotions such as anger, frustration, sadness, depression, fear, anxiety or loneliness;
- to 'silence' intrusive thoughts or feelings relating to past or still-current abuse;
- to feel more alive rather than numb and shut down;
- to punish themselves because of their perception that they are essentially bad. (This may be linked with past abuse or some other trauma. It could also be a reaction to parental separation or death of a family member for which a young person feels – irrationally but powerfully – that they are to blame. Or it could simply be that they have a highly distorted perception of themselves, resulting in their unconscious destructive thoughts leaving them feeling far more 'bad' than 'good'.)

Adolescents who cut themselves are often grouped together because of this commonality, yet each young person will have a particular family and personal context, a unique internal world and their own conscious and unconscious motivations for self-injuring. We, too, will have context-determined reactions. Our initial shock can be eclipsed by anger, impatience or critical thoughts. The self-injuring behaviour may be seen as 'teenage theatrics' or 'attention seeking', initial responses which defend against fear about where it might lead and whether or not it can be successfully stopped. The ethnicity, class and reputation of the student who is self-harming will also colour our response. If someone close to us has self-harmed or even committed suicide, our reaction is bound to be shaped by this. Until we talk with the young person and learn more about them, we have only collective or individual fantasies and subjective responses to go on.

School staff hearing about acts of self-injury may unconsciously feel the 'attack' is, in part, directed against them. It is a common human response to wish to distance oneself from any kind of violence or to find a way to quickly put a stop to it and 'get things back to normal'; to have to think about it and try to understand it can feel overwhelming or deskilling. It is not within the remit of school staff to deal with this level of acting out or to contain and process the countertransference feelings which are aroused in them. Most lack the training required to provide pastoral care to adolescents who are self-injuring and are rarely offered support to help them deal with such distressing presentations. As Ron Best (2006, 173), a professor at the School of Education at Roehampton University, points out,

> It is arguable that teachers and other 'front-line' workers need the kind of systematic clinical supervision which is built into the professional structures within which counsellors, psychotherapists and psychiatric social workers are expected to operate . . . While it might be unhelpful to 'medicalise' teach-ers' pastoral roles too much, recognising that, like workers in the physical and mental health services, they have a 'case-load' to carry may encourage the provision of such support.

As therapists, we are trained to be aware of our subjective responses and to 'hold' them, but that doesn't mean that we lack feelings. However, in our profes-sional role our task is to think about the feelings we have as useful information that provides us with insight into how others might be reacting and what the client stirs up in the adults around them.

Eating disorders and body image

Eating disorders are considered another form of self-destructive behaviour that at their most extreme can be life-threatening. Much has been published on the subject, some of it very accessible and written from a social/political context, such as Susie Orbach's earliest book on the theme, entitled *Fat Is a Feminist Issue*, reissued in 1998 with an additional section which includes helpful psychologi-cal exercises (Orbach 1998). Orbach's more recent book, *Bodies* (2009), covers issues arising for both boys/men and girls/women on how we view and treat our bodies including raising questions about societal influences and proposing theo-ries on how we become embodied.

Contemporary psychoanalysis also gives consideration to our relationship with our bodies. In *Internal Landscapes and Foreign Bodies: Eating Disorders and Other Pathologies* (2000), Gianna Williams develops Klein's model of projective and introjective processes and Bion's theory of the relationship between container and contained to help us to better understand body-related dysfunctions. Ales-sandra Lemma explores psychoanalytic perspectives on body modification in her publication *Under the Skin* (2010), examining the motivation behind why people pierce, tattoo, cosmetically enhance or otherwise modify their bodies, including the unconscious phantasies that underlie the desire for these modifications.

We know that our relationship to our body carries the hallmarks of our ear-liest relationships in infancy, primarily our experience of, and relationship with, our mother's body. As well, our mother's conscious and unconscious feelings and thoughts about feeding and intimately caring for her baby, including dealing with bodily wastes, will leave an imprint. How a mother experiences her baby's needs and how she feels about being responsible for feeding and nurturing her child will be unconsciously communicated through touch, vocal tone and gaze. The child too will have a response to what the mother is 'putting into him or her', literally and metaphorically. The history of the infant's relationship with feeding includes potent feelings linked to being dependent upon an external object – the mother – who may be experienced almost simultaneously as nurturing as well as envy provoking, or as selflessly giving while at the same time setting limits. The subject of eating disorders is far-reaching as it touches on so many aspects of these experiences including the primitive acts – and associations with them – of 'taking in' and 'expelling' as well as the inner parallels of being 'fed' psychic material which can be felt to be nourishing or, conversely, toxic.

When adolescents' bodies go through physical and hormonal changes, their intimate relationship with their physical self can also shift. Girls, and increasingly boys too, may try to halt growing up by severely limiting their food intake so their body remains 'under their control' and the evolution into a sexual being with 'appetites' can be denied or repressed. Or the opposite could be the case – they might 'comfort eat' to keep anxiety away as well as ensure that they are protected from anyone getting too close, warding off what might be the frightening prospect of sexual engagement or exploration.

When exploring eating disorders and ways in which the body is used symbolically, there is much to be thought about from the perspectives of psychoanalytic understanding, gender politics and social conditioning. This chapter is only headlining the more common themes; articles, books and information available online can easily be accessed on these subjects. The main aim here is to support therapists in their thinking and to provide some ideas of how to work with the everyday realities of sitting in a room in a secondary school with an adolescent who is – or may be at risk of – using their body as a vehicle for the expression of, or reaction to, unmanageable, unbearable, unarticulated or still-unknown feelings.

Assessing risk

Most school therapists view the first one to six sessions as an assessment phase for all their clients; this is especially important when we are referred an adolescent who is considered at risk of self-injuring (or already is engaging in this) or exhibits another form of self-destructive behaviour. All self-destructive behaviour has at its core the attempt to get rid of emotional and mental pain as well as thoughts – both conscious and unconscious – that are considered shameful or unbearable in some way. As has been described in earlier chapters, adolescence is a time in which moods may swing dramatically, unpredictably and frighteningly. Young people can misinterpret their own sexual stirrings and reawakened Oedipal urges, experiencing them as profoundly disturbing or shame inducing, or even overwhelmingly terrifying. Their fantasies about their bodies, their relationships and who they are or may be becoming can be in constant flux. One way to deal with this potent mix of feelings is seemingly to attempt to master them by blocking them out altogether. Self-injury, promiscuity, substance misuse and eating disorders are often misguided attempts to achieve this, giving a false sense of being in control or at least distanced from feelings of helplessness, the fear of growing up and the infantilising wish to be looked after by adults once again. As noted above, these forms of self-destructive behaviour will have a unique meaning for each young person and will act as a defence against underlying anxieties, conscious or unconscious.

In the therapy room

If the school gave the self-injuring or self-destructive behaviour as the main reason for the referral, then the therapist may choose to bring it into the first session, perhaps going in slowly and trying to get the young person to acknowledge it themselves. After introducing herself or himself and the service offered simply and briefly, the therapist might invite the client to start, saying, *Tell me why you think the school feels it is important for us to meet.* If the young person accurately identifies the reason for the referral, then the therapist could go on to say, *I imagine things might be difficult for you, and this is your way of coping. I hope that by working together, we can better understand what's happening and that you'll come to see that hurting yourself (or restricting what you eat/comfort eating/engaging in experimentation that is bordering on self-destructive and so on) will gradually seem a less attractive option to you. Maybe you can tell me in your own words what you think started this off . . .* If the young person is able to open up, then the therapist might affirm them as they go along, making gentle observations now and again such as *That sounds painful . . . It's been hard for you, hasn't it? . . . It takes some courage to talk about these experiences openly . . . Maybe you're wondering if I can understand where you're coming from . . . I get the impression that no one has been there for you . . . It sounds like you've been alone with this . . . (and so on).* At some point in the session, the therapist might need to remind the client that she or he shares the responsibility for their well-being with school staff, and confidentiality may have to be broken. A way of conveying this is to say something such as *You know that the school is aware of these issues and will want me to tell them if things become worse. If I do need to pass anything onto the school, I'll talk to you about it so that you know who I'm going to speak to and what I will be telling them.*

If the young person is wary or shut down and claims not to know why they have been referred, the therapist will need to decide what angle to take. Some choose to lead into the reason behind the school's referral rather than stating it outright. There are various ways of encouraging the client to open up, as the following example illustrates. *The school tells me they think you're having a tough time, and they'd like you to feel better in yourself. What's causing them to feel concerned about you?* If no response is forthcoming, the therapist might move on to address this, saying, *I get the sense that coming here wasn't your idea – perhaps you feel the school is asking you to come against your wishes. Is this how it is?* Whether or not the client replies in the affirmative, the therapist might continue with *It may be hard to believe that the school and I really do want you to feel supported. I'm here to help you think about what's going on for you. It takes time to get used to talking and to trust that what is on offer here could work for you.* At this point, it might be helpful to continue on a less threatening level, saying, *Why don't you tell me something about school or home life, past or present? It might be something you enjoy or an experience that was important for you . . .*

On the other hand, some therapists will elect to be transparent from the start. Here is how they might open up the first session after introducing themselves and their service: *Tell me why you think the school feels it is important for us to meet . . .* (The client claims not to know.) *You're not sure why the school referred you? . . . No ideas? That's interesting because I've been told it's come to light that you've been cutting yourself when things feel too much. When young people use cutting in this way, it's usually because they're convinced they don't have any other means of making themselves feel better and comforting themselves. The school is concerned and wants to support you. I'm hoping we can talk openly here about what triggers your urge to cut yourself. Maybe a good place to start is for you to tell me how the school came to know about this . . .*

Following on from here, the therapist might choose to ask the young person a few questions such as when the cutting first started, what triggered it in the beginning and what triggers it now. If drawing the client out is proving a little difficult, the therapist may want to take the pressure off and move on to say, *We know the school recommended we meet because of the concerns we've just been discussing; however, there may be other things that you want to bring here; we can make time for these issues too. Does anything come to mind just now?* Depending on how responsive the client is, the therapist might decide to introduce the theme of family relationships, perhaps saying, *I really don't know much about you at all. The school simply told me why they have concerns, which is what we've been discussing so far today. I'd like to get to know you better. Can you tell me about your family? Who lives at home?* The therapist could at this stage invite the client to draw a genogram or family tree as described in Chapter 20 to get a better idea of the family's relationships with each other, significant events and current circumstances.

If the adolescent has been referred for another reason altogether and then introduces the theme of self-injury or another form of self-destructive behaviour, the school therapist needs to use professional judgement to assess the degree of risk. If, for example, a young person talks about being drawn to the idea of self-harm, but there is no firm evidence of such action having been taken, it may be of greater therapeutic value for the therapist to 'hold' the information, treating it as confidential and then discussing it in supervision and working out whether or not the school needs to know at this stage. If it is felt that there is no immediate risk and the client's interest in the idea of self-harm is not going to be shared with the school at this point, it enables the therapist to work with the issue, and trust can be preserved. However, even if the client has not acted on their fantasies of self-harm, there may be times when the therapist feels it is necessary to break client confidentiality, especially if the student in question is extremely vulnerable. Making this judgement often relies on what can be unearthed in the 'here and now' through sensitively exploring how the client got this idea in the first instance (if it is self-injury), when it started, in what particular situations the young person feels drawn to this kind of acting out, what the deeper meaning might be, how receptive the client is to talking about it and whether or not they have told anyone else. Throughout, the therapist will be keeping track of the mood or ambience of the session, including their own feelings, and watching for any changes which might indicate the beginnings of trust or, conversely, signs of retreat.

The threat of self-harm or low-level self-destructive behaviour may naturally diminish as thinking becomes more possible, although trying to talk about mental pain can have the opposite effect and clients may want to rid themselves of any reminder of it by shutting down, actively avoiding or resisting any attempt at understanding. The degree to which the young person is able to discuss the subject and to stay with the feelings or mental states aroused will influence whether or not the therapist feels that the disclosure of a wish to self-harm must be treated as a serious safeguarding issue to be passed on to the school or whether the client is sufficiently psychologically minded to explore it and arrive at a point where it can be seen as an untenable option.

There are no easy answers to this dilemma. Many young people feel greatly relieved when they articulate a wish to harm themselves or are able to admit to an eating disorder or some other form of self-destructive behaviour. Their relief is deepened if the therapist is not overly alarmed or panicked and does not pathologise it but takes it seriously and is able to keep thinking, using the opportunity to reflect with these clients about the feelings stirred up as well as the meaning behind the acting out. It may be appropriate to balance the exploration of the symbolic meanings and the underlying emotions with a 'fact-finding' discussion to discover how serious the issue is. The conversation can be broken down into a sequence of events or thoughts. For example, the therapist can ask the young person who is toying with the idea of self-injuring what they have been thinking of doing, where on their body they imagined they would cut themselves and how far they had gone in their plans. When the therapist can contain the often strong feelings stirred up in response, it is then possible to acknowledge the client's pain, talk about its possible sources and also explore with the client their fantasies about the therapist's possible reactions to the potential for self-harm. For example, the therapist might ask the client, *What do you imagine my thoughts are about what you're telling me?* As therapists, there are times when we may even choose to be transparent but in a thoughtful and measured way, saying to our client, *Naturally, I feel concerned and a little alarmed by what you're telling me. I know from working with teenagers and from research that self-harm isn't the answer. It might seem to help in the short term, but in the longer term, it affects self-esteem and can even be life-threatening. I also feel that if we talk more about it and explore your feelings sensitively, it might be less necessary for you to do this to yourself (or to think about doing this to yourself).*

It is the therapist's responsibility to let the client know that self-harm could potentially be dangerous and that there are real risks involved, including the risk that the act might become habitual or ritualised and hard to stop. For instance, the therapist can say, *You probably know that self-harming like this can come to seem the answer whenever feelings get too much, but it has consequences. Research shows that it can become addictive and therefore dangerous as it can be hard to stop. Maybe there is a part of you that can hear what I'm saying and does know that I have your best interests in mind.*

The majority of therapists will assess each referral on its own merit, thinking carefully about the client's history and current circumstances, including whether or not there are some support structures in place for the young person such as a close friend, friendship group or school staff they can talk to in between sessions or someone they are close to within their family circle. The phenomenon of young people being drawn to the idea of self-harm is perhaps more common than society would like to think; therapists are advised to be prepared for this issue to come up when working in schools and to be aware of the need to keep an open mind rather than to react with too much – or too little – concern or anxiety.

Some thoughts about self-destructive behaviour in general

The focus of this chapter has been primarily on self-injuring; however, everything discussed so far is applicable to any form of self-destructive behaviour. Young people may feel reluctant to talk to adults about these tendencies, at least initially. As a means of widening and contextualising the conversation, it can be useful for the therapist to, for example, describe the unhelpful dualities or 'splits' which are common in our society as reflected in the use of labels such as healthy/unhealthy, normal/abnormal or well-functioning/dysfunctional. It is tempting for everyone to assign the description of 'other' to those who are perceived to have traits we prefer to distance ourselves from or disown. All of us can 'tell ourselves a story' about what are, in fact, our own unhealthy habits, comparing them to more extreme examples so that we can reassure ourselves that we don't have a problem with food, drink, intimacy or other lifestyle choices. In fact, our society frequently conveys a skewed view of what is considered 'normal', often dependent on status. A celebrity's standing, for example, is generally not impacted by revelations of self-destructive behaviour – on the contrary, there are contexts in which their status is actually perceived as enhanced by such disclosures.

It can be interesting to talk more generally with our young clients about how we all have a relationship with our bodies, which is reflected in how we treat them. Some aspects of this relationship will be good and fulfilling, while others will be less so. Any of us can use food or drink or sleeping or exercise or sexual engagement in a way that crosses a line and begins to work against us. A way to further develop this kind of conversation is to focus on creating a whole picture of the young person's relationship with their body by identifying how their body serves them well, reminding them of the physical health they might take for granted, exploring the different ways in which they take care of the body and so on, before moving into conversation along the following lines: *I'm getting the impression that a part of you does care and that there are times when you understand your feelings – we've been talking about them here, and I can see that you take in what I say. But another part of you easily feels overwhelmed. When that happens your 'coping part' is silenced and you listen only to the part of you that feels over-whelmed. Naturally it then feels too much, and you think you have only one way to make yourself feel better and that is to cut yourself.*

Perhaps explaining 'self-talk' at this juncture could be useful, that is, raising the young person's awareness of their internal voice and explaining how this inner monologue usually focuses on the negative rather than the positive. Any of us can tell ourselves, for example: 'Things are never going to improve'; 'Everyone else's life is much better – it's so unfair'; 'I'm no good at anything – there's no point trying'; 'No one will ever really like (or love) me' and so on. Sometimes these thoughts are on the edge of consciousness, just outside of awareness; it can be helpful if the therapist asks the young person to monitor their thinking between sessions to see what their 'self-talk' is telling them. Therapists can then help their clients to challenge this kind of 'all-or-nothing' thinking and also to reinforce a more positive self-image by balancing the negative with the positive in a realistic way. These techniques are probably most readily associated with cognitive behav-ioural therapy, but the basic principles can also be used in psychodynamic therapy.

With regard to critical self-talk, it can be useful to help clients to identify whose 'voice' or 'views' they have internalised. It is very easy for children, for instance, to misinterpret a parent's look and, based on this emotionally charged moment, lay the foundation for a core belief which goes unchallenged into adulthood. We may, for example, imagine our parent saw us as 'a disappointment', 'an academic failure', 'unlikely to amount to much' and so on. Children internalise their often distorted or exaggerated 'felt experience' of their parents' responses to them as well as the words actually spoken; together these can feed into self-talk and amplify negative beliefs. As well, children may cast themselves in a poor light because of the hostility or destructive quality of their unconscious reactions to parents or siblings, experiencing themselves as mostly – or all – 'bad' because of these phantasies and developing negative self-talk as a result.

Agreeing to offer regular sessions to a self-harming adolescent

At times, we may agree to see a client who is known to be self-injuring on a fairly regular basis and who refuses to go to CAMHS or attends a few sessions but disengages. The therapist may need to monitor the young person's self-harming, looking out for times when what's being discussed could provide the context for an informal 'check-in', saying, for example, *You've just been talking about a friend standing you up. In the past when you've felt rejected like this, you've had a strong urge to self-harm. What went through your mind on Saturday when you realised your friend wasn't coming and hadn't called or texted you?*

When working with a client who is known to the school as a self-harmer, the therapist may make an agreement at the start of the work that she or he will tell a designated school staff member about every self-harm incident or, at the very least, the most serious incidents. Alongside the therapist's work with the client, it is recommended that a school staff member such as a mentor, form tutor or head of year tries to maintain contact with the parents themselves, even undertaking to do some basic work with them if they will not engage with CAMHS.

Defining the boundary and scope of the therapy service

School therapists need to give careful thought to the boundary and scope of their service. Whether or not they agree to see students who are at risk of – or already engaging in self-destructive behaviour – will reflect their level of experience and their skills. Some may wish to let the school know that they will not take referrals of adolescents who fall into this category and recommend that they be referred straight on to CAMHS. They will also make it clear that if this kind of behaviour is revealed once work is underway, they will bring the sessions to a managed ending.

The school therapist, in consultation with their supervisor and, if relevant, with their organisation, may decide that the provision will not include students with presenting problems which could bring up safeguarding concerns or issues that fall into a mental health category. It is never easy to juggle the inherent tension between what the school ideally wants from the therapist and what the therapist feels equipped to deliver; however, it is important to be clear about what is being offered. An explanation of the service limits could be included in a handout for school staff outlining guidelines for referrals. The information provided can emphasise that students about whom staff have safeguarding concerns should be referred directly to CAMHS for assessment and possible treatment.

The therapist's context will affect the decision about whether or not to work with students who show a tendency towards self-destructive behaviour. A therapist whose service is embedded in the school and who has good relationships with key school staff, or who is new but is working with an agency, organisation or team that is well established in the school, and who also has a good working alliance with a senior supervisor, will be in a very different situation from the therapist who is a new trainee or is setting up a service for the first time.

Conclusion

This chapter has provided an overview of how, as therapists, we might think about self-destructive behaviour and ways it can be worked with in the therapy room. There are many related themes which have not been highlighted here as the aim is to empower school therapists in their role by providing examples of how they might draw their clients out and the kind of language or approach they may wish to use. The issue of power dynamics is one which is implicit in all forms of acting out. Unconsciously, adolescents may be in battle with adults, both wanting to strike out on their own, symbolised by taking full and absolute control of their bodies as 'their sole territory', and also wanting to export anxiety by locating it in the adults around them rather than owning it and learning to manage it.

Every school therapist will evolve their own way of working with clients whose acting out borders on, or seems to indicate, a more serious mental health issue. The main task – and it is not an easy one even for the experienced therapist – is to hit the right note with the adolescent. Too much focus on self-destructive behaviour can inflate anxieties and alienate the client; too little can be experienced as colluding with the young person's wish to avoid the subject and may even be considered a form of professional negligence. The therapist will always think carefully about the adolescent's context – there is a world of difference between the student who makes light scratches on her arm because 'it's the trend and all her friends are doing it' and the one who comes from a family where domestic violence, substance abuse or sexual abuse occurred or is still a feature. Every young client needs to be taken seriously, but the issues which are to be addressed are bound to be very different.

The conundrum all school therapists will face at some point or another is whether or not they will agree to continue to work with a student who is dangerously and persistently acting out if the adolescent refuses to attend external appointments offered by CAMHS or the equivalent mental health service for children and adolescents. We need to be conscious of the fact that we may be the only professional the student is willing to make contact with, as we are working on the school site and therefore perceived as less threatening. In addition, the school may actively encourage the young person to continue appointments with us. At times all of us will feel out of our depth, no matter what our experience. It can feel very stressful to work with self-destructive clients as they may be disowning their anxiety and passing it on to us, leaving us feeling entirely responsible for their well-being. It is important to know that this is a dimension of the unconscious processes at work and that as therapists based in schools, we are not the only adults who have a duty of care. It goes without saying that having weekly supervision with a senior practitioner who has some experience of working in schools or at least with adolescents is vital; we need to create a network around ourselves and our clients that is thoughtful and robust enough to hold the difficult material that inevitably comes our way. We are well placed to support adolescents who are self-harming, or at risk of it, if we can truly listen, observe and feel, helping them to give words to the stories they are 'writing' on their bodies.

Study questions

- What are your own associations or experiences with self-injury and self-harm in general?
- What are your anxieties about working with adolescents who self-injure or who act out self-destructively?
- What degree of self-destructive behaviour are you willing to work with? How have you arrived at this decision?

References and recommended reading

AnyBody www.anybody.squarespace.com

Best, R. (2005) 'An Educational Response to Deliberate Self-Harm: Training, Support and School-Agency Links'. *Journal of Social Work Practice,* Vol. 19, No. 3, pp. 275–287.

Best, R. (2006) 'Deliberate Self-Harm in Schools: A Challenge for Schools'. *British Journal of Guidance & Counselling,* Vol. 34, No. 2, pp. 161–175.

Farrell, E. (2001) *Lost for Words: The Psychoanalysis of Anorexia and Bulimia.* London: Process Press.

French, L. and Klein, R., eds. (2012) *Therapeutic Practice in Schools: Working with the Child Within.* London: Routledge.

Lawrence, M. (2011) *The Anorexic Mind.* London: Karnac.

Lemma, A. (2010) *Under the Skin: A Psychoanalytic Study of Body Modification.* London: Routledge.

McDougall, J. (1989) *Theatres of the Body: A Psychoanalytic Approach to Psychosomatic Illness.* London: Free Association Books.

Orbach, S. (1998) *Fat Is a Feminist Issue.* London: Arrow Books.

Orbach, S. (2009) *Bodies.* London: Profile Books.

Vivyan, Carol (2010) adapted from Lee, in Gilbert (2005) at www.get.gg © Carol Vivyan 2010 'Thought Record Sheet (critical voice)' Permission to use for therapy purposes www.getselfhelp.co.uk

Williams, G. (2000) *Internal Landscapes and Foreign Bodies: Eating Disorders and Other Pathologies.* London: Duckworth.

Chapter 9

The bereaved adolescent

Jo Evans

In a large secondary school, it is likely that there will be young people who have experienced a recent bereavement or are struggling with the after-effects of a significant past loss which has not been fully mourned or even properly taken in and understood. For these adolescents, the common teenage feelings stirred up by their move away from childhood into an increasingly independent lifestyle may be jostling with the strong conviction that there is 'no going back'. A feeling of emptiness or a sense of having no anchor points may dominate as if their past life really has been lost forever. Adolescence can be deeply confusing and profoundly unsettling for the young person who is confronted by a real bereavement with all its inherent losses. This chapter will focus on the impact of the death of a family member in adolescence and consider the changes or adaptations the school therapist may be called upon to make. Much of what is discussed will also apply to the diverse forms bereavement takes such as losing a parent through divorce or separation, never knowing a birth parent or leaving behind a foster family.

Thinking and talking about death

Most of us struggle to talk openly about death and can find it difficult to articulate what we feel or think about the subject. Being able to speak about our own or another's bereavement can be equally challenging. For those of us who have experienced the death of someone close, we know that there is no right or wrong way to grieve; we all have to work through the tasks of mourning in a way which makes sense to us. Every loss is unique to the person who is experiencing it as it will be contextualised by internal and external circumstances with conscious and unconscious ideas and fantasies playing their part.

Any death is both a sobering reminder of our own mortality and a hard-to-admit-to relief: we're still alive. Even though Shakespeare advises us to 'give sorrow words', it is not easy to create meaning out of what will always be a completely individual, and often solitary, experience of loss. However, as therapists we need to build the skills to speak about death more freely and to explore different ways of thinking about it.

When working with bereaved adolescents it is important to be flexible in our approach so that we can respect their pace and their own processes. Some adolescents may feel that just a few sessions are all they need or are comfortable with around the time of their loss, but then request to return at a later point. Others benefit from being able to sustain a regular connection with a school therapist over a considerable period of time. Working in the school setting means that we can also provide a more intermittent type of support where 'check-in' appointments can be offered if this is all the adolescent can manage.

On receiving a referral which mentions a recent death, a therapist new to the role might picture a tearful teenager showing up for their first appointment and feel anticipatory sympathy and compassion, imagining that the young person will be grateful to have someone to talk to. Often this is far from the reality. For example, a young man whose father died could be annoyed or resentful about being referred to the school therapist as if he is expected to feel sad and upset when in fact he has different feelings altogether. Maybe his father left when he was very young, and he is still carrying strong feelings about being abandoned. Or perhaps his father had an untreated addiction which meant he was emotionally unavailable most of the time or verbally and even physically abusive. In such instances, it is likely that the death will stir up a complex mix of feelings including triumph and relief. As well, guilt linked with unconscious Oedipal wishes to kill off the father will be present in some form, which may be combined with a confusing sense of loss and primitive rage for what was missing from the relationship and now can never be realised.

Another client may have an overwhelming sense of wanting to escape from any attempt to focus on what to them seems unthinkable. In these instances the adolescent may find it seemingly impossible to hold in mind the concept of death in its enormity or to get in touch with their intimate experience of it while it's still so recent. If the timing doesn't feel right and the sessions simply cannot be used, we can acknowledge this and name some of the feelings, as well as let them know how support can be accessed in future.

It is not possible to work through a death to a final endpoint as feelings and thoughts about the deceased will resurface at different points in the life cycle with varying degrees of intensity. This could include missing the now-dead parent at a milestone birthday, at a graduation ceremony or at a wedding. Or it may mean missing a sibling who could have been there to talk to about difficulties with parents, teachers or friends. Death signifies the end of a life, but it does not mark the end of a relationship. The degree to which earlier mourning processes relating to primal losses such as weaning and separation have been worked through will contribute to how equipped any of us is for coping with loss and will determine our capacity for sustaining good internal relationships with those now dead.

The therapist who has no personal experience of death to draw on may be better placed to hear the adolescent's story more objectively. Those who have experienced a significant bereavement will be aware of not wanting to over-identify with the bereaved young person as this could impinge on, rather than helpfully inform, the work. If the therapist carrying a personal experience of loss has been able to think carefully over time about her or his own grief experience, this can then be held in mind but kept in the background, to be drawn on implicitly and explicitly when useful. What and how the adolescent communicates will then be less likely to be filtered through the therapist's own take on events, which means the adolescent may have a deeper experience of being heard, related to and understood.

Working with the grief experience

The therapist's reaction to what the adolescent is telling and showing her or him will impact consciously and unconsciously, triggering feelings and thoughts both known and unknown. This transference/countertransference experience will shape the therapist's understanding of what the adolescent is going through and what their unacknowledged feelings may be. Descriptions of the stages of grief give names to common feelings linked to bereavement while also capturing in a general way the main features of mourning. A chronological order can be implied, starting with shock and denial before progressing to anger and guilt, despair and depression, and then acceptance. No two people will experience these feelings in the same way; their strength and the order in which they surface will vary considerably. From moment to moment feelings might conflict or overlap. Numbness may suddenly give way to outrage, bewilderment to embarrassment, loneliness to guilt, anger to anguish and so on.

In every sense, the individual will be struggling to adapt to a new reality against the continuing backdrop of everyday routines, which are a constant reminder that the world keeps revolving regardless. Familiar tasks such as getting to school on time and managing a busy academic timetable may now seem overwhelmingly taxing and even pointless. The ripple effects of a death can spread through different areas of the adolescent's life. This may include the necessity of having to move home and/or school due to financial constraints resulting from the death or perhaps having to stay temporarily with friends or relatives; or the young person could even be placed in care, separated from other siblings. Previously held views that everyday life can be taken for granted are, in such instances, shattered.

During this upheaval the adolescent may also feel that he or she is expected to behave as if nothing out of the ordinary has happened. However, we know that no matter what role the parent or family member played in the life of the young person, the impact of their death will always resonate. When someone close or significant dies, it is as if a border has been crossed into a new internal landscape. Death clearly demarcates a 'before' and 'after'. The known geography of everyday living has been permanently altered, and it can feel extremely difficult for the adolescent to retain any sense of stability as there is no return to what was once familiar territory.

Death of a parent

In the school setting, the death of a parent is the most common bereavement experienced by adolescents. A referral for therapy may take place as soon as school staff become aware of the situation. Alternatively, it may occur at a later point, especially if the adolescent initially seems 'fine' but subsequently presents with an uncharacteristic change in behaviour. Quite often, very little is known about the circumstances, and the only piece of information the therapist might receive prior to the first session is that 'this student's father has died'. In such instances, the therapist needs to progress sensitively as she or he will not know whether or not the adolescent lived with or had regular contact with the father, what the relationship with the father was like, what kind of person the father was, what the adolescent's unconscious feelings about the father might be, whether or not there is another father figure in the adolescent's life (e.g. a step-father or an uncle or male friend of the family) and so on. It is always useful for the therapist to gather a little more information beforehand if possible. If there is no time or opportunity to do so, the therapist will need to go into the first session with an open mind and put aside any preconceived views of how the death of a parent might be experienced. This creates a space for the young person to give words to what may not yet have been communicated, and where their thoughts and feelings can be heard and thought about in the presence of an attuned therapist.

Even when the therapist does know what has happened and has been given some information about the adolescent's life history, it is still important for the client to have the opportunity to recount their version of events with no expectation or censorship being conveyed by the therapist. It may also be worth considering certain questions to hold in mind, whether or not they are articulated or the answers forthcoming. These could include questions about what the relationship was like with the person who died and how the person died: was it a long illness where the death was anticipated, or was it completely unexpected? Was the person murdered, or was the cause of death suicide? Were they involved in an accident? How was the client told about it, and how has it been talked about in the family? Did they attend the funeral? What does it feel like talking about it now?

Some adolescents will feel the need to fill the session with a detailed description of their experience, however distressing and painful, as if they want to get rid of the memory of it and push it into the therapist. This could also be seen as a defence against thinking more deeply about what it means to them, or as an attempt to fill with words what is felt to be an unbearable hole left inside by the bereavement. Other adolescents will only be inclined to talk about the bare minimum, leaving the therapist in touch with the emptiness these young people feel but cannot put into words yet or alternatively shutting the therapist out in the way they feel shut out by the death they've experienced. Over time, some young people are able to gain an awareness of what they are feeling and can be helped to reflect from different perspectives on their loss. Others prefer a more indirect way of communicating, such as using metaphors to verbalize their experience, or expressing themselves via sharing the lyrics of songs that speak to them, or making up stories or poems and/or using art materials.

Working with the adolescent whose parent is dying

The adolescent who has a parent who is terminally ill will present other challenges. We might be working with them through the build-up to the death and be alongside them when the parent dies. During this time the therapist might need to find out sensitively what the adolescent is witnessing at home or in hospital. Questions arising in the therapist's mind might include 'What are they being exposed to day in and day out? For example, have they taken on the role of carer, which might necessitate administering medicine? What does it mean to go and visit the parent in the hospital? How is the illness talked about? What does the adolescent know about the funeral arrangements, and do they have a role in making them?' The therapeutic aim is not to obtain information for the sake of it but to construct a better picture of the young person's circumstances so that they do not feel so alone or isolated and, over time, to enable them to identify what they are feeling or thinking about the impending death. Even if the therapist does not find a way to articulate the questions, holding them in mind is still important as it keeps us in contact with the feeling of uncertainty the young person may be left with.

Some adolescents may feel that their life is being eclipsed by the parent's terminal illness and that little or no attention is being paid to them at a time when they most need it. What about me? feelings can mask deeper anxieties about the future which may be too painful to face directly, worries such as who will be there to meet their needs after the parent's death, which can evoke anger and guilt. The young person may also feel an unbearable but unacknowledged sense of revulsion towards the parent whose condition is deteriorating, alongside feelings of injustice and powerlessness at what they might be witnessing. They may be incensed with their own inability to save their parent from dying, or they may feel responsible. Some may have a father dying in another country, perhaps one they have never met. Here the task may be to acknowledge the anger at not having a birth father in their life as well as mourning the loss of what could have been.

An ill and dying parent and the aftermath of a parent's death will resonate unconsciously on many levels for the adolescent and also for the therapist. For the young person, this could be the fulfilment of the unconscious Oedipal wish to pair with the surviving parent, having successfully 'killed off' the dead parent. However, the wished-for experience of forming a couple with the remaining parent is very different when real life creates these circumstances. Following the death of a same-sex parent, some adolescents may feel that an unwelcome role has now been foisted upon them, especially when they are unconsciously cast as the 'replacement'. This may be understood as a defensive reaction on the part of the family to quickly fill the void left by the now-dead parent.

The adolescent might also unconsciously try to manoeuvre the therapist into the role of 'provider' and 'rescuer' in the transference, to counter the sense of loss and deprivation. The therapist in turn, perhaps desiring to make things 'better' for the client, could find herself or himself under pressure to be more available by extending session times or letting the client take materials from the session to 'make up for' their loss. The therapist may not talk about all these aspects of the experience with the young person, but by thinking about them and discussing them in supervision, she or he will be bringing the experience alive in her or his mind, and the client will sense this and feel better understood.

Death of a sibling

Less common are referrals for the death of a sibling, but this occasionally occurs, especially if the sibling attended the same school. The death of a young person will always be deeply shocking for those within their immediate and wider environment, no matter how they died. It could be that the young person was the victim of a stabbing or shooting that was the result of either gang warfare or being in the wrong place at the wrong time. Or the young person may have had a prolonged illness where the likelihood of survival was known to be slim. Some may have lived through the pendulum swings of a sibling's bouts of remission following treatment, allowing for a sense of temporary optimism.

Where does this leave the remaining sibling(s) in their grief? What was the relationship with their sibling like? It could be that the adolescent wants to share with the therapist their painful sense of loss over a relationship which, following the death, has become idealised and is described as full of fondness and affection, apparently lacking in conflict. However, it's useful to bear in mind the more complex nature of sibling dynamics, which are commonly tempestuous and intensely competitive. The occasional or frequent enmity strongly felt between siblings is tempered by the conscious or unspoken knowledge that there will be future opportunities to come together in more loving ways or to resolve differences. But with the death of a sibling it can seem as though any opportunity for this relationship to survive and develop further is prematurely and permanently severed. Cruel words once spoken in fury may now come under harsh scrutiny and take on a new meaning. The adolescent may be left with feelings of ambivalence, confusion, remorse and even triumph towards the dead sibling. These feelings might remain unvoiced or be banned from conscious thought but will nonetheless have an impact on the young person's sense of self and their relationships with those around them. For instance, an adolescent might become preoccupied with the notion that the sibling who has died was the 'favourite'. This can occur particularly if the idealisation of them becomes fixed in place rather than being an initial reaction which is replaced over time with a more realistic picture. The bereaved adolescent may harbour feelings of intense envy and resentment that this sibling has now become 'forever perfect' in their family's eyes.

Or the young person might wonder why their sibling died while they themselves survived, questioning whether their own life can be justified in light of their sibling's death, thereby triggering a form of 'survivor's guilt'. They could convince themselves that they were responsible for their sibling's death because of things they said or did. There are instances when the mother or both parents might put an adolescent under pressure to 'become' the kind of person they wished the dead sibling could have been. This might be their way of compensating for the earlier loss as well as manoeuvring the young person into being an idealised version of what the parents would like to have become themselves. These perceptions are not necessarily voiced by the therapist but can provide a background framework for thinking alongside the more explicit content of the session. If the therapist can develop the ability to think 'around' the adolescent's experiences and reflect on all the different ways they might be feeling or reacting, playing in her or his mind with possibilities while simultaneously following what the adolescent is talking about in the here and now of the session, this will give more depth to the client's experience of being heard and understood.

It is part and parcel of human nature to feel powerful emotions in all of our relationships, especially in the family. The fantasies these feelings evoke are held in the unconscious mind and take more primitive forms such as a wish to 'do away with' a sibling who is getting more attention than we feel we are, or to 'kill off' a parent who frustrates us or whose powerful position we want to occupy. The guilt these fantasies engender and the threat they pose to our idealised image of ourselves as 'good' mean that we often keep them out of conscious thought. However, the real experience of a death in the family can cause these fantasies to come closer to the surface and result in either crippling or self-punishing guilt and self-destructive behaviour or the opposite: a manic need to deny any feeling whatsoever.

Ending therapy with a bereaved adolescent

Ending will be a potent theme for the bereaved adolescent. It is helpful for the therapist to be alert to what is communicated before and after breaks, and to the significance of the final ending, as all will carry a symbolic association with death. The school therapist will need to prepare herself or himself for the unplanned-for or premature ending as well as for what might come up if the adolescent can stay the course and work towards a planned ending.

Conclusion

This chapter has highlighted how conversations about death can be better facilitated when the young person has a sense of being in the presence of a therapist who is able to 'hear' their spoken and unarticulated narrative and to 'take it in' in whatever form it might be expressed. We also need to be alert to what comes up in the here and now of the session in terms of the transference and countertransference feelings whilst also thinking about unconscious processes which underlie this dynamic. Whenever possible, it is important for the adolescent to have a rounded experience of therapy which not only encompasses their past or present losses but also explores other aspects of their current life, identifying what is going well for them in addition to making time for their more everyday teenage concerns. One adolescent I worked with said in her final session that she would take with her 'the memories I can now create'. This insight touchingly and poetically sums up how we try to help clients give words to unconscious thoughts and feelings that are difficult to own or stay in touch with, bringing together the fragments to create a more coherent picture of their past and present life that they can carry in mind and continue to build on in the future.

Study Questions

- What are your experiences of bereavement or significant losses?
- How did your family deal with losses, absences or bereavements?
- In what ways might your own experiences colour how you react to a bereaved adolescent who is seeing you for therapy?

Vignette 1

You're told by the Head of Year that a Year 9 boy's mother died over the summer break. In the first session, when asked why he thinks the school recommended that he see you, he says it's because he's always getting into trouble. *What would you say?*

Vignette 2

You have been working for a while with a young person whose mother recently died. During the work, you have felt under pressure at times to become the 'replacement' maternal object in the transference. After this student leaves the session you notice that a felt tip pen from your art resources that she had been using in the sessions is missing. The next week she produces this same pen and uses it in front of you with no explanation. *What would you say?*

Vignette 3

A student turns up at a different time from her scheduled appointment in deep distress. She strongly identifies you as someone who will take care of her and seems to expect that you will be able to see her then and there. *What would you do?*

Vignette 4

A student is very resistant to sharing or exploring his experience of bereavement with you. He cuts you off if you try to offer your thoughts, saying things in a mocking or derisory tone such as 'What could you possibly know about what it's like?' and 'What makes you think you have all the answers? You're just another stupid adult trying to make me feel better, and it's not going to work!' *What might you say?*

Sample responses

Vignette 1

You might start by asking, *What kind of trouble?* before linking this with his bereavement by saying, *Young people may not know how to put feelings into words and sometimes act them out through strong behaviour instead. I get the sense from what you've told me that you've had times when you've become quite angry with adults, especially female teachers. I know that your mother was ill and that she died not so long ago. Perhaps some of the anger comes from this. Even adults find death brings up strong feelings that can be hard to face. Often when situations frighten us, we react by getting angry – that feels safer and it can feel like we're more in control.*

When you see how the adolescent responds to your reference to his recent bereavement, you can decide how you'll progress. For example, if he looks extremely uncomfortable, you could say, *We don't have to go into this now – it's something we can return to later. I'd also like to hear about what's going well for you. How have you found secondary school in general? What do you enjoy about it?*

Or if he seems relieved that you've mentioned the death, you may choose to open up the subject a little more by saying, *A death in the family is a very difficult experience to go through. Maybe you can tell me what happened – was she ill, or did she die suddenly?* As you go along, the client will probably find it helpful if you acknowledge what he's saying with brief observations such as *It's hard to talk about his but you're managing. I can see that it's upsetting – that's entirely natural. Your loss is recent – it's no wonder you're feeling it so strongly. You've managed to tell me about your mum, and that's not easy. It takes courage to talk about what's happened to you* and so on.

Vignette 2

You try the following approach: *I can't help but notice that you're using a pen that belongs here. I saw it was missing last week. Often it helps to have something that is a reminder of this time with me. You probably know that the pen needs to stay here. Maybe near the end of the session, you can make something or we can create something together that you can carry with you such as a little 'hello/goodbye card' the size of a business card that you can keep with you as a reminder that even though we say goodbye every week, we're going to say 'hello' again the following week.*

Vignette 3

You could say, *I see that you're upset, and I want to hear about it; however, I can't see you until Period 4 when we're booked to meet. I'll be here for you then, and we'll be able to talk about what's distressing you. It's not easy to wait until later, but you know I'll be here for you.* If the student seems unable to manage her feelings, you can go on to say, *Why don't you go to the school reception and ask if you can sit there for a while until you feel better? They will understand and will tell your teacher. I have another appointment now, but I will be here for you in Period 4.* (In these situations, it is likely that she wants you to hold the feelings that are hard for her to stay in touch with such as powerlessness, helplessness, confusion and guilt.)

Vignette 4

You could start with *Until you've experienced it, perhaps it's hard to understand how talking with someone like me can help. Sometimes we don't know what we think or feel until we try to put it into words. I don't have the answers, and I can't change things for you, but I will listen and I can offer you my thoughts on what you're going through.* He may react with continued scorn, saying, *This is pointless. Can I go back to class now?* You may need to demonstrate that you can tolerate his rejection of you (the negative transference) by saying something like *It's difficult for you to be here, isn't it? Maybe you feel you had no choice. It takes time to get used to seeing someone like me. I'd like to hear about all parts of your life, not just your recent experience of loss. Maybe you can tell me what you like best about school or about your social life. I'm curious and would like to get to know you better.*

The young person may not be ready to talk and may resist this invitation too. You could say, *Let me tell you what I know about loss and bereavement. Some of what I say might make sense to you, or you could feel quite differently.* Describe in simple terms the cycle of grief. If he cannot stay focused, you might choose to end the session early, saying that you'd like to meet again next week just to see how he feels about things then, adding that sometimes a week can make a difference. Then give him an appointment time for the following week. Acknowledge again that it's not easy to come to see someone like you but that if he sticks with it, it can get better.

Chapter 10

The pupil at risk of exclusion

Akin Ojumu

School therapists frequently work with young people who have had a short-term exclusion or are at risk of permanent exclusion (expulsion) from school. Such referrals are often made at a point of crisis, when the school feels that a young person's behaviour is particularly problematic. There can be a great sense of urgency to get the pupil the appropriate support, especially because a permanent exclusion has a significant impact on a young person's life chances. As well as reducing their chances of leaving school with any qualifications, evidence suggests that school exclusion is a risk factor for youth crime and unemployment (The Social Exclusion Unit, 1998).

While the threat or experience of exclusion can have a profound effect on a young person, it can also provide an opportunity for them to think about the underlying causes of their behaviour. A young person might well be feeling vulnerable, rejected or humiliated; some, on the other hand, might appear to consider an exclusion as a badge of honour.

The school context

There are various types of exclusion that schools are able to use as sanctions. External exclusions require a formal process and take place within a legal framework. A fixed-term external exclusion stipulates that a young person is not allowed to attend school for a specific time period; a permanent exclusion is invoked in the most serious circumstances, when a pupil is expelled from school without the possibility of returning. Schools can also decide to use an internal exclusion in which a young person is removed from class and taught separately from their peers on the school site for a period of time. The vast majority of all exclusions, both external and internal, take place in secondary school.

Depending on the individual school's ethos and behaviour policy, there are different criteria for excluding pupils, but an exclusion can only be used for disciplinary reasons, that is breaking the school rules. The Head Teacher is responsible for the external exclusion of a young person for a fixed term or on a permanent basis. The latter sanction is relatively rare and according to official guidelines should be enforced only when allowing the young person to remain in school would harm the welfare or education of other pupils.

Secondary schools are large institutions which rely on rules and discipline to create a safe environment in which learning can take place. As has been discussed in previous chapters, adolescence is a developmental period of transition that frequently involves testing boundaries and challenging authority figures at home and in school. Exclusions are a powerful sanction, sending a strong message to pupils and their families about what is deemed unacceptable by setting limits to enable the school to carry out its primary task of teaching young people. From a therapist's perspective, a young person's behaviour problems are generally a sign of emotional disturbance, so this can be an opportunity for the pupil, together with school staff and the therapist, to think about what might be behind the acting out that is leading to the exclusion.

What kinds of behaviour lead to exclusions?

Put simply, pupils are excluded or face exclusion when they break the school rules. If we think of the rules as a form of contract between the school and pupil, these violations signify a tension in the relationship. Of course, many pupils will break the rules at some point, but a young person who has been excluded or is under threat of exclusion has generally transgressed to an extreme and worrying degree. Thinking about the types of behaviour that lead to exclusion provides a clue as to what might be troubling the young person.

The most common reason for exclusions is 'persistent disruptive behaviour' (Department for Education, 2013). Some young people struggle to function within the boundaries set by the school. There is a strong correlation between having a statement of special educational needs (SEN) and being excluded: these pupils are seven times more likely to be excluded permanently than those not on the SEN register. This suggests that despite the contemporary focus on inclusive education, young people with learning difficulties struggle with those issues as well as the emotional strain of feeling different from (and being treated differently than) their peers. As the emphasis on attainment increases when pupils progress through secondary school, disruptive behaviour – challenging teachers and interrupting the work of their peers – can be seen as a reaction to feeling unhappy about their own difficulties, which may well come from feeling bored and/or frustrated during lessons.

Violent behaviour is another common reason for exclusions. Violent, threatening or bullying behaviour is clearly not acceptable in schools, but when a young person gets into trouble for those reasons, it is necessary for the therapist to look at the triggers for the behaviour. A psychodynamic approach might focus on the idea that some young people were not helped when they were younger to understand their more vulnerable or aggressive feelings. Infants rely on their parents and/or carers to pick up on their different emotional states and respond to them in a sensitive and appropriate way, enabling the young child to learn to tolerate their own varying moods and develop a sense of emotional regulation. Young people who don't have enough of these positive experiences of emotional containment can develop violent or aggressive ways of dealing with difficult situations. As relationships to peers and teachers become more complicated in secondary school, adolescents can find it hard to manage their emotions in a way that fits in with the school's standards of behaviour. Particularly for those with a fragile sense of self, the experience of being humiliated, ridiculed or rejected can be intolerable if they haven't been adequately helped to deal with their feelings at an earlier stage in their lives. The young person who feels threatened in these ways can retaliate violently, turning the tables on their 'tormentor', projecting onto them all the intolerable emotions they cannot bear to feel themselves.

Some young people find it hard to respect the authority of the school and so appear disobedient. The culture of a typical secondary school is quite different from the generally more pastoral and forgiving environment of primary schools. Managing the transition from primary to secondary school in a thoughtful way can be a protective factor against future emotional disturbance. Some young people struggle to respect their teachers or take in anything useful from them. This might be because they lack positive examples of boundaries and limit-setting at home and struggle to engage appropriately with the authority figures in school. Some young people who do not have sufficiently good experiences of adult figures in their lives find it hard to take in the learning and other opportunities for personal growth that are offered in school.

Boys and exclusion

School therapists know that boys and girls often present with different issues in secondary school. Boys are likely to externalize their problems and 'act out' against others in possibly aggressive or violent ways, while girls tend to turn against themselves and/or their bodies, for example through cutting and eating disorders. There are, of course, examples that refute this delineation, but this remains generally the case. Because of the common tendency to act out, boys are three times more likely to receive an exclusion, either for a fixed period or permanently, than girls (Department for Education, 2013). Similarly, boys are more likely than girls to receive a diagnosis of attention deficit hyperactivity disorder (ADHD) or a conduct disorder, which relates to impulse control and behaviour.

One of the developmental challenges for an adolescent boy is to create an identity for himself as an independent young man while having to remain dependent on his parents and/or carers as his primary source of emotional support as he negotiates his way through these often tumultuous years. Similarly, in school, there is a conflict between valuing the stability provided by the institution and wanting to assert himself by testing boundaries. An added dilemma could be that among his male peers, academic success and good behaviour might not be seen as valued attributes.

Adolescent boys are more likely than girls to have lost meaningful contact with their same-sex parent. Why is this important? On one level, the experience of having a father who can provide a model for his son of how to manage himself in the world is valuable. The paternal role includes a limit-setting function; if the father is comfortable owning the natural authority invested in his role, it usually means that a young man will not be so eager to assert his masculinity in negative ways. Unfortunately, many boys experience their father as an absent figure, literally and/or emotionally, and the sense of rejection this creates can impact heavily on their self-esteem. The lack of a father who affirms and takes pride in him can be an intensely painful experience for an adolescent boy at a time when he is going through a period of major, often unsettling, physical and emotional change.

In psychodynamic thinking, there is an idea that the two parental figures, even if not necessarily in an intact heterosexual couple, provide a framework in which a young person has to navigate a three-person relationship. This is an important precursor to dealing with complex relationships throughout life.

Tarik was a 15-year-old boy who had been referred after several fixed-period exclusions for challenging behaviour that included fights with peers and a defiant attitude towards his teachers. He lived with his mother and younger sister; his estranged father had died a few years earlier in a tragic accident. Well-dressed and charismatic, a leader amongst his peers, he had relationships outside school with older males who were involved in local criminal activity. He presented as confident, sometimes arrogant, but generally respectful and keen to be liked by his male therapist.

Tarik could regale his therapist with tales of his (sometimes) illegal activities and his appeal to the opposite sex. His violent side came out in impulsive outbursts that he frequently recounted, which usually occurred when he felt threatened or undermined, causing him to lose self-control in episodes that subsequently left him feeling anxious. He was able to talk about his more vulnerable side: the shock at the sudden loss of his father and the mood changes that precipitated his violent acts. But it was difficult for Tarik to reflect on his actions or begin to understand the feelings that triggered his actions. At times he felt uncontained and uncontrollable, which is certainly how the school experienced him, but he could also appear to be a lost little boy in search of his father.

Social and cultural issues

Evidence shows that those young people particularly at risk for school exclusion include pupils with SEN, those from some black and minority ethnic (BME) groups and adolescents from low-income families. When a young person has more than one of these characteristics, the likelihood of exclusion increases greatly. They often carry with them into school additional pressures such as poor housing and financial stress within the family, which are known to be potential barriers to learning and healthy emotional development.

There can also be powerful inter-generational beliefs about school that are inherited from parents who struggled at school and found the learning environment intimidating. In such families, low aspirations and anxieties may be passed on to the children. Moreover, when difficulties arise these parents might not feel able to form a productive alliance with the school to consider the best interests of their child. Another source of personal anxiety and disaffection is the shadow of economic austerity and uncertainty under which young people are growing up, which is occluding their ability to see anything positive in academic achievement or 'staying out of trouble'.

What exclusion means for a school

Schools are under increasing pressure, particularly in the form of league tables and assessment targets. Even so, there will be varying degrees of tolerance of and understanding about 'disruptive' behaviour, depending on the culture of the school. Since exclusion represents a crisis point for the school and the young person, an exclusion or the threat of one can generate considerable anxiety in the system. When this happens, the school is able to draw on a variety of interventions, including counselling or therapeutic input.

There are a number of ways schools can react when faced with a possible exclusion. They might feel frustrated but determined to support a bright young person who has had persistent disciplinary problems. A Special Educational Needs Co-ordinator may have an understanding of what the pupil is contending with away from school and can see therapy as a way of providing emotional support. Alternatively, a teacher might find a young person's behaviour so difficult that he or she struggles to see the young person as separate from the problems they pose for the school. Therapy can be seen as a last resort in these cases, and a therapist will have to guard against unrealistic expectations as well as helping the school, if necessary, to think about the wider context of the young person's difficulties. This can put the therapist in a delicate position, balancing the school's ideas and fantasies about what the therapy should be about and the young person's thoughts about the work. At such times there is a risk that unconscious sabotage from the school will put the therapy in danger.

What exclusion means for a young person

The prospect of exclusion can stir up a variety of emotions in a young person. It is clearly a punishment, but of a particular kind. An external or even internal exclusion can feel like a sort of banishment. A pupil might feel emotionally rejected from the mainstream life of the school, cast apart from their peers. This sense of rejection will be particularly difficult for young people who, for whatever reason, already feel loss or rejection in their lives. For internal exclusions, the location of the room used for this purpose can indicate something to the young person about how the school views pupils who are sent there.

In contrast, some pupils seem to see their exclusion as a status symbol for which they earn kudos among their peers. Even in these cases, though, we should also be aware that underneath that attitude there might be more uncomfortable feelings of hurt and rejection.

When a young person is referred because of an exclusion, they might have set ideas about the purpose of therapy. They won't have self-referred themselves, and they may believe the therapy is part of their punishment, or something that they have been offered purely because of their bad behaviour. Many young people view therapy as a form of anger management, which for some, especially boys, is more desirable than being asked to see a therapist to deal with their emotional difficulties.

Thinking about starting the work

Although the school might have an idea of how therapy will be useful for a pupil, the young person might have different ideas about what they want, if indeed they do want therapy. Therapy might have been offered following a post-exclusion meeting – a delicate time to start working with a young person as there will be a high level of anxiety in the school system. It seems especially important to develop a therapeutic alliance when working in these circumstances, which can be difficult if the young person feels strongly ambivalent about therapy as something being imposed on them.

It is important to explore with the young person what they believe are the reasons behind the school's decision to seek a referral, then to invite them to think about what they would like to get out of the work. Their goals may be quite different from those of the school. This conversation can provide the opportunity to explore any negative ideas the young person has about their referral.

The offer of a thinking space to explore the feelings behind their behaviour will be a new experience for many young people, and it can be useful if the therapist is able to convey the idea that it is an opportunity to think about themselves and their actions in a fresh way. The therapist will be looking to see how much curiosity the young person has about themselves and how thgether they can use this reflective capacity to enhance the therapeutic process.

If a young person believes they have been referred for anger management, a therapist might respond by saying that their anger is one thing that can be explored together but that there are usually many different factors that make someone angry, and it would be interesting to see what sorts of things in particular make them angry.

The client might try to downplay the significance of their behaviour or even deny they did anything wrong. A therapist should be empathetic and perhaps not seek to challenge the client's defences too early as this could harm the developing therapeutic relationship. But as the work progresses, the therapist will be more able to judge the young person's emotional resilience. Gradually they should try to take up a stance that is supportive without colluding with the young person's more unhelpful defences.

Conclusion

Working with a young person when an exclusion, or the threat of one, is involved in the referral process presents a particular set of opportunities and challenges to a therapist. Since the pupil will often believe that the exclusion is the reason for the referral, the therapist has to work carefully to try to engage them in the idea of working together on aims that go beyond the immediate problems that are being presented in school. The therapist's challenge is to maintain a delicate balance in thinking about what the school and the young person might want to get out of the therapy when the objectives of both parties might be very different. Despite the anxieties that the prospect of an exclusion raises in everyone involved, the therapist will have to use their assessment skills and therapeutic judgment to gauge what is the most useful approach to take with a young person who, possibly despite their insistence to the contrary, is facing a crisis in their school life to which they are particularly vulnerable.

Study questions

The vignettes below explore some of the themes highlighted in this chapter.

Vignette 1

James (14) has been given a number of internal exclusions for 'persistent disruptive behaviour' in class. He is talented at sports but is on the school's SEN register and receives free school meals. He tells you that he has been referred unjustly because some of the teachers have been picking on him unfairly. *How would you approach James?*

Vignette 2

Sam (15) has just served a week-long exclusion for attacking another boy in the playground after a disagreement. Sam says he was provoked, and although he regrets injuring the other boy, he still thinks that he couldn't ignore what the other boy had said to him. *How would you approach Sam?*

Vignette 3

Lee (16) is an African-Caribbean boy who is a high-achieving student, predicted to get good grades in his GCSE exams. The school is concerned because he is often 'disrespectful' and 'angry' in front of teachers and has recently been asked to leave the classroom on several occasions. *How would you approach Lee?*

Sample responses

Vignette 1

You know, I think you are telling me that sometimes it can be really difficult for you in the classroom, and I'm sure that you feel that things are unfair. In fact, maybe it feels unfair that you have to come to see me today as well, and I can understand that. But maybe we can talk about some of the things that have been going wrong for you at school recently and think about what has been happening for you, then see if there is anything that can be done to make things feel better.

Vignette 2

It sounds like you were in a really difficult situation with that boy. Maybe part of you regrets what happened, but another part of you thinks that you did what you had to do, even if things went too far in the end. I can see how that must be a bit confusing for you, having those two different ideas in your head. It sounds like in the moment you just didn't know what else to do. It might be useful if we can think about what that felt like for you and why you felt pushed to do something which actually ended up getting you into a lot of trouble.

Vignette 3

I get the impression that some things are going really well for you in school and some things not so well. That's really interesting, and I was wondering why that was happening right now – obviously I know that you have a lot going on at school at the moment. Maybe you too have been wondering about what has been happening to you. Perhaps thinking a little about all this is something we can do together.

References

Department for Education (2013) *Permanent and Fixed Period Exclusions from Schools in England: 2011 to 2012*, London: Government of the United Kingdom.
Social Exclusion Unit (1998) *Truancy and Social Exclusion*, London: HMSO.

Chapter 11

The impact of internal and external authority figures in adolescence

Myra Berg

Adolescence is a process rather than a state. As already described in previous chapters, the search for a separate and new identity can entail not only acting out the more destructive drives of impulsivity, omnipotence and instant gratification but also getting in touch with creative drives such as concern for others, a growing interest in justice and a draw towards good causes in general. This search inevitably generates inner turmoil and uncertainty about all aspects of identity as well as one's future place in society.

Who am I and what will I become? is a question that often underlies the emotional upheavals. For some, the question is so terrifying that they unconsciously use the omnipotent defence of 'stopping time', acting as if the future will not happen and the present is all that counts. Despite being cognitively aware they are in transition to adulthood, for such adolescents their powerful unconscious anxieties and wishes may drive them down paths which deny this fact of life. Sometimes this takes the form of delinquency.

As adolescence is a time of change and transition, it naturally brings about the need to re-negotiate positions with internal and external authority figures. This has been described as having to accommodate the co-existence of a strong push for independence along with the simultaneously felt desire to be reassured that dependency needs will still be met (Bradley 1998). The ways in which adolescents manage these conflictual drives and needs by testing out their relationships with authority figures will be explored in this chapter. In keeping with the overall theme of this book, the authority figures considered will be parents and teachers. As will be illustrated, the extent to which adolescents are able to contain their emotions will reflect the quality of their early internalisations of these figures.

Conscious and unconscious representations of authority figures

Margot Waddell notes, "When the strength of internal structures is being so severely challenged, external structures acquire enormous significance" (2002a, p. 145). Our work with adolescents includes thinking about whether or not these external structures are experienced as supportive or undermining and what – or who – authority figures represent for the adolescent. The internal turmoil of the adolescent is holistic, encompassing physical (hormonal/pubertal) aspects as well as psychological shifts and changes. This creates tremendous confusion and internal contradictions which may result in an impossible double bind: authority figures can be viewed as domineering if they set limits and rejecting if they don't. The unconscious conflict of the adolescent is often projected onto the external world. For example, teachers may be experienced as subjecting them to the constraints and rules of the educational system, which can be felt at one and the same time as controlling and as containing. Parents provide financial support, which both satisfies dependency needs while also giving them power over the adolescent.

It is common for adolescent students to rebel against school rules by, for example, repeatedly arriving late, not doing their homework and truanting from lessons. However, they may complain if their misdemeanours go unnoticed and unpunished, especially if this leads to heightened feelings of insecurity. Equally, while adolescents frequently feel their parents are withholding money and freedom, a young person who is given unlimited resources and has no restrictions placed on their movements may experience this as a form of neglect or rejection and might demonstrate their hurt feelings by showing aggressive contempt for adults in general.

For example, Alex, aged 14, was brought up in a permissive household where he was given trust and freedom by his parents and had an equal say in his life with them. However, he began to demonstrate emotional and behavioural difficulties at school, following only the rules he felt to be appropriate. He was unable to view staff with anything other than contempt if they attempted to enforce their (and the institutional) point of view. This is one way in which the traditional adolescent complaint of being 'misunderstood' can be thought about as a projection of internal confusion. It can lead to distorted internal representations of the actual external parents/teachers, with the consequent 'acting out'. As Waddell (2002a) invites us to ask, what qualities do the internal parents/teachers possess? And are these qualities projected onto the actual parents/teachers?

Another student, 15-year-old Fred, was having significant behavioural difficulties in school, treating staff and occasionally his parents as enemies. In individual therapy sessions he revealed that he viewed all adults as 'not caring about children' and trying to 'humiliate children'. He was the son of very successful parents; his own envy of adult potency as well as his hatred of vulnerability was given expression in his critical view of adults.

If the authority figures are viewed as abandoning, a punishing/aggressive response from the adolescent may be acted out. It is likely that Fred's aggressive attitude towards school staff came from an unconscious denial of his own vulnerability, compounded by the fact that authority figures had begun to see this tall teenager as potent and intimidating. Thus his actual dependency needs and vulnerability were, in reality, 'misunderstood'. Fred's story highlights how difficult it can be for authority figures to keep hold of the fact that it is often anxiety and vulnerability that fuel young people's aggression.

The punishing position that the adolescent may adopt can also take the form of self-harm or suicidal ideation, which provokes anxiety in authority figures and leads to greater attention being paid to the adolescent. It is particularly true when the self-harm is very evident, for example in the case of eating disorders and suicidal ideation (overdosing, verbal threats). If the authority figures are viewed as being oppressive or domineering, the adolescent may act out of a fight-or-flight state of mind, using polemical arguments, delinquent behaviour or withdrawal. In these states of minds, authority figures are seen as having stale or outdated ideas or as being hypocritical and thus open to criticism.

Why adolescents might have difficulties with authority figures

The general anxiety about change and growing up, as well as the possibility of losing relationships which they had depended upon, creates immense pain and confusion in most adolescents. The psychological defences of splitting and projection are often used to alleviate emotional discomfort, leading them to act out the internal conflict in preference to trying to resolve it, replacing thought with action. The defence of splitting encourages idealisation (of themselves and/or peers) and denigration (of the adult world and authority figures). This is linked to the passion with which adolescents can embrace 'good causes' (idealism) and also argue polemically against the attitudes and values of authority figures (denigration).

A 16-year-old called James frequently used his therapy sessions to rage against the poor management of the world by numerous world governments. He felt that wars were caused by politicians forcing ignorant adults to kill other people in order to gain power or territory. He himself came from a family with a history of domestic violence and not only internalised this conflict but identified with the role of the aggressor and had manifested aggressive behaviour towards authority figures since reaching puberty. However, his engagement with his therapist enabled him to externalise his difficulties through talking about wars which were ineffectively managed and to receive support from his therapist in thinking about these themes. Following an exploration of his projections, James became able to understand both his exploitative and exploited parts, both of which fed his aggression.

Others use the defence of projective identification with adults to avoid the threatening experiences of adolescence. When this occurs, they assume a clever and superior persona to distance themselves from feelings of vulnerability or dependency. They may then look down on adults and denigrate authority figures, thinking they know better, and in the process project their own vulnerability onto parents and teachers. The clever 'know-it-all' in class can thereby make their teacher feel deskilled or ignorant. These omnipotent defences lead to a denial of pain but also contribute to more general communication difficulties with adults.

How this plays out in therapy sessions

A major aim of therapy is to help the adolescent take back some of their projections. The therapist needs to be a containing object in order for the projective mode of functioning to diminish. The therapeutic relationship allows the adolescent to investigate their own feelings in a person (the therapist) who is felt to be resilient enough to contain them. Bion (1962) used the term 'reverie' to describe this therapeutic endeavour. In much the same way as the mother (or primary carer) is single-mindedly focused on the infantile states of mind, the therapist becomes the maternal container for the state of mind of the client. In this way, the confusions, conflicts and contradictions of the adolescent can be re-experienced using the relatively safe space of the therapy sessions. The therapist and client work together to try to make sense of both the client's external and internal worlds. This thinking/containing process is then 'taken in' or introjected by the client. When this kind of enhanced understanding can be achieved through the vehicle of the relationship with the therapist, and through the experience of the therapist having a mind which can contain and reflect, a parallel process takes place resulting in a shift in the client's internal relationships. It probably goes without saying that this can be a profound and lengthy process.

James, mentioned earlier, came to an understanding of his vulnerability following 18 months of weekly therapy at school. He began having nightmares in which he dreamed he was being chased by an invisible but huge, dark figure. He could not see the figure, nor did he wish to. In therapy sessions we were able to think of these nightmares as possibly reflecting his wish to understand and integrate his vulnerable and domineering states of mind. The therapist's containing mind was used as a third position to help him do this. Following sessions exploring these aspects of his internal figures, the nightmares ceased. In his daily life, James was also more able to 'walk away' from conflict without feeling like a coward. The therapeutic process can make it possible for the adolescent to give up their omnipotent defences against emotional pain and to better tolerate conflict and confusion without resorting to the acting out of splitting and projective processes. Linked to a balance between projective and introjective process, it involves 'letting go' and mourning the loss of childhood but also brings excitement about potential future opportunities.

Many adolescents who agree to embark on therapy initially view it as supporting their stance and grievances against the adult world, which means that a complex dynamic can be in the mix even before the first session. As described earlier in this chapter, the struggle between dependency and independence creates a natural ambivalence in the adolescent's mind. This can be played out in a number of ways:

- Erratic attendance
- Poor punctuality
- Disregarding or rejection of therapist's ideas
- Acting out, such as risky behaviour
- Continuous flow of speech, making it difficult for the therapist to speak
- Silence.

The fact that they attend sessions at all implies the desire to take up support and is likely to relate to a more realistic and mature part of the adolescent's mind; the part that is beginning to balance introjection and projection and accept vulnerability. Of course, attendance may also indicate a more infantile, needy aspect, which might show itself by the client attempting to seduce the therapist into taking the role of protector. It is not difficult to distinguish between these two, since the former will be in the depressive position in which they will be able to think and tolerate difference.

However, the 'attacks' on the process are a clue to the young person's often unconscious aggressive drives, where the therapist is viewed (like the parents and teachers) as a domineering or rejecting figure. When this occurs, the therapist has to experience, via her or his counter-transference, the rejection, anxiety, frustration and confusion of the adolescent. It is only by gradually 'feeding' interpretations of the counter-transference back to the adolescent in a neutral and non-persecuting way that client may introject these experiences and thoughts.

For example, a 13-year-old girl, Mary, often arrived 10 minutes late for her therapy sessions and then proceeded to talk rapidly and continuously about grievances with teachers or parents. It was very difficult for the therapist to take in, let alone have a voice in this volume of information. The counter-transference experiences of intense confusion and frustration were very useful in helping the therapist to better understand Mary's internal world, as well as in informing the interpretations, some of which took forms such as the following: *I think you want me to know what it is like to have no voice and not be allowed to speak. You want me to experience what it is like to be someone who is not really noticed and is just kept waiting on the sidelines.* And *Such a lot going on, such strong feelings – how confusing.*

This is the container-contained relationship, as described by Bion (1962). It is the fundamental core of all human relationships and, as in the infant-mother dyad, needs to be repeatedly replayed in the therapist-adolescent relationship. Through this process, the therapist may then be valued and gradually internalised as a 'good object', which supports a shift from the internalised domineering or neglectful adult to the thoughtful one. This, in turn, is likely to allow truth and reality to permeate the internalisations of the actual parents and teachers in the mind of the adolescent. Through this, the client may begin to see himself or herself as a 'work in progress' and as 'growing', which in turn lays the foundation for the capacity to use the positive aspects of adults that are based more in reality than phantasy.

For the therapist, understanding the meaning of the attacks is essential. Here is a short-hand overview of frequent ways that young people act out:

- Non-attendance or lateness: can be interpreted as 'killing off' the therapy or therapist and is linked to the destructive drive;
- Risky behaviour: provoking anxiety and links to neediness or fear of loss;
- Confusing narrative or changing the subject: this is an attack on thinking about helpless, vulnerable states.

The constant analysis of our counter-transference is thus necessary in order to ascertain who we may be in the transference as well as what the quality or state of mind being projected onto us tells us. The interpretations (based on counter-transference experiences) need to be given very sensitively, taking on board the fragility of the adolescent personality and their tendency to feel persecuted.

How does the therapist position himself or herself?

The position the therapist takes up requires careful consideration as, for reasons previously stated, she or he may easily be experienced by the adolescent as taking sides. Also, it is easy for the therapist unconsciously to fall into the role of an authority figure. As Bradley (1998, p. 53) comments, "Therapeutic work with adolescents is likely to take in some of the characterisation of adolescence itself." This means, practically, that splitting and acting out are common pitfalls for the therapist to be aware of.

Fred (aged 15), who was previously mentioned, described an incident in which he and a group of friends had been rolling cigarettes outside a classroom. A senior teacher walked by and asked them to show him what they were holding. Fred walked away past the teacher, 'brushing' the teacher's arm.

The therapist felt alternately shocked (at Fred's audaciousness), angry (with Fred's inability to see his own unreasonableness, despite a number of therapy sessions) and sympathetic (to the plight of the teacher). It was very difficult for the therapist to resist acting out and 'explaining' to Fred the error of his ways, and so behaving like a teacher or parent. It was possible to maintain the therapeutic position only by pausing to think about Fred's projections of impotence and frustration. Therapists will often experience an internal pressure to act, but it is important to resist this and to think with the client about the meaning of the behaviour and what might be going on in the therapeutic relationship.

For example, Millie, a 14-year-old, disliked attending class registration. She explained to her therapist that 'nothing happens except cussing and it's only ten minutes'. Millie engaged well in her therapy sessions, and both she and her therapist related positively. Millie said that she would rather spend the 10 minutes with her therapist as 'I've got more to say and I get more out of this than registration'. As may be imagined, it was difficult to resist the feeling of being valued as well as the probable accuracy of Millie's comparison. However, using the therapeutic concept of boundaries and understanding the importance of an adolescent's need to experience realistic frustration helped the therapist to maintain her position and to reflect on why it was actually more helpful developmentally for Millie to attend registration.

The pressure may not come only from the adolescent. The therapist working in a school is frequently requested by staff to 'do something'. This is usually in relation to a concern about the behaviour or risk status of a particular student. It can be common for therapists to be asked by school staff to raise certain topics in sessions or to reinforce the school's perspectives. For example, a therapist who was working with Stevie, a 13-year-old, was asked by his Head of Year to use part of the session to go over a recent episode when Stevie had pushed a member of staff and had to be disciplined. The Head of Year wanted the therapist to ensure that Stevie understood the school's rules.

In this example, the boundary between the role of school staff and that of the therapist was being blurred. Taking on board the projection of anxiety alive in the network (in this case, school staff), the therapist may want to remind the Head of Year that her client will be best helped if she can be seen as more objective or 'neutral'. That way, Stevie will have the experience of a facilitating adult who is able to help him to think things through rather than of one who is taking up the authority which adults naturally possess and seemingly 'siding' with school staff. The therapist might want to reiterate that an aim of the sessions is to help her clients to understand and think about their difficulties in general and that this kind of work should, over time, enable them to take more responsibility for themselves as well as be able to judge future situations more accurately and appropriately.

Conclusion

If one is able to manage the complex external and internal boundaries inherent in being a school-based therapist, it is likely the adolescent client will learn a great deal about inter-personal relationships. As Waddell states, "The struggle towards an internal capacity for intimacy is what the adolescent has been working toward all along" (2002b, p. 176). Here, intimacy is being taken as meaning a more realistic relationship, one which necessitates the client relinquishing both the denigrated and idealised versions of their own selves and also of their relationships in favour of reality. It is about the letting go of desires and beliefs that were merely illusory. This kind of work has been illustrated in this chapter, most notably in the case of James. He had an idealised self-image of being omnipotent and invulnerable but gradually became able to let go of his phantasies through accepting his vulnerability and dependency needs. This development allowed him to become a more integrated, happier and functioning adolescent. The ability to evolve in this way is fundamentally linked to integration, which depends on acceptance of aspects of oneself and one's states of mind. It is, of course, precisely the goal of psychodynamic psychotherapy.

Study questions

- How would you describe your current relationship to authority figures? What about when you were an adolescent?
- What kinds of defences might you adopt when beginning to work at a secondary school?
- Where do you place yourself when a Head of Year and a client are in conflict?
- How can you help staff to see aggression in terms of managing anxiety?

- How do you help clients view teachers as being supportive rather than 'the enemy'?
- What might you say if a client asks you to side against school rules?
- How does the client 'see' you ? As a judge or enemy? As easily intimidated, too weak or too strong?
- What might you say to a teacher who asks you to discuss a school rule with your client?

Further reading

Bradley J. and Dubinsky H. (1994) *Understanding Your 15–17 Year Old.* London: Rosendale.

References

Bion, W. (1962) *Learning from Experience.* London: Heinemann.

Bradley, J. (1998) Chapter 4, "Confrontation, Appeasement and Communication" in *Facing It Out.* Ed. Anderson, A. and Dartington, A. Tavistock Clinic Series. London: Duckworth.

Waddell, M. (2002a). Chapter 9, "Puberty and Early Adolescence" in *Inside Lives.* Tavistock Clinic Series. London: Karnac.

Waddell, M. (2002b). Chapter 11, "Late Adolescence" in *Inside Lives.* Ed. Temple, N. and Waddell, M. Tavistock Clinic Series. London: Karnac.

Chapter 12

Relationships, sex and sexuality

Lyn French

Secondary school sets the scene for far-reaching social and personal changes: existing friendships may be tested or replaced, new possibilities for different kinds of relationships will come to the fore and unspoken questions around every aspect of sexual identity and intimacy in general will be in the very ether. To become the architect of their own life depends on the adolescent having the capacity to make increasingly more conscious choices about how they shape their identity, how they manage their relationships and how they view their sexuality. Many adolescents do not have the internal scaffolding to provide them with the support needed to take on a more autonomous role. These pupils in particular benefit from having access to on-site therapy sessions which offer an opportunity to reflect on their experiences as well as discover a language with which to express themselves.

Recognising what it means to have a mind

The move towards creating an increasingly private life naturally begins to encompass the adolescent's inner world too. Most young people wouldn't necessarily describe it as such, but what they discover is a new way of using their mind as a 'place' in which to stand back and look in on life from a distance, even if only fleetingly. This internal space forms the foundation for the development of autonomy and self-agency; without conscious intentionality, the adolescent gradually takes over thinking and decision-making processes from parents and other adults, ranging from the everyday – how to style their 'look', for instance – to decisions about the kind of life they want for themselves. Becoming aware of a 'place in the mind' is also key to developing the capacity to understand more fully that others have minds too and will, therefore, have their own perspective on things which will need to be taken into consideration.

In tandem, young people begin to recognise that they have views on life which have been unconsciously formed or absorbed from those around them and may, for the first time, question them. Many will become more conscious of how their family defines themselves in terms of social class, cultural identity, generational histories, assumptions or beliefs about the world, and articulated as well as unspoken family 'rules' or ways of being. Relationships within the family will in all likelihood be re-configured, shifting either subtly in small, incremental moves or suddenly in seismic lurches. These changes may leave in their wake degrees of confusion, hurt feelings, anxiety and a resonant sense of loss for everyone involved as the realisation that things may never be the same again takes hold.

For some, the necessary separation process from parents, and often from the general family culture (that is, 'the way this family does things'), can only be managed psychologically and emotionally if a clean break is made. It can be overwhelmingly confusing for many young people to struggle with ambivalence or grey areas. To defend against this, differences can be amplified so that what is being left behind or separated from is no longer seen as meaningful or desirable. The parents' ways of being and thinking are labelled as 'out of date' or simply 'wrong', making it possible to downplay the loss implicit in separation. This also ensures that the imaginary line separating adolescents from their parents' generation as a whole is clearly demarcated rather than blurred or muddled.

Internal worlds

All of our everyday relationships in the real world have internal representations called 'internal objects' in psychoanalytic theory. This language reflects the fact that we are the subject of our lives and those around us are the objects of our attention. Internal objects comprise not only conscious memories and impressions of our past and current life but also the meaning that we gave to these experiences at the time and the stories we've subsequently told ourselves about them. These narratives are driven by unconscious agendas, influenced by different aims such as the wish to safeguard the beliefs and norms that are important to the family or to hide shameful parts of family history. For example, emotionally potent experiences buried in a family's past, such as rape or incest, domestic violence, a stillborn baby and so on, may be enshrouded in silence, but the attendant feelings, in particular burningly strong ones like shame and guilt, which may not have been digested, 'tell' the story. These feelings can be toxic, leaking out and unconsciously damaging a young person's perception of what adult sexual relationships encompass. Frightening impressions of the power of sexual desire and of what human beings are capable of in general will be churned up on conscious and unconscious levels. Working with adolescents, especially those bringing complex and painful family histories, inevitably means that, in one way or another, we are in and out of touch with the more disturbing sides of sexuality, albeit often in symbolic or unarticulated forms.

At the same time, the adolescent's burgeoning awareness of what it means to be a sexual being will be influenced by other, perhaps less uncomfortable impressions, such as how sexual relationships are thought about within their home culture as well as by their peers and the media. This often means that there are tensions to be borne as parents' spoken or unarticulated but powerfully conveyed views about sexual choices, the age at which sexual experimentation can begin and what sexual acts are deemed permissible may differ from, or significantly clash with, the adolescent's.

Opening up exploration

There can be tensions to be managed and 'blocks' to be negotiated within the therapeutic relationship as well. Not only do some adolescents have a degree of ambivalence about or resistance to openly exploring themes relating to sex and sexuality; therapists, too, may have reasons for being reluctant to move into this territory. At first, many of us may not have the language or the ease with which to express ourselves. Or we may be worried that talk about sexual interests could spill over into disclosures of recent sexual activity which can bring up dilemmas about the need to share such information with the school. School therapists can find themselves in a situation not dissimilar to parents, who might also have to gauge whether or not an adolescent is psychologically and emotionally ready to experiment and how best to support the young person in this crucial phase of adolescent development. Although dilemmas around confidentiality can be thrown up, it is important to note that generally school staff will already be aware of which pupils are the most vulnerable. If the therapist does need to break confidentiality, it usually has a positive outcome, leading to the young person receiving more targeted support.

Openly discussing sexual identity can be another tricky subject to navigate for both the client and the therapist. The contemporary world is changing rapidly. For example, in Western countries, teenagers may not feel they need to define themselves early on, or indeed ever, as either heterosexual or homosexual but can instead move between the two positions, choosing their relationships on priorities other than gender. This kind of lifestyle choice isn't restricted to urban settings; the internet links up teenagers around the world while also providing ready access to sites which might explore these subjects. As therapists, we need to have thought through what informs our own views on adolescent sexual experimentation and sexual identity, as each of us will have a particular take on these subjects, influenced by religious or cultural beliefs, our gender, our personal experience and our own values. Our aim is to facilitate a spirit of enquiry and exploration which is not distorted by assumptions or agendas on our part.

Some parents' faith or culture of origin includes strict conventions around how to live and even what can and cannot be done or spoken, which may leave their adolescent child caught up in a confusing or even hostile or punitive culture clash. Powerful transferences can be activated in therapy sessions. The school therapist could, for example, be idealised as 'the other' who represents a more lenient culture, or conversely may be denigrated as powerless, stuck in their own belief system defined by their profession or rebelled against as 'old and out of touch' – or simply blanked out and ignored.

Supporting this kind of student, the therapist will be concerned with containing the underlying anxieties which feed such views by sensitively naming and addressing them, challenging black-and-white thinking and re-framing the young person's story. Facing social choices and opportunities for new relationships can be daunting for even the most confident adolescent. When confronted with a culture clash in a client's life, the therapist can usefully bear in mind that some of what is being presented will be a manifestation of more general adolescent fantasies and anxieties about their own bodies, what it means to be intimate with another and the kind of primitive feelings that are evoked, echoing back to infancy when the body played an important role in the relationship with the mother or carer. At the same time, we can't underestimate the reality of clashes sparked by a historical family culture coming up against a dominant 'lived-in' culture represented by everyday life, the media and social networks. In these instances, the young person is faced with what can feel like an impossible choice: either to conform to family expectations and limit life choices or to break away, which may feel akin to severing all family ties and striking out on one's own.

Questions which the therapist may choose to reflect on include: What, or whose views, might I represent for my client? How can the potential for, or the reality of, splitting (that is, seemingly taking one side or another) be thought about and addressed? What is this client most conflicted about?

Accounts of sexual experimentation

It is the exception rather than the norm for adolescents to share accounts of sexual exploration with their therapist. We know that the first forays into adolescent sexual investigation bring up a mix of responses ranging from excruciatingly intense embarrassment to a sense that entry into the adult world has finally been gained. Young people who are referred to the school therapist may not be able to articulate what they are thinking or feeling or, if they can express themselves, might find it counter-intuitive to reveal sexual fantasies, wishes or actual encounters. Sometimes sexual experimentation is alluded to. When this happens, the therapist may want to signal that the client is still considered too young to be engaging in sexual relationships by saying something like *When you are older, you'll need to feel comfortable about your choices. It's not just a matter of saying 'yes' or 'no'; you can suggest to your partner that you take your time. As you get older, you'll need to be sure that you feel ready and that you're not being pressured into something you're not sure you want to do.* This kind of observation conveys to the client that they may still be too young or may lack the emotional maturity to be engaging in a full sexual relationship.

If the client acknowledges that sexual intercourse is a tempting possibility, the therapist may want to open up the conversation, perhaps saying, *Let's think about how it feels with this boy (or girl). Tell me more about the relationship. What do you do when you spend time together? How does s/he show you s/he respects you as well as likes you? What do you have in common?* Depending on their age, their maturity and the context, the therapist may need to remind them of the legal framework, saying something along the following lines: *You probably know that sex under 16 is illegal in this country, and there is a reason for this. Young people need time to develop and mature, not just physically but emotionally too.*

The young person who starts talking about an active sex life may need to be stopped so that the therapist can say, *You may remember we talked about confidentiality when we first met. You probably know that I'm going to have to pass on to the school what you are telling me. I want to talk you through what I suggest we do to best ensure you are supported.*

Questions for the therapist to bear in mind when deciding what to do with the information disclosed include:

- How old is the client? *(Is this pupil mature enough and close enough to the age of consent [16] to be safe? Is the relationship a healthy, established one with a young person who is known to the school or to the family?)*
- What are the past and present family circumstances? *(How vulnerable is this student? Are the parents in a position to support the adolescent appropriately and mindfully?)*
- Do you have an idea of what the school's view is? *(Have you heard from the school that this young person has already had sexual encounters? What else is in place to support the pupil?)*
- Is the young person taking too many risks? *(Are they at risk of being drawn into something they aren't ready for because of lack of affection or love at home? Are they mistaking sexual interest for a form of love?)*
- What is the social context? *(Is the partner also a pupil in the school? Or have they met outside of school or via social media?)*
- If it is a same-sex partner, what has led up to this choice, and what is the social context? *(What are the young person's fantasies about how peers and family will respond?)*

Sexual acting out

We know that some young people are left with unmet needs from childhood and are looking to compensate for this through seeking out opportunities for what they believe will be intimate encounters. Their need to have the experience of being wanted can be great and may override all other considerations. Sexual acting out often has its roots in a deeper, unmet infantile need to be held, stroked, cared for, regarded as special and loved unconditionally. While these are usually experiences that have been missing in the lives of both boys and girls from complex family backgrounds, girls, perhaps more than boys, are drawn to the idea of engaging in sexual acts as a means of experiencing what they sense they have lost out on. Unconsciously they might crave being touched or cuddled or held as they imagine a young child would be; alternatively, they may be looking for someone to replace an absent father. It is sometimes the case that they feel so disempowered in their own lives that they are seduced by the idea of having power over another, even if it is only for the brief moment when they experience another young person desiring them. Some may also be caught up in unconscious rivalry, wishing to triumph over or displace their mother.

Girls who are vulnerable in any of these ways may be exploited by individual boys or occasionally groups who might take advantage of the girl's neediness even if she presents as full of bravado and 'street attitude'. Boys as well can come under the sway of similar unconscious motivations, but it is more likely that they will be driven primarily by their bodily urges. Often a wish to master their fear of sex propels them into action. Competitive striving amongst their peer group may also play a part.

Sexual acting out can take different forms. Examples are given below:

- Promiscuous behaviour (e.g. brief one-off or very short-term sexual encounters, one swiftly followed by another) may be a form of mania not dissimilar to the young child who is rather frantically trying to engage an unresponsive mother. It can also be used to defend against fear of abandonment. Or it could be a defence against making attachments and having any kind of meaningful emotional experience. For some young people, it may serve as an effective distraction, blocking out greater anxieties about course work, assessments and exams or the future once they leave school.

- Getting involved with a much older boy or girl or one from a gang could be a sign of wanting to leapfrog over adolescence and into adulthood, or it may represent an unacknowledged desire to be looked after and protected from taking on more adult-like responsibilities. The gang element, as discussed in Chapter 15, may represent a substitute family which offers a sense of belonging where loyalty is both demanded and offered.

- Taking repeated risks such as having sexual encounters without using any form of contraceptive or when under the influence of drink or drugs is another form of sexual acting out. In such instances, a kind of chaos is created which makes it possible to sidestep any responsible decision making. Young people who may be very anxious about breaking family rules or are frightened of any form of intimacy might unconsciously choose to numb themselves and even deny their intentions or refuse to own responsibility for their actions. Failing to use any kind of contraceptive can be another form of denial; it is as if the young person wants to convince themselves (and their internal parents) that whatever took place was out of their control. There can be a self-destructive tendency running through this type of behaviour as well.

Many of the most vulnerable young people turn to sex to compensate for the real or imagined losses of childhood. As school therapists, we will want to make links, at least in our own thinking, between the kind of behaviour a young person is engaging in and their own history. Crucially, however, we must break our client's confidentiality if they disclose this kind of behaviour and we consider them to be at risk of harm, especially if they are under 16. Our aim is to sustain the therapeutic relationship and to keep appointments open for the young person even if their initial response is to feel that we have betrayed them. We also continue to process our responses to their disclosures and to 'digest' the material they have left us with, using our own supervision and personal therapy to help with this.

Fear of pregnancy or actual pregnancy

Some students might reveal that they fear being, or that they actually are, pregnant. One of our roles is to support them through this experience. We begin by handling their disclosure sensitively. We tell them that we cannot keep this information to ourselves but that we will be sharing it with a school staff member who will need to know and who can help. We might ask them if they understand why this is necessary and then explore their fears or concerns about this with them. We could explain to them that adults have different roles in the school. The role of the school therapist is to think about the feelings and thoughts towards the possible (or real) pregnancy and to process the experiences. It is the role of the school to deal with the practical side. Often it will be a learning mentor, the Special Educational Needs Coordinator (SENCo) and perhaps a Head of Year who will get involved. The school nurse may have a part to play too. We ensure that our client understands these role divisions.

Based on what we feel in the here and now of the session, and on how receptive the client is, we may open up the conversation, perhaps asking them questions such as the following: *How sure are you? Have you told anyone else? What were your first thoughts about it? How did you think I'd react? What do you feel about me sharing this with the school? Would you like to be there when I talk to Mr/Ms X?*

There is much to explore and to think about when a young person goes through this experience. It is always best if they are willing to continue with the sessions so that we can help them process what is usually a distressing, confusing and frightening experience. Questions we might be thinking about in supervision include:

- What might this pregnancy represent for this particular client? *(Are they an only child or one of many? Do they have a sense of family? Do they have an experience of being fostered? Are they adopted? Has there been a recent death in the family? What does the boy's family represent for your client?)*
- How can we manage our conversation with them so that they don't feel we are taking sides?
- What feelings come up for us, and for the client, if the young person is intent on keeping the baby?
- What feelings come up for us and for the client if a termination is the preferred option?
- How do we help the young person process the experience so that it does not cause lasting damage and impair future sexual relationships?

This can be a challenging issue for the therapist to work with because of our own transferences to teenage pregnancy which can resonate on so many levels. It is rare that a client being seen by a school therapist makes a disclosure of this kind; however, it is best to prepare for this eventuality and to be clear which staff members in the school would need to know.

Relationships and the role of social media

Used creatively and positively, social media open up the possibility of building on and enriching existing relationships and developing new ones. For example, young people can sustain contact with their peers during holidays or if their friends move away. Having their friends easily accessible may feel less isolating if their family circumstances are unfulfilling or even negligent. Sometimes it can be easier to share things electronically that might be harder to talk about face to face, such as struggles with sexual identity. Young people may also be able to find virtual friends who might share their circumstances, such as dilemmas around their sexuality or problems at home, including a parent who misuses substances or one who is in prison or perhaps a very ill or dying family member.

On the down side, social media can inflate peer rivalry and amplify a young person's sense that they are unpopular or socially excluded or in some other way an outsider. There are also instances when they unwittingly or innocently expose too much personal information and this backfires. Or they may develop 'friendships' based primarily on information-sharing via social media sites, texts, messaging and so on, which can easily become too competitive or lack authenticity. Young people whose social world is dominated by online media may miss out on developing their social skills and find that it becomes that much more difficult to engage in face-to-face conversations where, for example, sympathy, empathy and understanding are shared.

The school therapist can usefully help clients to think about the role of social media in relationships in general. For example, exploration might be opened around the following themes:

- What issues are the easiest/hardest to convey in texts, emails or messaging?
- What do you prefer to talk about in person?
- How do you protect the privacy of your relationship if your friends want to see texts sent by your boyfriend or girlfriend?
- If most of your conversations take place online, what do you miss out on? What does it actually feel like to be with your boyfriend or girlfriend?

More specific questions can be posed around the theme of exchanging photographs:

- What kinds of photographs of yourself are you happy to circulate?
- What images would you consider private?
- What are the risks of sending a boyfriend or girlfriend intimate photographs of yourself?
- What are the risks of putting photographs of yourself and your boyfriend or girlfriend up on social networking sites?

We know how easy it is for adolescents to make contact with young people or adults whom they have met online, as has been discussed in Chapter 4. However, if the school therapist is working with a client who is engaging in relationships with people they've never met, some additional questions to think about with a client might include:

- What can we really know about someone without meeting them?
- What kind of picture are we giving of ourselves? How reality based is it?
- Is there a plan to meet up? If so, what do you need to do to keep yourself safe?
- Who else knows about this relationship?
- What do you hope will happen with this/these relationship(s)?

More positively, social media can open opportunities both for socially active young people and for those who are shy or perceive themselves as different or whose social field is limited, enabling them to link up with others in ways that weren't possible before. However, young people are particularly vulnerable to being swept along by fantasy and may not pause to think about the risks they could be placing themselves in if they arrange to meet someone they have been corresponding with.

Conclusion

Relationships are the fabric of everyday life. Thinking about how we live and work alongside others, how we form our intimate relationships, how we perceive ourselves and how we shape our identity, which is at the core of every relationship we have, is the very essence of therapeutic practice. Just as relationships offer opportunities for establishing deep connections and making discoveries about ourselves as well as others, they also stir us up, provoke us, confuse us and bring to the surface difficult feelings which can be hard to manage. Adolescents can be the most challenging of client groups to work with, as they are at an age when sharing aspects of their lives with an adult may feel counter-intuitive. Moreover, talking about the most intimate sides of life – deeply personal relationships, sexuality and sexual encounters – can be especially difficult for both the young person and the school therapist, who will need to be thinking of the levels of meaning in what the client is telling her or him as well as holding in mind her or his duty of care. There are no easy answers to any of this, and the work needs to be thought about on a case-by-case basis. Sometimes young people who do broach the subject of sexual engagement will need to be passed back to the school or referred on. At other times, the adolescent might continue to work with the school therapist while also seeing a learning mentor, the school nurse or a professional outside of school to deal with their lifestyle choices. Weekly supervision is absolutely essential, as is forming collaborative working relationships with key staff in the school with whom one can speak confidentially about clients who raise concerns.

Finally, working with adolescents will inevitably take us back to our own teenage years and put us in touch with the highs and lows of being on the cusp of adult life. None of us will remember that phase of our lives without mixed feelings.

For some of our young clients, this passage is an extremely painful and confusing one, marked less by optimism than by confusion, fear, loneliness and acting out. As school therapists, we have an invaluable role to play in supporting all young people. Our work in secondary schools is particularly important, and its impact is not to be underestimated.

Study questions

The subject of sex, sexuality and relationships is a potent one for all of us. Questions that can help us prepare for work with young people around these themes include the following:

- What aspects of your own relationship history stand out?
- What was most challenging for you when you were a teenager?
- What are your feelings and thoughts about same-sex relationships? Bi-sexuality? Trans-sexuality?
- What do you think are the biggest challenges facing young people today around the subjects of sex, sexuality and relationships?

Chapter 13

The nuances of difference in the therapeutic relationship

Reva Klein

Difference is as ubiquitous in the human world as in the world of nature. There are the obvious disparities of race and colour and the various mixtures and gradations within those distinctions. There are, too, the often less apparent distinguishing factors of culture, religion, nationality and class. As school-based therapists working with adolescents, we will be aware of how, as cultural theorist Stuart Hall (1996) has put it, different groups have different repertoires of meaning.

Negotiating our way through and deciphering those various and often complex repertoires is something we do consciously and unconsciously as a matter of course many times a day in our interactions with our clients, with school staff, with colleagues, with supervisors, and with family and friends as well as whenever we read a book or take in information from the media or watch a movie. The lens through which we experience the world and interpret meanings is defined by our experiences, which are determined to a large extent by our personal and collective history and how we see ourselves in relation to others in light of it.

While we all live with a sense of our singularity, which includes our differentness from everybody else, some of us identify with otherness or being outside what we perceive to be the mainstream more strongly than others. Working in inner-city schools, we as therapists more often than not come from a different class, race and culture from the young people we work with. However 'other' we may feel ourselves in relation to the school hierarchy or ethos or indeed to a class-conscious British society because of our national or cultural backgrounds or other orientations, we are likely to be perceived by our clients as insiders, in positions of power and authority. It is also sometimes the case that a therapist who presents as ostensibly from the same racial or cultural background as the client may be seen as someone who will better understand the client or who will even take sides with him or her against the school or a particular teacher in contrast to someone who is obviously different.

In our increasingly diverse society, assumptions about otherness are constantly being challenged, if not upturned. We all, to some extent, are the bearers of hyphenated identities that make us who we are, as complicated and sometimes conflicted as that may be. The young people we work with will often have multiple identities that happily coexist with each other. It's not unusual for young

Muslims, Hindus, Sikhs and Jews who go to religious school to have big family celebrations over Christmas. They may call themselves Turkish or Afghan or a multiplicity of other nationalities but are also confident in their identities as Londoners or Brummies and so on. We are also likely to have clients who are in a state of conflict between their home culture and the peer culture they so much want to be part of. Whether the family is rooted in traditions of religion or culture or neither or both, these situations can cause enormous heartache and splitting in the young person who is trying to find an identity for themselves while being torn between these two powerful influences.

In 'Working with Difference' in Volume 1 of *Therapeutic Practice in Schools*, Akin Ojumu discussed many of the ways in which cultural, racial, social and age differences impact on the therapeutic relationship. The present chapter will be looking at some other manifestations of difference that are present in our work with young people.

The differentness of adolescence

As has been discussed in previous chapters, adolescence can be a time of enormous emotional volatility, introspection and self-criticism. It is a confusing time, riven with contradictions. While still needing the boundaries of a secure home environment, teenagers feel compelled to disown that need by testing, pushing, rebelling. But not only are these needs and desires contradictory, they are often incomprehensible to adolescents and those close to them. When they say, as they often do in therapy, that 'nobody understands me', we are confronted with a number of emotional truths: that their internal chaos is distinctly and horribly *theirs*, making them feel atomised and cut off; that their sometimes narcissistic preoccupation with themselves makes it difficult to believe that anyone else could possibly have an understanding of what they're going through; that their identity is in a state of foment so that the 'me' they believe nobody can understand is not understood by them either; and that, in the transference, the therapist is just like 'the others', possibly an echo of an internal object who is well-meaning but ineffectual.

Working with these levels of adolescent alienation and their concomitant effects can sometimes be extremely challenging. These clients' sense of unease with themselves, sometimes accompanied by a strong sense of hopelessness, may be projected onto the therapist, making it difficult for us to think or believe in our ability to work with them. Robert, a 14-year-old African Caribbean boy who was referred to the school therapist after he was 'caught' downloading pornography via a school computer that hadn't been firewalled, spent many sessions sitting across from his therapist, face down and in almost total silence. He had one brother in prison, and his father had been killed when he was still in primary school; both had been involved in gangs. While he saw his downward trajectory as a hereditary fait accompli, his high-risk high jinks with the school computer seemed a promising signal to the therapist that he wanted some help. But what did he want? Did he have a fantasy that he could be rescued from his circumstances?

What form did he imagine this rescuer would take? And did he really want rescuing if it meant having to separate psychically from his father and brother?

His therapist came from an alien planet as far as he was concerned: white, middle class and speaking with a different accent from the heavy street dialect that he clung on to as if for his very existence. Hanging heavily in the air was the question: 'What's the point?' When the therapist reflected this back to him, he would smirk and sink further down in his chair. Robert was caught in the internal double bind of adolescence: a strong need to be held/contained and the hatred of that need. In the end, he said that he wouldn't come to the room anymore, that he hated being there and it was a waste of time. His therapist admitted to her supervisor that it came as a relief, albeit one swathed in regret that she couldn't shift his position and concern about what would happen to him. Soon after leaving the therapy, he was excluded.

The numbing pain of adolescent alienation, the push and pull of competing forces, can be enacted in myriad ways. For Rose, 13, her sense of being on the outside was accentuated by events in her rapidly changing family. The eldest of three and the only girl, her desperation to remain her father's favourite after he had moved in with a new partner was killed off when they had a baby girl. Not only did Rose feel that her position had been usurped, but it was also as if her identity had been stripped from her. From having been 'daddy's little princess', she was now expected to be a kind and loving big sister to the new rival who was infinitely more adorable and sweet than the surly teenager she had morphed into. Her mother couldn't be confided in because of her own malign feelings towards her ex, and she didn't dare express her vulnerability to friends for fear of appearing 'lame' and mean-spirited. So Rose turned her fury and pain in on herself, somatising and cutting. That way she could at least control the pain and at the same time re-enact being comforted when she was ill, as she had been when she was little.

Her therapist worked towards helping her understand that her feelings of displacement in her father's affections were tied up with her ambivalence towards growing up. Together they explored the complicated fantasies she had in which being an adult meant heartache and loneliness and where the only comfort to be had was rooted firmly in childhood.

The micro-culture of families

What we see in our work is that along with the various cultural, racial and socioeconomic differentiations that our clients come with, there is the highly individualised, often febrile realm of adolescence that they inhabit. How they negotiate these often challenging positions will be influenced to a large extent by the family culture in which they have been raised. Every family, whether it takes the form of a dyad or consists of two parents with or without other siblings or is a group that includes extended family members, comprises its own unique world. We know from our own childhood and adolescent experiences of spending time at friends' houses the extent to which it could feel like entering a parallel universe where, despite some familiar conventions and dynamics, there would be sometimes surprising differences from the way our own family lives were led: how people spoke to each other; rituals, traditions and conventions that were or were not followed; prohibitions and liberties; attention given to the physical environment of the home. While these distinctions are difficult to separate out from the larger cultural, religious and national traits of the family, there are those that go beyond these signifiers.

We know how powerful the effects of inter-generational phenomena can be. A woman who lacked a good enough experience of mothering may well struggle with meeting the emotional needs of her children. The man who was beaten for not complying with his parents' demands may become a father who lives by the dictum of 'spare the rod, spoil the child', resorting to harsh discipline to keep his children in line and out of trouble. The couple who have migrated to this country to escape poverty or oppression may find it difficult to let go of their insecurities, consciously or unconsciously passing them down to their children, who become enveloped in a smothering cocoon that keeps them separate, different and, in the parents' eyes, safe.

Take the case of Joshua, a 13-year-old whose parents had fled political strife in a West African state. Joshua was born in this country but lived a life that in some ways resembled how his parents were raised. He had to do chores before and after school, and if they weren't carried out adequately or on time, he was hit or else deprived of watching TV for a week at a time. There was no computer at home because the parents were fearful that he might misuse it, and he wasn't allowed out to play because their estate was known to be rough. Joshua was strongly resistant to the therapy for the first four months, speaking little and instead ritualistically drawing highly stylised pictures of superheroes, one after the other. He then moved on to playing hide and seek, which he and his therapist did over and over again. He took great delight in outfoxing her, and she would comment on it; but while he listened and seemed to take it in, he didn't respond. It was after a couple of months that he started talking about his home life. It was like a dam had burst. He was finally able to disclose painful experiences after years of complying with his parents' demands to keep 'family business' private, thereby suffering in silence. With his consent his therapist met with the father to discuss, among other things, alternative ways of keeping children safe and disciplining them. The hide-and-seek games soon petered out, and Joshua said that the atmosphere at home had improved.

Home culture can be oppressive when boundaries are lacking as well. Leaving young people free to watch TV, play games and/or engage in social networks without limits can take its toll. Mandy, 15, regularly comes to sessions tired with big shadows under her eyes. She says she's 'addicted' to instant messaging and is on it through the night. She has a TV and computer in her room as well as her phone and says her mum doesn't know that she never shuts them off because she keeps the sound low. She knows she's not doing herself any favours, but she says she just can't get out of these habits that have become her life for the past two years.

She is insecurely attached to her mother, who uses alcohol and is not consistently available to her practically or emotionally. Mandy has conflicted feelings towards her mother: she believes she's responsible for making her mum's life so difficult that she's turned to drink and feels guilty about it; she feels furious with her that she can't be a proper mother; and she is deeply embarrassed by her disinhibited behaviour, which prevents her from having friends around. When she feels abandoned by her mum, she can temporarily override her loneliness by texting and 'BBMing' away, whether it's about her emotional state or 'just gossip'. Her therapist has been able to work with her on her desperation to be in constant contact with her friends and the outside world to counteract the feelings of isolation she feels at home with a mother who isn't present for her. They have also been able to explore and challenge her own identification with addictiveness.

There are also those family cultures that, while distinctive, are not objectively problematic but give us pause to consider how best to help the young person to understand them. Katie, 12, is the youngest of three children. She is an eccentric girl whose mind meanders into the wonders of physics and biology, where, possibly, she feels more at home than in the strife-ridden and impoverished here and now. Her mother died when she was a baby, and since then her disabled father has been the sole carer. In his desire to make things better for his children, the father has shared with Katie a succession of elaborate fantasies for the future, all of which involve moving to other countries and starting all over again. Katie has bought into these convoluted projects, staunchly supporting her father in his various attempts to realise them.

In sessions, both fantasy and science are interwoven into Katie's narrative seamlessly and persistently, flooding the space in an attempt to keep the therapist's thinking at bay. She is aware of the symbolic roles she oscillates between in the transference: a consistent, present maternal object and, at the other extreme, an agent from the real world (social services, school) who has the potential to wreck her father's dreams. She is conscious of the need to tread carefully: Katie's eccentric singularity and consequent isolation make her identification with her father strong to the point of being merged. To let the therapist in is an enormous compromise that threatens the shaky edifice of their lives. So she patiently works on making small interventions that show that she understands why Katie is communicating in the way that she is, in the hope that his trust in her will build and with it will come a loosening of her defences.

These snapshots offer just a few examples of the way the adolescents we work with, whatever their background, bring their distinctive family identities into the therapeutic frame. Sometimes we will have strong counter-transference to what we perceive to be irresponsible parenting. When we hear about how poverty impacts on the family's ability to house itself adequately, we will feel anger on their behalf and also, perhaps, hear alarm bells when a 12-year-old girl tells us she shares a bedroom with her 16-year-old brother. Whatever the circumstances that are brought into the room, we need to be thinking about context and content as well as the unconscious communications that underlie the spoken narrative.

Conclusion

Going beyond the usual meanings of diversity, what we as therapists find in our day-to-day work is a panoply of ways in which our clients are different – from us, from their peers, from their schools, from their view of conventional society and sometimes from their families. That sense of otherness can be experienced in ways both constructive and otherwise. In young people with robust egos, their singularity will be something they may well pride themselves on: it's a mark of resistance to the desperate conformity so prevalent in adolescence, which means they may genuinely enjoy the distinctiveness that marks them out. For others, the ravages so often part of the maturation process during the teen years can be compounded by feelings of being on the outside, unloved and unlovable.

As therapists, our challenge is not only to find a way of relaxing the defences that adolescents erect around themselves but also to be mindful of the many guises of differentness. We must also remember that to make assumptions based on race, class, religion and other distinguishing marks may not only distort our clients' complex realities but occlude our thinking on other forms of difference that are at least as powerful.

Study questions

- Thinking back to your teenage years, how did you place yourself in relation to peers you identified as being part of 'mainstream society'?
- Are you aware of making assumptions about clients during their first session on the basis on their accents, race or religion?
- How do you imagine you're socially placed by your clients? By staff in the school? How does it tally with the way you would define yourself?

Reference

Hall, S. (1996) 'Who Needs Identity?' in *Questions of Cultural Identity*, ed. Paul du Gay, 1–18. Thousand Oaks, CA: Sage.

Chapter 14

Bullying
The real and the virtual encounter

Margery Craig

Fear of bullying is a frequent anxiety raised by Year 6 pupils when they are preparing for their transfer from primary to secondary school, and not without reason: being bullied, or taking up the role of the bully, is a recurring theme in secondary schools. This chapter explores some of the forms bullying takes, including cyber bullying, as well as ways in which bullying may be presented to the school therapist and thoughts about how we might work with those who have found themselves in the role of either the bully or the victim.

Forms bullying can take

Bullying can be the primary reason a student is referred to us. In such cases, it is worth giving thought to what this means consciously and unconsciously to both the school and the young person. For example, a referral might tell us that a young person has been a victim of a particularly traumatic bullying incident and that the school wants to offer them the opportunity to process this in an attempt to make good the injury. Perhaps at an unconscious level the school wishes to 'tidy the incident away', preventing emotions from spilling out and damaging the school's reputation. The young person might welcome the chance to see a school therapist as it can give them the time and space to heal and move on. Or they may fear that seeing the school therapist might keep them in a victim position. Some might worry that they may experience a re-traumatisation of the original event if they have to talk about it.

In other instances, a referral might arise because the school is perplexed about what to do with the student who often finds himself or herself at the centre of bullying incidents. Though this young person may often come off worst, the school can hold on to the impression that he or she is an 'agent provocateur' and may struggle with the recurring problem of how to apply sanctions fairly. In this case the school may want the therapist to uncover 'the truth' about the young person's role, and the pupil, aware of the school's mistrust, might approach the therapy very defensively.

Sometimes the school refers someone whom they identify as a perpetual victim. Compassion may have turned to frustration, and the school could feel it has exhausted its powers to protect the young person. In this case, there can be relief that the problem has now become the therapist's responsibility and a hope that it will drift into the background before disappearing altogether. The young person may interpret the suggestion that he or she see the school therapist as further reinforcement that his or her peer group problems cannot be resolved within the school's normal structures, increasing a sense of helplessness.

For perpetrators of bullying, it may be the school's policy to offer therapy to provide them with a thinking space. For example, staff might refer a student whose bullying behaviour seems out of character or someone who is aggressive towards others and is at risk of exclusion. In each case the school may have a sense that all is not right with the young person's emotional life and hold out hope that the school therapist will be able to get to the root of the problem. While the pupil who is acting out of character may be relieved that their distress has been noticed, the delinquent young person may arrive at the school therapist's door with the impression that this is their 'last chance' to keep their place in a school they already feel ambivalent towards; if the destructive drive dominates, such a pupil may attempt to 'fail' to make effective use of the therapy in order to be free of the school.

When the therapist is alerted to bullying in the school's referral of a student, it is likely that there will be access to further information such as the school's version of events, the student's general attitude and the defences he or she may already be displaying, which could form a starting point for the work. Sometimes, however, the subject of bullying can take time to emerge as the young person will need to feel sufficiently comfortable with the therapist to be able to disclose a traumatic or shaming incident in confidence. Once trust is established, the therapist may then begin to hear about the existence of material that is considered 'taboo' personally or socially. This might include themes touching on the young person's sexuality, family deprivation or low academic or social ability in relation to peers.

Not all bullying will have taken place in school or will involve peers from the young person's school. He or she might want to discuss incidents that involve others who have no relationship with the school, including incidents which may call for multi-agency support. Though the work within the therapy room may be similar, thinking about practical support will vary, depending on whether the bullying is taking place within or outside the school boundaries or, as is increasingly likely, within an un-boundaried virtual domain.

The impact of social media and new forms of bullying

As young people's involvement with digital media has grown, so has the potential for new forms of bullying. Cyber bullying refers to incidents when the internet, mobile phones, online games or any other kind of digital technology is used to manipulate, threaten, upset or humiliate people. It is a particularly insidious type of bullying as it reaches young people wherever they go, contaminating their most intimate spaces. Young people who are bullied in this way can experience it as an overwhelming intrusion and feel that nowhere is safe. For most adolescents, the computer and personal phones represent virtual retreats from the adult world and are considered absolutely private. When bullying is perpetrated via internet pathways, young people often feel that they cannot turn to the adults in their lives for support for fear that an anxious and protective parent will withdraw their online freedom and thereby threaten their social life. The fear of being forced offline can leave them feeling very isolated.

Cyber bullying has many features in common with face-to-face bullying, with some key differences. In a face-to-face incident in school, the perpetrator's behaviour is likely to be modified not just by the presence of others, or the potential for other students or teachers to suddenly appear, but also by the visceral experience of the victim's reaction. In cyberspace, however, without the threat of authority figures in the background or the 'hit' of a real emotional reaction, the bully and any onlookers can become increasingly disinhibited and excitedly vicious, possibly tapping into destructive unconscious fantasies. The virtual world is at one remove from lived experience, which means that bullying can escalate at a dizzying pace and rapidly spread to involve others. In contrast, some young people may find cyber bullying easier to deal with than face-to-face incidents; rather than be forced to live out and embody their humiliation in public, they can delete messages and bar access. But even with the ability to block out the hurt literally, they will be emotionally impacted by the experience and their self-esteem may take a serious knock.

Cyber bullying can be perpetrated by an individual or a group, by strangers or by those known to the young person. A group may feel sufficiently defended to allow at least some members to reveal their names, but the young person does not know who else is bearing witness to his or her humiliation and can feel ganged up on. For individuals, anonymity can be easily achieved: a bully, for example, might set up fake accounts and hide their IP address or block their mobile number before targeting their victim. This can leave the victim feeling even more vulnerable. If they take action to block or change their account they are still left wondering whether the bully is someone they know and trust. This undermining of trust is a side effect of any bullying but can be particularly pernicious in cyber bullying, and at times it is the central purpose of such bullying.

Adolescents are especially vulnerable to cyber bullying because at this stage in their development there is such a strong drive to forge an identity, and cyberspace affords the perfect forum for this kind of experimentation. And yet these newly hatched 'ideal selves', untested by reality, are immensely fragile. The online image is an adolescent's own creation, and they are likely to be devastated if it is spoiled by mocking or abusive comments, which they often read when they are alone in their bedroom. The effect can be profound, and they may well struggle to return to school. Sometimes they will want to make visible the unseen damage by self-harming or expressing thoughts of suicide. As therapists it is likely that we will be referred these pupils only when the after-effects start to become apparent and school staff become concerned.

Avoiding a polarised approach

Bullying incidents can provoke a binary mentality in individuals and systems. There are those who hold the view that all victims are innocent and powerless and all bullies are powerful and inherently 'bad'. If a culture is organised around this view, action will be taken to protect the victim by identifying and making an example of the bully. At the other pole is a belief that 'bullying is a fact of life', and that a developmental task is to build the emotional resilience to be able to confront and resolve a bullying situation. If this is the predominant belief, then there will be a reluctance to act.

Adopting a polarised approach is a human reaction to an anxiety-provoking situation. It represents a wish for a clear and immediate resolution to what can sometimes feel unbearable. Deep-seated beliefs embedded in school or home culture can reinforce this stance, providing respite from complexity and painful thinking. If the therapist is to be of help it is important to be aware of the dominant belief systems at school and home and of the pressure the young person may be under to conform to them. Powerful unconscious forces will be in the mix. The adolescent client might, for example, try to position the therapist in such a way that she or he takes up the role of the critical outsider whose value system is at odds with the home culture. It is vital to remain objective, open and curious rather than being experienced as joining forces with the young person and seemingly ready to assign blame. A more neutral stance will allow the therapist to identify and gently challenge what might in fact be a 'victim's' passive aggressive provocation or to take up the sadistic element of a feisty client's 'button-pushing' interactions with his or her peers.

Why some young people become bullies and some are bullied

Few people are unaffected by bullying. Many of us can remember the powerful emotions associated with being victimised and also the experience of having bullied others. Fear of bullying may have inhibited our own range of activities at school and beyond; for example, we may have wanted to avoid 'sticking our neck out' for fear of attracting notice. Or it may have contributed to other defensive strategies that limited our adolescent experimentation.

If we do experience bullying, the level to which it feels damaging will relate not only to the severity, length and public nature of the bullying but also to the strength of our own self-esteem and the resilience and quality of our internal objects. Bullying which accurately targets our unconscious insecurities will 'hit home' and will be far more damaging than attacks where we can confidently dismiss what comes our way or see it as belonging to the bully, who is only trying to get rid of it by projecting it onto us. Unfortunately, it is often apparent to others which personal qualities, physical traits or ways of being we are uncomfortable with or try to deny. Those who cannot face their undesirable parts are the most highly defended and are, paradoxically, the most vulnerable to being damaged by bullying.

Gender divide in bullying

Adolescents are often intensely focused on every aspect of their identity: how they look, talk and think; how they come across to their peers; what social status is accorded them; who they want to be versus who they still are; their sexuality; their perceived 'desirability' and so forth. To a certain extent, these common teenage preoccupations will have a gender bias.

Boys, whatever the stage of their physical maturity when they start secondary school, will be moving from the relative safety of childhood into a world where masculinity is a hot topic. There are many ways in which they will be challenged to see whether they are 'man enough to take it'. Even teasing banter can take on an incessant quality to test their endurance. Showing off physically may take centre stage amongst some boys. For example, status may be achieved by asserting what is stereotypically seen as masculine power, and aggression can be acted out in different forms, often very publicly and sometimes very dangerously. Those who do not wish to get involved learn to don a mask of bravado or find a means to compensate via their quick-wittedness, humour or, in some instances when driven by desperation, even bribery.

For adolescent girls, at least until the focus shifts to sexual relationships, prestige is more likely to be gained through popularity with other girls; the spotlight is turned on who is 'in' or 'out' of groups as well as what personal attributes girls can offer to their friendship group in terms of their 'social capital'. Although girls may physically enact envious and aggressive feelings, bullying more often takes the form of attacking the links formed between others. For example, they might undermine another girl's confidence in her established friendships and attempt to plant the seed that 'no one really likes her' or try to make her doubt her personal attributes.

Insiders

The human tendency to form exclusive social groups can be understood as rooted in primitive survival instincts. To thrive physically, emotionally and psychologically, we need to be part of some type of kinship or social group. The primal terror of being left out, left behind, overlooked or forgotten lives on in all of us and can be acutely felt by infants and young children, who are totally dependent on adults for their very survival. In adolescence, 'survival' takes on a different meaning. The small child's fear of abandonment may be rekindled and played out on the social field. Teenagers can experience even seemingly small rejections or brief spells of losing their place 'inside' a friendship group as a kind of social death. Peer groups provide a temporary replacement 'family' for adolescents to take refuge in as they negotiate their move away from their parents, and for this reason peers can assume a huge importance in adolescents' lives.

Forming and sustaining peer groups, each of which will attract varying levels of status, will often rely on splitting and projection. Not only will disowned feelings be split off and projected onto the outsiders, but those on the inside will unconsciously harbour paranoid fears of being pushed out themselves if they do not fully comply with the group and show unwavering loyalty. Splitting and projection and the attendant paranoid anxieties rooted in the fear of some form of retaliation or of the tables being turned often have a central role to play in contributing to a culture of bullying behaviour.

Another example of this primitive defence in action can readily be seen in those young people who suppress fear and shame about their own sexuality. To distract their peers' attention from it, they will often seek out a substitute who can be 'accused' of having the same disowned desires and thereby becomes the focus for denigration and bullying by the group. In such an instance, the young person fearful of his or her own sexuality does not come off unscathed. Instead, the unconscious conviction that his or her sexuality is 'bad' or 'shameful' and cannot be admitted to will be reinforced when his or her peers join in the attack. This leads to a form of internalised discrimination and is a significant factor in why young people who are lesbian, gay, bisexual or trans-sexual are at a much higher risk of suicide than their heterosexual peers.

Outsiders

Not all adolescents will seek refuge in the group, nor will they be accepted into an inner circle. This may be because of straightforward reasons such as preferring the company of a best friend or enjoying solo activities. Those with something which visibly sets them apart, such as disability, a cultural difference or being new to the school, may be branded as outsiders. This can be an isolating and acutely painful experience that the school can go a long way towards addressing by promoting inclusive practices.

Other young people take up an outsider position, seemingly unmotivated to make friends or share interests and apparently disregarding the good opinion of others. At its worst, this 'anti-developmental stance' can be deeply disquieting to parents and teachers who long for such adolescents to build healthy relationships. Such pupils can be emotionally challenging to their peers, particularly when they make their vulnerability apparent by engaging in self-harming, risk-taking behaviour or a studied lack of self-care. This strategy of adopting an attitude of shamelessness can be enacted as an extreme form of victimhood. It can also be seen in those who take up the role of the bully, operating independently or with a gang, who callously act out their torturing behaviour without any conscious feeling of empathy towards the victim. Such young people who appear to be announcing that they have 'nothing to lose' are externalising what has been called a negative sado-masochistic object relationship, in which "a wilfully misunderstanding object" (Bion 1967) has breached all the protective layers of shame, leaving them feeling irredeemably despicable and destructive. In another words, they hold on to their 'power' by stubbornly refusing to let themselves experience their own dependency needs even for the briefest of moments or to feel any degree of human compassion towards others. If no value is placed on human relationships (including the relationship with the self), this effectively puts them outside the reach of feelings of shame or humiliation. An extreme presentation such as this bears the marks of disturbing early experiences and a damaged mother-baby relationship that went undetected and untreated.

Working with the bully: fear and power, and fear of power

Strong feelings can be stirred up when working with young people who bully, and we may find we approach the work with trepidation. Indeed, some young people do attempt to unsettle and intimidate their therapist with whatever means they have at their disposal. In these moments it can be hard to hold on to thinking, let alone curiosity, about why they need to resort to such an omnipotent display of power over adults. Even before the work begins, the transference feelings of the staff member who refers such a pupil may colour what is passed on to us. We might get the sense that the adolescent is perceived as a 'real handful', someone who is complex, emotional and confusingly difficult to understand. Similarly, we may pick up that there are endless stories in circulation about the young person featuring reckless behaviour and uninhibited aggression, sparking both perverse admiration and the belief that they will come to a bad end. The pupil may have built a reputation as a character to be feared, secretly admired and harshly judged in equal measure.

How do we work with this kind of presentation? Do we seek to understand the young person and feel compassion for them by seeing their recklessness, rebellion and open aggression as exaggerated forms of the kinds of feelings we all have but may seldom act on, and in the process overlook their real source? Do we concentrate our energy on 'liking them', excusing or minimising their more difficult behaviour by choosing to see them solely as a victim of a complex family background? Perhaps we relish the experience of being 'the one' who can form a good relationship with this wild and often difficult-to-reach adolescent. Or maybe we find ourselves enjoying the cut and thrust of the sessions; the image of ourselves impressively parrying their sarcastic remarks, attacking scorn and belittling accusations, might make us feel potent and powerful. If we are drawn into positions like this, we are stepping out of our role and getting caught up in enactments. Such stances distract us from the serious issues and risky behaviour that threaten the young person's future in the school and beyond. The therapist's task is to resist this push and pull while attempting to retain objectivity and consistent boundaries. We can be helpful by calmly but repeatedly conveying our wish to understand their past and present circumstances and what they are defending against. We try to stay in touch with reality instead of taking up a position that might play out aspects of their internal drama; at the same time, we attempt to make contact with the part of the young person that may be very frightened and will have concern for themselves and their future. We might also choose to acknowledge the adolescent's skill with words by saying something like *You're fast at responding and also clever with words. But I'm left wondering what's happened to the part of you that is worried about your future.*

What we encounter in the consulting room can give us an idea of what happens at home, where vulnerabilities and any sign of dependency may be quashed with scorn, derision and denial. Unfair comments such as *Who do you think you are?* can be delivered by a parent in such harsh and critical tones that they simultaneously wound deeply and trigger instant rage. This feeds into a cycle sparked off by the young person's immediate retaliatory attack, followed by hostile withdrawal, residual rage, plans for an even more hurtful attack to be launched later (of the *I'll show her!* nature) and the sense of being both persecuted and persecutor. The yearning for mutual tenderness, the wish to be understood, the desire to be forgiven and the need to allay the fear of abandonment are buried so deep that the therapist may find it takes some time to get even a fleeting glimpse of such feelings.

For these adolescents, who have made what could be described as a deadly alliance with the despised and destructive parts of themselves, this work can feel particularly heart-breaking, as we must endure attacks on our attempts to know them, trying to tolerate their hostile 'shutting-us-out' silences and other enactments of their hatefulness. To progress they will need to witness our capacity to survive such attacks and experience our willingness to maintain a readiness to relate. They will also need to understand, at some level, our fundamental belief that relationships that are more creative than damaging are possible and that change can be achieved, albeit slowly.

Another persona that can be adopted by some clients is being a 'good person' and a high-achieving student. This could be because they experience the love of their attachment figures as conditional on their behaviour. These young people may act out their unconscious resentment and anger at always having to be 'perfect', or their envy of those who are loved unconditionally, by engaging in different forms of bullying. This could lead towards the disapproval of loved or admired teachers and peers whose respect is important to them and who, they suspect, now see them as remiss in their treatment of others. Being convinced that they have lost the positive regard of others, and with little or no experience of ruptures being repaired or the 'good' being resurrected, they may feel devastated. Slow, careful work could be required of the therapist to demonstrate to these clients that all parts of their personalities are acceptable and can be thought about. This may, in fact, form the main focus of the work.

Understanding and working with the victim

Each victim of bullying will tell us a different story, which, in turn, will call up feelings in us. As therapists, we may, for instance, find ourselves being pulled into a role equivalent to the victim's, feeling stuck, powerless, deskilled and unable to think. This can reflect our client's vested interest in either pairing with us as a 'partner victim' or leaving us carrying their victim feelings. Alternatively, we may be able to think freely and to come up with important insights which the young person recognises as valid, but end up feeling frustrated by their seeming determination to hold on to their role. At times, we may even feel uncomfortably sadistic in the counter-transference, wanting metaphorically to shake our client to startle them out of their passive and seemingly helpless stance.

For those young people whose internal world is populated by hostile figures, taking up a victim's role provides them with a much-wanted opportunity to disown or distance themselves from their own aggression and their persecutory fear of retaliation. Being an 'innocent victim' may be their only way to get in touch with a 'good self'. Often such adolescents are part of a family system which employs a similar strategy. Such families may be carrying powerfully felt shame from past and present sources. Perhaps the family history includes more than one generation marked by domestic violence, substance misuse, psychiatric admissions, prison or suicide. When a young person comes from a family such as this, where rage, disappointment, shame, guilt and depression about the seeming impossibility of reparation dominate, hostility is easily aroused, and revenge looms large in their unconscious fantasies. Being 'the victim' at school may be the only way that they can experience themselves as worthy of understanding, comfort and protection. If attempts are made to initiate a dialogue with the family about the adolescent, the parents may unconsciously identify with their child and project their own 'bad' parts onto the school, relishing the opportunity to be seen in the role of loving protectors, taking their child's side against the school, which in this scenario can only be seen as 'bad'.

In working with such a young person, though they may initially present as relieved and gratified to have been recognised as a victim, the therapist is likely to find a negative transference developing and may soon be seen as a persecuting object. The young person may defend against any exploration of their internal world by increasing this defensive strategy, saying or conveying, for example, that the therapist is trying to blame them or is trying to 'catch them out' in some way. Time and the therapist's consistency in tone, manner and presentation are important. So too is the therapist's focus on building trust by taking in and thinking about, but not reacting to, these projections. This approach can result in a thinking space being opened up.

Sometimes a young person will present an experience of being bullied in school from which they can't seem to move on. When the young person describes the incident, the focus may be on one aspect or detail that seems to them especially humiliating, to which they repeatedly return. This could be recognised as a screen memory behind which lies a much deeper, perhaps infantile wound that was re-opened when the bullying took place. The therapist needs to decide how appropriate it will be to explore more deeply. Raising the adolescent's awareness that we can all assign too much meaning to some of our more difficult experiences can be helpful, perhaps explaining that this usually happens when the present pain touches on an old hurt that we may never be able to track back and identify. In such instances, we need to do our best to explore every aspect of the painful incident and then try to let go of it.

When young people are being bullied because of difference we may feel especially powerless. We may, for example, find ourselves hopelessly wishing that we could wipe away a disability, or we may feel angry towards the bully or society at large for harbouring such attitudes. But not all young people who are different experience bullying, and it is important to try to get underneath the situation to see what the young person's attitudes towards their own difference are while being mindful, too, of what we and school staff make of it and the responses aroused consciously and unconsciously.

Young people can be bullied despite having characteristics seen as admirable by their peers. Here envy is likely to be at least part of the story. A securely attached young person with a stable sense of self and supportive others may well be emotionally bruised, but they can usually make use of therapy to help recognise what belongs to the bully and to affirm their own strengths and ability to recover. It is important not to pathologise a young person who has been the random victim of a bullying attack: sometimes just one or two sessions may be enough.

Other pupils who might be expected to shrug off a bullying incident may in fact be presenting a false self, their bluster masking a very fragile self-esteem. Being the target of envious bullying may be particularly difficult to recover from, provoking immense anxiety about unlovable aspects of their personality. Thinking about a bullying incident may be just the starting point for a much wider-ranging therapeutic encounter.

Conclusion

We know that no school will ever be free of bullying behaviour. As this chapter has illustrated, bullying has powerful unconscious motivations and agendas. All schools work hard to ensure that such behaviour is managed and that the message is given to young people that it will not be tolerated. However, bullying often takes place on the edges of school life, away from the reach of staff. When our clients bring accounts of bullying to the sessions, we need to think about what we are being told from a number of perspectives, as the examples provided in this chapter show. As therapists, we can work alongside staff to help create a school ethos which promotes compassionate understanding and reflection and a culture in which both 'bully' and 'victim' are thought about using a wider lens that takes in each young person's circumstances, both internal and external.

Study questions

The questions below are designed to aid self-reflection on our internalised attitudes and our key anxieties around bullying.

- What are your own experiences of having been bullied within the family circle, in the community or at school? How was it resolved? Do you feel there were any lasting effects? What emotions are evoked when you think of these experiences?

- Can you remember having bullied others, either as an individual or within a group? How difficult was it trying to admit to this? How do you understand your behaviour now?
- What are the first feelings that come up for you when someone tells you that they are a 'victim'? Where do you think your feelings stem from?
- What are the first feelings that come up when you meet someone who has a reputation as a bully? What informs these feelings?
- How comfortable and knowledgeable do you feel around the use of the internet and social media? Do you know where and how to find out more?
- What do you know about the attitude to bullying in the school in which you work – not just what is contained in its bullying policy but how it is implemented? Is there a consistent ethos within the school, or are you able to detect some aspects that are being disowned?

Reference

Bion, W. R. (1967) 'A theory of thinking', in *Second Thoughts*. London: Heinemann: pp. 110–120.

Chapter 15

Understanding peer relations in adolescence – group or gang?

David Trevatt

Why do young people form peer groups?

This chapter looks at the importance of good peer relationships for young people's emotional health during the years of adolescence and at how some relationships are not mutually supportive and may be detrimental to emotional health. Peer pressure, whether from a group or an individual, can lead to bullying and victimization. Young people need to learn to recognise the difference between friendships that can enhance their feelings of self-worth and relationships that undermine their capacity to think and act independently. Furthermore, because of the significant role relationships play in healthy development, concerned adults need to develop ways to support them in making good judgements.

Human beings are essentially social animals, and, reflecting this, society has developed from earliest times through the sharing and exchanging of ideas and of the means of support for the wider survival and security of the majority. The family has developed as a part of this process and is a group that most people have an experience of belonging to that provides a template for future interpersonal relations. The family can also be seen as a part of or as belonging to a community, a wider grouping of families who share an environment and a set of beliefs and values. Young people grow up, learn and socialise in various groupings within this context.

As children mature into adolescents, friendship groups play an increasingly important role in their lives. Close relationships with peers enhance adolescents' feelings of self-worth and assist the development of their interpersonal skills as well as providing positive role models. Early adolescents tend to engage in friendships not as stable dyadic pairs but as members of larger groups that can have a shifting membership. In later adolescence, friendships can become stronger, and the emotional ties may be closer. Along with sexual development, pairing is more prevalent at this time, and a more intimate type of relationship is common. Every young person has had their own particular experience of family and peer relationships, and while the majority may have developed connections that are stable and sustaining, many adolescents will have experienced deficits or difficulties at points in their development, such as problems arising from parental separation or a family moving home and the subsequent loss of valued friendships.

Research has typically focused on either friendship dyads or networks of friends, but young people can also participate in other types of peer relationships, such as cliques, which are exclusive, tightly knit groups, or else more loosely associated networks, often referred to as loose groups or liaisons (Cook et al. 2002). There are, however, many young people who have difficulty joining any stable friendship groups for a variety of reasons. These teenagers can experience high degrees of isolation and loneliness that also may leave them victim to various types of bullying.

Here is an example:

> Sam, aged 15, was having problems with his peers in school. He had few, if any, close friends and thought he did not 'fit in' with anyone. He was intelligent and able to do his schoolwork well, but his class peer group was not motivated to achieve academically, and he felt this set him apart from them. They teased him a lot for succeeding in schoolwork, and in order to stay on reasonable terms with this group (and not become a target for their hostility) he felt he had to join in with them and the activities they enjoyed. He said he was aware that they looked for 'fun', which included taking drugs and drinking alcohol when they went out at night. Sam told his school counsellor that he had no choice; if he did not go along with them he would have no friends at all. At the same time he was not sure what this group really thought about him. He felt he had to invent things he had done in order to impress them, but at the same time he was worried that they would find out and humiliate him publicly.

The role of the peer group in adolescence

Friendships with peers are a key feature of social and psychological development in adolescence, which is a time of actively 'separating' from parents in both practical and emotional ways as the peer group becomes especially important as an alternative means of emotional support. The peer group is sometimes characterised at this stage as a surrogate family, where strong ties are made which may become lifelong, or sometimes more temporary relationships as young people continue to develop and explore their potential in different directions.

Where the child had previously sought comfort, advice, guidance and support from parents and family, now the peer group is where many adolescents seek these things. This is not to suggest that the family and parents are redundant, even if some parents sometimes feel like this. Far from it; many young people continue to value and draw on the support of family and parents, even when there may be tensions around particular issues. Usually, even those teenagers who choose to spend their time with friends rather than with parents and family will not have rejected their families entirely. They may take the support of parents for granted, while showing no overt sign that they value having a family. It is likely that they are responding to the developmental needs that every adolescent experiences: to undergo a gradual process of separation and individuation.

At the same time, there is also a desire and a need to belong, to find others who share the same perspectives and with whom emotionally valuable relationships can be made. As part of this process the adolescent friendship group helps teenagers to manage this transition to more independent activities and independent thoughts and feelings. What friends think and like, how they speak and dress, all may become more important to the teenager. School-based friendship groups are particularly important because such a large part of adolescent's day is spent in school, and groups may influence students' academic performance and behaviour. Whatever the context, adolescents form friendship groups in the main with those who appear to share certain values and opinions. They can be thought of as a subculture with shared norms, almost speaking its own language with slang words that can only be understood by the members of the group.

The impact of school and the formation of roles within peer groups

The transfer to secondary school at the age of 11 is a significant milestone in the development of most young people. Children usually go to secondary school with friends they made at primary school. But sometimes they can find themselves separated from their friends if they do not all gain a place at the same school, and this can lead to feelings of isolation and vulnerability. In these situations, not only have they lost the emotional support of their familiar group, but it may not feel easy to make new friends if everyone appears to already be in groups.

As the young adolescent moves through school from year to year, there may be a reorganising of the peer group depending on a number of factors. In the first year of secondary school there is the arrival at the new institution and an introduction to the various classes and subject groups that each young person becomes familiar with. In the second year there are often changes in groups as new friendships are developed and often exchanged for others. There are many accounts from young people of friends they had with whom they fell out and who became 'worst enemies'. The group can develop in different ways with these changes and move from including to excluding particular members who may have fallen out with the 'leader'. With the advent of social media there are now many more opportunities for opinions to be shared amongst a wide population of young people. Sometimes they can find themselves the subject of comments, accusations and rumours that can have a powerful impact on their self-esteem, whether or not they are true or malicious. In a very real sense the welcoming social group can at times turn very rapidly into an aggressive one 'ganging up' on an individual. What these actions show is the prime importance of friends and friendship groups for most adolescents, who, like the rest of us, are by nature social animals requiring the support and co-operation of others in order to survive.

When a group may become a gang

How does the therapist working with a young person in school distinguish between the description of a 'normal' group of friends and something that may appear to be of more concern, such as a gang? Canham (2002) makes a distinction between group and gang states of mind that can be seen as active in the individual as well as in the functioning of a group. In one state, which he associates with Klein's depressive position, there is the individual or group that can 'tolerate, explore and value difference, alternative viewpoints and the tensions and potential for creativity these throw up'. There is a healthy interaction that promotes growth and development where the young person can learn to be empathetic towards others. Alternatively, for an individual or group in the grip of a gang state of mind,

> the defences and organization of the personality are more akin to the paranoid-schizoid position described by Klein (1946). In it there is a gathering together in a malignant huddle of parts of the personality in a very particular constellation. The dominant and destructive parts of the self take hostage what they feel to be those other parts that would expose them to feelings of neediness, littleness and ignorance and they do so by imposing a reign of terror on these other parts. There is therefore a submission to tyranny by a leader. This dynamic process happens within gangs but also can effectively structure the personality of individuals through an atmosphere of intimidation, fear of reprisal and a coercion to conform.

The word *gang* can have a different meaning in different contexts. It can be seen as a harmless description of a group of friends who share an identity, perhaps quite innocently, for example 'our gang'. But there is a much more threatening and worrying understanding of the term – 'violent' gangs, which have a long history, from highly organised criminal gangs that use intimidation to extort money to relatively unorganised street gangs that keep to their home territory or postcode.

There are frequent reports in the news of teenagers being stabbed or shot, sometimes fatally, by other young people. Many adolescents know they have to be careful where they go to prevent themselves from becoming targeted. To be seen in an area where you do not live means running a considerable risk; to be outside your postcode may result in finding yourself in the territory of another group. Many adults are unaware of the potential threats young people face as targets of other youths organised in a gang.

Gangs in London are many and sizable, but it is hard to establish who is in one and who leads them. Members will often deny they are members; it is not something to talk about with anyone outside the group itself. But if you live in a gang area you are more likely to know that they exist and are very influential and powerful. Young people who are identified as suitable members may be enticed or threatened to join the gang. Sometimes it can be difficult to say no if threats of violence are made against family members. Those who confront gang members can find themselves in such danger that they feel it necessary to move home, sometimes with their families, at a moment's notice.

However, gangs have different functions for the people who comprise them. They often provide alienated young people with a place and a role, a sense of belonging and of being a part of something that is strong and effective. Gangs thrive on deprivation and fear, and young people have to know that they are a force to be reckoned with. But how does this description vary from a description of how other groups operate? There are some similarities among different groups' forms and functions based on a strong code of values and criteria as to who is accepted into the group and who is excluded. The idea of grouping together is to find strength and support from like-minded people, with influence exerted on members that binds them to the shared code and shared interests. However, it is worth bearing in mind that families, too, can operate in a rigid and intolerant fashion. Harris and Meltzer (1986) described the 'Gang Family', noting that in this organization the family is intransigent, disregarding evidence that does not accord with its views.

A psychoanalytic understanding of the group

Bion (1961) referred to the recurrent emotional states of groups as 'basic assumptions'. He states that in every group, two groups are actually present: the work group and the basic assumption group. The work group refers to the conscious reason why the group was initially set up, or its primary task. Often groups that have an objective can stray from it because they are powerfully influenced by the unconscious forces of the basic assumptions. The basic assumption group refers to the underlying assumptions on which the behaviour of the group is based. Bion identified three basic assumptions: dependency, fight-flight and pairing. When a group is under the influence of any one of these basic assumptions, it interferes with the task the group is attempting to accomplish.

There are many examples of young people who are victimized by a group of peers either because they are different or, sometimes, because they are very needy. Children who have experienced some form of emotional deprivation are less able to recognize when they may be being misused, or even may be prepared to tolerate what appears to be misuse in order to avoid isolation. To be included, even as a scapegoat, may feel like an acceptable compromise compared to being repeatedly ostracized and excluded.

So groups and gangs can have some common elements, but there are of course important differences. Where, for instance in healthy friendship groups someone is able to join or leave at will, leaving a gang is often not an option (because members fear, perhaps justifiably, others 'knowing too much'). Despite the significant differences between them, it is helpful to visualise groups and gangs on the same continuum of relationships. A gang is a group, but it is at one end of a spectrum, an extreme representation of a group that has dysfunctional relationships at its heart. At the other end is the functional group, where members freely join, participate and leave if they choose to. In between are groups that may embody aspects of these two extremes as young people learn from each other about what they can expect from the rest of the group. Even for so-called normal functioning there are 'abnormal' elements that occur within groups. It is natural for unacceptable parts of the self to be projected onto a group, or for one group to project these elements onto another group. Take an example such as a group of football supporters who see their neighbouring rival team in opposition to what their own team stands for. All the bad elements are routinely and partly consciously, partly unconsciously, identified as belonging to the other team and its sorry band of supporters, while the home team is idealised as the epitome of excellence.

How does a young person understand and negotiate what can seem like a threatening primitive jungle of different groups and relationships? It seems to be common sense that it is better to belong to a group than to be on one's own and therefore potentially exposed and vulnerable to everyone. It is basic human nature to want to be with others and to join forces for mutual gain. Bear in mind the saying 'My enemy's enemy is my friend'. The school playground may look like a pleasant place to spend recreational time, but it is also an area which may be subtly demarcated into areas for young people with different interests and relationships. Many parents will hear from their teenager about bullies and bullying in both primary and secondary school. As discussed in the previous chapter, some young people can find themselves standing out for some reason and become an easy target for others to treat as a scapegoat. This can take the form of verbal as well as physical ill treatment. Young people with special needs can be especially vulnerable to this kind of behaviour. Parents of young people with autistic spectrum disorders are often aware that their teenager can find it particularly difficult to join a group because of a difficulty in reading the social cues that would enable them to fit into the group.

Leadership and followership within peer groups

The peer group is often subdivided into those with leadership skills and those who follow. However, leaders are not always the most balanced and at ease with themselves. In fact, they can be driven by a need for others to do what they say, perhaps because they find intolerable the idea of being told what to do by anyone else. So leaders may not fit easily into a group and may be in some way outside it or even on the periphery. They exert their influence by daring, charm, threats or promises. They have to maintain a kind of dominance over those who prefer to follow or put up with the shortcomings of the bossy leader. Leaders are also constantly vigilant for challenges to their leadership and may seek to expel or subdue any challenges from within the ranks. By accepting the dictates of the leader and his or her inner circle, the follower is protected, but sometimes the costs of followership are high. It may require delinquent activity or behaviour, which possibly involves having to discard some of the closer ties of family.

Conclusion

Children are of course dependent on parents or carers to protect and educate them. When a child reaches puberty it is common for the emerging adolescent to withdraw emotionally from the bonds of intimacy with parents and parental values and standards in order to make the transition to independence. This can take the form of an extreme withdrawal, with adolescents finding it hard to talk to their parents. At the same time, there is often an increase in social processes with contemporaries. Teenagers who are apparently awkward and inarticulate with adults can be surprisingly communicative with those with whom they feel more comfortable. The friendships that develop with contemporaries who are going through similar daily challenges and experiences, in which adolescents can share observations, find out new information, test each other's resolve and compare strengths and weaknesses, can offer more mutual understanding and be more immediately rewarding.

With all the changes going on, it is not surprising that adolescents can have lots of insecurities about themselves. These can be framed as questions such as Am I normal? Why am I bigger/smaller than my friends? Do I have the ability to make it to adulthood? Will I be able to reach my goals? Will anyone like me and accept me for who I am? The questions may not be the same for every young person and may not be as clearly framed as these, but they are common worries. Having friends who share the same challenges and who struggle to some extent to meet the same expectations provides reassurance that the individual is not alone and that there is support from others who 'understand', when it might feel that adults cannot and do not.

Study Questions

- What were your own adolescent friendships like?
- How did they influence you?
- What are your thoughts about gangs?
- How could you help young people at risk of joining a gang – or who are already members – to think about this aspect of their life?

References

Bion, W. R. (1961) *Experiences in Groups*. London: Tavistock.

Canham, H. (2002) 'Group and gang states of mind'. *Journal of Child Psychotherapy*, 28(2), 113–127.

Cook, T. D., Herman, M. R., Phillips, M., and Settersten, R. J. (2002) 'Some ways in which neighbourhoods, nuclear families, friendship groups, and schools jointly affect changes in early adolescence.' *Child Development*, 73(4), 1283–1309.

Harris, M., and Meltzer, D. (1986) 'Family patterns and educability'. In *Studies in Extended Metapsychology*. Strath Tay, Perthshire: Clunie Press.

Klein, M. (1946) 'Notes on some schizoid mechanisms'. In *Envy and Gratitude and Other Works, 1946–1963*. London: Hogarth, 1975.

Chapter 16

Working in schools with teenagers on the autistic spectrum

Tamsin Cottis

'Autistic spectrum disorder' (ASD) is a term that therapists working in schools are likely to come across. ASD is a condition with a triad of impairments. Individuals diagnosed with ASD have difficulties with communication, social interaction and behaviour (National Autistic Society, 2013),[1] which are explained in more detail in this chapter. However, because ASD is a spectrum disorder, the nature and extent of impairment in each domain can vary enormously. It is useful to think of the diagnostic label as a flexible framework when it comes to getting to know, and making sense of, the young person who is referred for therapy in a school context. Being on the spectrum is no barrier to individuality. As with any client, your main task will be to get to know them and find ways of imagining what it feels like to be them in order to facilitate a relationship between you. In this way, therapy, and the therapeutic relationship in particular, can help the client with ASD to make the most of themselves in the world.

Defining ASD

Diagnostic criteria for ASD

School therapists will not be expected to make a formal assessment of their clients, but it is useful to know how the criteria are defined. Functional impairment is broken down into two main categories:

1   Social communication/interaction, including

- difficulties in 'back-and-forth' conversation, in initiating conversation and in sharing attention or sharing emotions and interests with another
- severe problems in maintaining relationships, evidenced by a lack of interest in others, in pretend play, or in adjusting to social expectations
- non-verbal communication problems, for example, with eye contact, facial gestures, voice and body gestures.

2   Restrictive or repetitive behaviours, which may be shown in

- speech
- motor movement
- the use of objects
- having strong routines and being very resistant to change
- having restricted interests, or interests which are abnormal in intensity or focus
- being hypo- or hyper-reactive to sensory input.

For a diagnosis of ASD to have been made, the difficulties must be serious enough to impair function. Sometimes a child's difficulties are apparent from infancy, though diagnosis before age two is extremely rare. Others may receive their diagnosis later in childhood when difficulties are identified at school. It is also the case that some cases of milder ASD are not diagnosed until adulthood. Sometimes a young person may have a diagnosis of ASD alongside other diagnosed disorders such as attention deficit hyperactivity disorder or an anxiety disorder. As a therapist, the diagnostic criteria may be useful. For example, knowing that there may be a greater than usual need for routines and predictability can help us make sense of why a client with ASD becomes so distressed when there is an unexpected change to the school timetable or to their session time.

The ASD client

Despite the facts, when we hear the term 'autistic', we may immediately make assumptions about the client we have not yet met. We might imagine a closed-off person, unable to relate to others and existing in their own separate world. We may feel worried that the client with ASD will exhibit mystifying or bizarre behaviours. Examples of 'autistic genius' are well publicised in fiction as well as fact. We may be told that a client is on the milder end of the spectrum or has Asperger's Syndrome. (It is worth noting that while this diagnostic category has been removed from the *Diagnostic and Statistical Manual of Mental Disorders*, the American Psychiatric Association's classification and diagnostic tool, it is likely to persist in school records and reports in general for some years to come.) ASD and Asperger's Syndrome are labels that may lead us to imagine someone who is perhaps fixated on one particular thing and who may be socially awkward and on the outside of the usual adolescent social circles.

As therapists beginning work with a client who has ASD, our primary concern is likely to be the inability to make therapeutic contact with them. However, even in the most extreme cases of autism, a person with ASD does not exist in a world devoid of human connection. Autism may make relationships different – including the therapeutic relationship – and in many cases more difficult. But a relationship is possible and can be an agent for personal growth and change. This is as true for the ASD client as it is for anyone else. The challenge for the therapist is in understanding how to do this and to what extent a relationship will be possible. An ASD diagnosis in and of itself may not tell us anything very helpful about how to build a relationship with a particular child or young person. In terms of social interaction, it is not that the ASD client is not interested in things; it is that they have difficulty sharing that interest with another person in the usual ways. Relationships are also just as important to them as to others; individuals with ASD do feel very strong love for and attachments to people in their lives, but the reciprocity of the relationship and the way their feelings for the other are expressed is likely to be unusual or impaired.

Autism is a complex and controversial condition, with many splits between those who feel it to be a primarily organic and perhaps inheritable condition (Baron Cohen 1988) and those who attribute it to environmental factors – most especially the relationship between a baby and its primary carer (Bettelheim 1967). Anne Alvarez (1992, 2012) says it may be more helpful to take an integrated approach and see autism as a 'double helix where heredity and environment twist around each other in an interacting spiral' (1992:187). As our interest in, and our understanding of, autism increases, many new sources of information have become available. These can be academic studies or professional 'how-to' books, or they can be personal testimonies from those who are on the spectrum and have described, filmed or written about how they experience their world. There has recently emerged, as well, a growing movement of self-organised 'neurodiversity activists' (Solomon 2012) who assert that ASD is a rich experience, not a disorder at all. There are also people with an ASD diagnosis who may have some, or little, or no self-awareness of their condition. It may cause them distress or relief, or, alternatively, it may have no obvious impact on their sense of self.

Some reasons why a young person with ASD may be referred for therapy

Emotional distress arising from the condition itself

The young person with ASD may have an awareness that they are different from others but without understanding the exact nature of that difference. They may feel lonely and isolated and have a desire for more rewarding relationships but be uncertain and confused about how to go about achieving this.

Behaviour problems which are a function of ASD

A young person with ASD may become angry when routines change unexpectedly or when others do not conform to what they need in order to feel safe and in control. Anxiety and fear are often behind such angry outbursts, but therapy can help the ASD client to make links between their feelings and actions. Therapy can help to regulate emotions so that, for example, angry outbursts can be better controlled. It can also help the client to find the words to explain what they are feeling, rather than reacting in ways which mystify others.

Emotionally distressing experiences such as divorce, bereavement and neglect

A young person with ASD may experience a range of emotions in response to challenging life events, just as any other young person might. However, difficulties in making sense of themselves in relation to other people can make the experience more confusing and harder to understand and process. Subtleties and nuances in both the expression of a relationship and the experience of it may be very difficult for a person with ASD to understand. Making sense of a suddenly absent loved one or the breakdown of a parental relationship can be very painful, and the effect of such losses highly traumatic.

Working with the client's care network

The assessment process for therapy is crucial. It will help the therapist to gain an understanding of what the presenting problems are and for whom they are a problem. If a person is quite severely affected by ASD it may be very difficult for them to explain the full story themselves to the therapist. For such clients, it is very important that the therapist is in contact with other significant people in the young person's life. If the client is known to the school and the teacher or teaching assistant has already developed a means of maximising communication, it is helpful for the therapist to find out what these are beforehand. Because so much of ASD presentation is enigmatic or confusing it is helpful for the therapist to be as well informed as they can be. Likewise, supportive parents can be a rich source of useful information that can help the therapist to develop a rapport and relationship with the client. Indeed, they may well be expert in attempting to do this. Members of the network can also be on hand to share information as the therapy progresses. This collaborative approach clearly has implications for privacy and confidentiality, important issues for the therapist to consider in supervision and with the young person's network.

If the primary reason for referral has been behavioural difficulties, the school's expectations of what therapy will achieve may be high. It is unlikely that problems will disappear completely, but it is reasonable to expect that over time the frequency or intensity of episodes of difficult behaviour will diminish. *Be prepared for progress to be slow.*

Therapy may go on for longer than with a non-ASD child, and it can help to raise this possibility at the outset – especially if there is pressure on the therapist to provide short-term therapy.

It can be helpful for the therapist to have updates from the client's teachers and Special Educational Needs Co-ordinator on how the client is getting on in class and elsewhere. As well, the presence of a therapist in a school can be a vehicle for developing understanding, knowledge and insight in others who work with the child, which in turn can help to improve the quality of school life and relationships for the young person with ASD.

None of the above replaces more general guidance about assessment, and, as with any client, the assessment process will involve the therapist looking and listening for unconscious communications from the client and their network, as well as for the affective and relational quality of what is said. Many parents, for example, will have experienced tremendous strain and difficulty in getting a diagnosis for their child and have had to fight very hard for the support and education they want for them. Others may have only recently received the diagnosis and will still be struggling to accept it. The diagnosis may have come as a relief, a terrible blow or a combination of both.

Thoughts about the label or diagnosis can form a part of the assessment process, which means trying to find out what the client knows about their condition, how they understand it and how it impacts on their sense of self. A significant issue for families may be the challenge of loving and caring for a child who may be able to show their love back only in limited or specific ways. It is not that the child lacks concern for others, or is unable to be distressed by another's distress, but rather that this capacity may lack sophistication or complexity: it can be seen as a level of 'mind-blindness' when it comes to understanding themselves and others. Arietta Slade (2008) has written extensively about the challenges for parents of building relationships with an autistic child. It is likely that the therapist too may experience some of these feelings in the context of a therapeutic relationship.

Issues in the therapeutic process

Crucially, the therapist needs to consider the work in terms of 'relationship' and the issues that impair or enhance the client's capacity for relationships – with himself or herself and with others. There are no hard-and-fast rules, but there are some things to be especially sensitive to:

Intimacy

Because ASD is a condition affecting social interaction, and because people on the spectrum find relationships difficult to manage, it may well be stressful for an ASD client to be alone in a room with another person. As psychotherapy is a very intense and emotionally intimate interaction and its purpose and effect are unlikely to be clear to the client at the outset, the process will need to be taken very slowly and gently, making the procedure as clear as possible.

It can be helpful to voice the possible confusion, uncertainty and anxiety that a client may be feeling in the room. At assessment it is vital to ensure that means are in place to prepare the ASD client for their session, so that they are not surprised or taken aback by it. It may be helpful to introduce yourself first, outside of the therapy room, and for the client to visit the room with a trusted adult before they are expected to be alone with the therapist. The client may prefer to know that another trusted and familiar adult is on hand, perhaps close to the therapy room. Working in this way may be an unfamiliar way of doing things for the therapist and will require flexibility. Putting thought into how you arrange your interactions is vital, however. A person with severe ASD may have little insight into why they experience the feelings they do. Because of this, their life is made safer, more tolerable and enjoyable if they are 'known' by those around them, and the safer they feel, the more possible it will be to build effective therapeutic rapport through which effective change can take place.

Non-verbal and unconscious communications

As with any client, the therapist will be watching very closely to see how the young person with ASD is affected by the therapeutic encounter, taking cues from signs of calmness, agitation, anxiety, distress or disengagement. When the client has ASD, you may see higher levels of avoidance or disengagement than with other clients. Pressing for eye contact may be unhelpful or even distressing for a person with ASD; eye contact can be alarming and unsettling to them. So by avoiding meeting your eye, they are not being awkward or difficult: it is just very difficult for them to do so. As many people with ASD cannot make good use of information provided by eye contact, they use other senses to make sense of what's going on. As one autistic boy says, 'What we're actually looking at is the other person's voice. Voices may not be visible things, but we're trying to listen to the other person with all of our sense organs' (Higashida 2013: 43).

Therapist as enlivener

Child analyst Anne Alvarez has raised the difficult but central task of the therapist providing 'live company' to clients with ASD. She writes, 'The major technical problem for the therapist is how to provide such experience (of live company) to children who have difficulty in assimilating experience in general and also a particular difficulty in assimilating the experience of a living human object' (1992:77).

I understand the term 'live company' to mean the therapist's active and alert mind being communicated verbally and non-verbally to the client. An autistic person finds it hard to read faces or to conceptualise feeling states in themselves as well as in others. Because of this, passivity or neutrality on the part of the therapist may be experienced as deeply confusing or even hostile.

Alvarez suggests that one of the main challenges in working with a client who is on the autistic spectrum is this: the person with ASD cannot conceive of a mutually rewarding relationship in which each party is affected by the other because he or she finds other people mystifying, confusing, alarming and so on. This being so, the idea of a positive two-way relationship which can develop and grow may have to be built from the very beginning.

A further challenge can be in keeping the sense of connection between therapist and client 'alive' during the session itself. Because of the nature of ASD impairment, the preoccupation may be presented in a very boring way, with little sense of how uninteresting it is to the other person. Similarly, people with ASD may have a flatness of delivery, so that the voice of the client is monotonous or hard to listen to or be engaged by: 'the words we want to say and the words we can say don't always match that well . . . there's a gap between what I'm thinking and what I'm saying' (Higashida 2013:33).

Working with what the client brings

A client on the autistic spectrum may have abiding preoccupations which they want to focus on to the exclusion of other things. This can make a teacher's job very difficult. However, as a therapist in school you are in a privileged position of being able to focus all your attention on the client and their world without pressure to meet other targets. For example, 14-year-old Danny is preoccupied with superheroes, particularly Batman, whose pictures and figures he brings to the sessions and who he loves to talk about. For me as his therapist, Batman is my primary source in building a relationship with Danny. As well as being alert, interested and empathic as to just how happy Batman seems to make Danny, I can begin to think about his choice of interest as perhaps telling me something about his internal world and his sense of self. For example, perhaps he is projecting onto Batman his wish to be all-powerful – a hero who is rewarded with admiration for his bravery and daring, rather than someone who is not used to being admired by others. I can play alongside Danny, mirroring his movements and words, and I may wonder out loud about his feelings about Batman. It is Danny's interests which are my starting point, and I would recommend this as an approach to working with ASD clients in general.

Art and creativity in therapy

Working creatively in therapy rather than relying exclusively on direct person-to-person verbal exchanges can be an effective approach with a client with ASD. It is, for a start, less intrusive: for a person who may struggle to know what a feeling *is*, it can be difficult to make sense of the question, *How do you feel about that?* Working creatively also encourages the use of imagination and the flexibility of thought that can help to develop the capacity of the mind. Working with metaphor, or indirect communication, can aid the development of being able to think 'as if'. For example, I may say to Danny, with strong affect in my voice, 'When you tell me about all the things that Batman can do, it's *as if* you'd like to feel as strong as him.'

Working indirectly in this way may feel safer for the ASD client. It can also allow for the expression and discharge of feelings such as anger, love and loss, even if they can't be interpreted, understood or talked about directly.

Assessing whether therapy is helpful and effective

The following is a checklist to hold in mind when thinking about how the therapy is progressing with clients with ASD.

Look for changes

In how the client engages in sessions and with play materials

Jayden, aged 11, lives in a stressful home environment where there is little money, many siblings and conflict between the parents. When he first came to therapy he used the sand tray to create battles between dinosaurs and monsters. He shrieked and yelled as he staged these chaotic fights, which never seemed to end or be resolved in any way. Penetrating this behaviour in order to build a relationship took many months. However, after a year of weekly sessions, Jayden's sand tray worlds became far more ordered places. For example, using bricks and plastic animals and people he created a town in the sand tray which had a factory, café, farm and block of flats with residents. In a children's playground he created a scene in which a boy asked a girl if she would play with him.

In how the client relates to you

Jayden became able to greet me and to say goodbye consistently and developed an increased awareness of when the sessions were going to take place. He was able to name feelings regarding my absence or presence.

In the client's capacity to reflect and make connections between feelings and actions

Jayden's capacity to describe difficult events or experiences improved, as did his capacity to link them with behaviour. After one confrontation in school he explained to me, 'I didn't have the right kind of crisps in the shop so I shouted and wouldn't eat my lunch and had to sit outside (the head teacher's office).' In the early days he had found it very difficult to reflect on his experiences in this way.

In levels of emotional distress

If isolation or unhappiness has triggered the referral, the experience of the therapeutic relationship can to some extent ameliorate these feelings. As with other clients who face adversity due to life circumstances it is unlikely that actual circumstances can be significantly changed by therapy. However, therapy provides a regular space where the young person with or without ASD can feel understood and have their distress witnessed without shame or blame or an overly 'corrective' or 'problem-solving' approach. This is in itself therapeutic, and people should not be denied access to this kind of support on the grounds that they have ASD, even if making use of the therapeutic relationship is a more complex process.

In the transference and counter-transference

Be acutely sensitive to your counter-transference. It may be that feelings of dread or boredom at the start of the therapy transform, in time, into more positive feelings of warmth and pleasure. Such change indicates a development in the reciprocal relationship and positive attachment. It is crucial to assess the therapy regularly in supervision. A feeling of 'stuckness' or deadness' can be part of the transference in therapy with autistic people. The therapist may carry these feelings for the client as projections and as a result feel that the client is not progressing. She or he may have to work extra hard to stay in affective contact with the client, and this can be draining and exhausting when the temptation is to shut down oneself or switch off.

Progress may be slow, and change incremental. However, it is important for the therapist to feel supported in the work in order to stay alert and remain in a state of consistent wondering about the client's communications. Feedback from others and skilled supervision to help untangle these complex transference communications is vital.

Issues to share with your network at assessment and at review

- A dialogue about what communications have helped
- A general reporting of evidence that the client has experienced new insights into previously mystifying events
- Supporting staff to see that behaviours may have an emotional component
- Witnessing and empathising with the network about the challenges posed by the ASD client

When to refer on

Not everyone is helped by therapy, and, as discussed earlier, complex transference communications can make it difficult to assess the effectiveness of therapy for a client who has ASD. However, the following indicators may help identify those times when therapy is not appropriate.

No change in the client's response to the therapy

The client may find the experience of therapy distressing and is not able to stay comfortably in the room after several sessions. Or, after some months, the experience of therapy does not seem to be impacting on the client's sense of self at all, or there is no change in their capacity to relate to the therapist and no change in behaviour outside the sessions; in this case it is possible that more behavioural interventions are appropriate.

Risky behaviour

If the stress of the therapeutic encounter is too great for the client with ASD and they become violent and aggressive, the therapist will be unable to create a safe therapeutic space.

The development of a sexual self in adolescence can be a very difficult and confusing time for the ASD person. They will experience sexual feelings but may not have an understanding of how the expression of them may impact on others. Sometimes this can lead to behaviours which are risky to others and which the client has difficulty controlling. In such cases it is important that a full risk assessment is carried out and specialist help is sought.

Undiagnosed ASD

It may be that a client's behaviour and way of relating make you question whether they have as yet undiagnosed ASD. In this case, it is important to raise your concerns with the school and recommend an assessment.

Conclusion

Although working with young people who have ASD can be challenging, it has been shown to be beneficial. It is vital that young people with ASD have equal access to therapeutic support. Working alongside the network may be particularly important when offering sessions to young people with ASD. As well, the therapist will need skilled supervision in order to understand and work positively with the complexities of the transference with these clients.

As an integrative arts psychotherapist with many years of experience in the field, I know that young people who present with ASD features or have an ASD diagnosis can make use of the therapeutic relationship, and most will value it. In writing this chapter, I discussed ASD closely with colleagues, in particular, Lisa Walters, who is a Child and Adolescent Mental Health Service-based child and adolescent psychotherapist. We both feel that providing therapy in the school setting to young people represents an important step in reaching pupils with ASD. School-based therapists have much to offer this client group and can also helpfully raise the awareness of the whole school community of how best to support these adolescents more generally.

Study questions

- What thoughts, feelings or mental pictures come to mind when you hear the words 'autism' or 'autistic'?

- How might these influence how you act towards or interact with a young person displaying autistic features?
- How might you explain autism to a parent or young person? Why would it be important to do this when making a referral for a formal assessment?
- David, 16, is estranged from his father, who has left the family home. His account of what has happened between them is repeated word for word each session, apparently without affect. You do not know if his account is true. How might you respond to this inside and outside the therapy room?
- Courtney, aged 12, brings her phone to sessions and, when asked a direct question, will often turn the volume up on her music, hold the phone close to her ear and sing along, effectively blocking you out. How might you respond?

Note

1. The fifth edition of the *Diagnostic and Statistical Manual of Mental Disorders*, published by the Americal Psychiatric Association in 2013, has made changes to the description and diagnosis of ASD. These include the grouping of social interaction and communication difficulties into a single domain, and the removal of Asperger's Syndrome as a separate condition.

References

Alvarez, A. (1992) *Live Company*. London. Routledge.

Alvarez, A. (2012) *The Thinking Heart*. London. Routledge.

Baron Cohen, S. (1988) Social and Pragmatic Deficits in Autism; Cognitive or Affective? *Journal of Autism and Developmental Disorder,* 18.3: 379–402.

Bettelheim, B. (1967) *The Empty Fortress*. New York. Free Press.

Higashida, N. (2013) *The Reason I Jump*. London. Hodder and Stoughton.

National Autistic Society (2013) *National Autistic Society* [online]. Available at http://www.autism.org.uk/about-autism/all-about-diagnosis/changes-to-autism-and-as-diagnostic-criteria/qanda-dsm-5.aspx [accessed 25/9/13].

Slade, A. (2008). Working with Parents in Child Psychotherapy: Engaging Reflective Capacities. In F.N. Busch (ed.) *Mentalization: Theoretical Considerations, Research Findings, and Clinical Implications* (pp. 207–235). New York. Analytic Press, Taylor & Francis Group.

Solomon, A. (2012) *Far from the Tree*. London. Chatto and Windus.

Chapter 17

Working with Year 7 pupils

Melissa Jones

Transferring from primary to secondary school is a significant stage in every child's development. Moving on from the relative security and familiarity of primary school to the unfamiliar terrain of a new secondary school can leave young people feeling both excited and anxious. The nurturing environment of primary school is often linked with childhood itself, while the entry into secondary school foreshadows adolescence and signifies the developmental stage that is to come, or indeed has already begun, signalling the unavoidable physical process of growing older, and all that this implies.

Some children may feel a real reluctance to leave childhood behind and even harbour a wish to regress to an earlier stage of childhood. For both those not ready to give up on being a child and those in a position to begin the task of mourning the loss of childhood as preparation for the move into adolescence, this period can be particularly painful.

Thinking about the Year 6/7 transfer from the perspective of attachment, this time of life can herald an acceleration in the separation process which may be hard for both the young person and the parent/carer to negotiate. It is not unusual for family members to be affected. Whatever position the child occupies in the birth order, his or her transition to secondary school will mark a significant event in the family's life cycle and can bring up difficult feelings. For example, when a family's youngest child starts secondary school, this may arouse uncomfortable feelings for the mother whose primary task has been a maternal one. She might feel her role becoming more marginalised, which could trigger anxiety about her future identity, her personal value and her purpose in life. Having her last child start secondary school may resonate on deeper levels too, reminding her consciously or unconsciously that her fertile years are dwindling and that it is unlikely there will be another baby to replace the one who is now growing up.

In addition to the emotional and psychological challenges linked to separation and individuation that define the Year 6/7 transfer, there are many other changes for young people to navigate, most seemingly practical but each resonating in different ways depending on the child's personal history. These include, among other things, having individual subject teachers for each lesson, moving around the school to different classes, needing to follow timetables and taking more responsibility for their own learning. As this chapter focuses on why some children may find the transition particularly unsettling, a more in-depth exploration of the differences between primary and secondary schools will not be offered, nor will the nuts and bolts of working in the educational context be considered. A useful book to refer to on these subjects is *Therapeutic Practice in Schools: Working with the Child Within* (French and Klein 2012), which provides an overview of key psychoanalytic concepts relating to child and adolescent development as well as covering the practical aspects of delivering therapy in the education sector and an understanding of the school context in all its complexity.

Especially in inner-city schools, there will be a significant number of children who have complex histories linked to an unstable home life: bereavement, separation or loss; changes in family composition or being a looked-after child. More generally, those experiences which leave children feeling different from their peers are equally impactful. This chapter begins with a detailed description of the kinds of experiences that might make the transfer from primary to secondary school emotionally unsettling, highly confusing or even distressing. This will be followed by a discussion of the invaluable role the school therapist has to play in supporting students who are experiencing difficulties and of what form a non-stigmatising, informal approach to this kind of work might take.

Home life

Some Year 7 students will have already experienced transitions and moves of various forms in their lives, whether between neighbourhoods or cities or across continents, motivated by a range of reasons. For example, parents' separation may lead to the main carer not being able to manage childrearing on their own, so the child is sent to live with the other parent or with grandparents. When parents' new partners come on the scene, this can add a further layer of instability to an already complex situation. Families may also have unresolved immigration issues and might not be able to access secure housing, making them reliant on relatives or friends for temporary accommodation; such arrangements can change quickly and can impact on a child's schooling. A child who is cared for by a parent who is physically or mentally ill may also experience instability at home. If a parent is hospitalised, for example, the child might be placed with family or friends or may be taken into care. Such experiences can leave behind unnamed, unprocessed or undigested feelings and sometimes quite acute anxieties about change and transition generally.

As well, instability of any kind will impact on the child's inner world. Those who have gone through many changes may have only fragmented experiences of consistency or of knowing what will happen next. This means that they may not be able to rely on the knowledge that they can cope with episodes of change or that the inevitable disruptions will settle down over time. Such 'not knowing' will intensify anxieties around uncertainty in new situations, including the move up to secondary school. It may be hard for these children to evoke the image of a good enough internal object, which could give them the emotional resilience to manage change with less anxiety or fear. They might defend against their own unmet needs and wariness of 'the new' with a particularly over-confident presentation, perhaps coming across as arrogant, dismissive, in control, street-wise, confrontational or provocative, giving the impression of being wholly self-sufficient. Such behaviour masks their fragile inner self and acts as a potentially impenetrable defence against being in touch with the reality of what transition and change entails.

Family bereavement

Bereavement is arguably the greatest challenge any of us experiences, and for children in the process of moving from primary to secondary school, it can shake their belief in a stable world. Any experience of death in the family, whether a grandparent or someone younger, will have an impact on everyone, but for the child who is losing the security and containment of the primary school setting, bereavement can tip the scales.

When children witness grief-stricken parents who have lost their own parent, a child or someone else close to them, their inability to relieve their parents' distress can lead to feeling powerless as well as fearful that they've lost contact with one or both of their primary attachment figures. Low self-esteem can also result as the child may form the belief that they are not, in themselves, 'enough' to draw the parent out of depression or to put the parent back in touch with loving feelings.

If a parent is consumed with the death of another child, it can be hard for surviving siblings to feel that they have a right to claim their place in the world. A bereavement of this kind might also cast a shadow that dulls or extinguishes hope in the family. Indeed, children may feel they are being disloyal to a now-dead sibling by planning future events and thinking about the opportunities they may have at secondary school. Such young people might also feel under intense pressure to achieve at secondary school and make up for the lost sibling. Alternatively, they could fall prey to 'survivor's guilt', irrationally punishing themselves for continuing to live. Many of the painful feelings associated with this kind of loss can come to the surface around the time of transition, when young people's thoughts about their future will stand in stark contrast to the sibling's life which has been cut short.

Separation and loss

When the move to a new school coincides with a parental breakup, it can feel particularly destabilising. Even the young person whose parents separated much earlier may find that the transfer to secondary school triggers memories of this period, reawakening feelings about, and associations with, past losses.

A young person's place in the world may feel under threat when secure structures both at home and at school are in flux. Children often feel in some way responsible for their parents' separation even when parents have taken care to reassure their children that it is not their fault. When a young person has yet to make sense of or work through these feelings, the capacity to form new relationships can be affected. Conscious or unconscious guilt about his or her perceived role in the breakdown of the parents' marriage can take the form of anxiety about the potency of his or her destructive or hostile feelings. All children have passing experiences of hating their parents and wishing the worst upon them, even wanting them dead, as well as times when Oedipal wishes take over, during which the child desperately wants to take sole possession of one parent or the other. When parents do actually break up, these wishes appear to have been fulfilled, representing a moment when fantasy and reality elide. This can be very unnerving and frightening on both the conscious and unconscious levels.

If a new relationship has already been established by one or both parents, the child may also have to rapidly adjust to getting to know another adult, one whom he or she may have very ambivalent feelings about. This can be more bewildering or confusing if the parent has moved on to a same-sex relationship or one with someone from a different culture.

For those who have left their country of birth, feelings of loss around times of transition can also be connected to leaving behind one's place of origin and having to adjust to a new culture. It is a situation that is not uncommon among young people in inner-city schools. Why and when the move was made, who was left behind, what the family's immigration status is, whether or not English had to be learned as an additional language, how different the home culture is and how the move affected each family member – the parents in particular – will all influence the child's internalisation of the experience. Transferring to a new school has the potential to revive memories of moving country and may spark a yearning not just for earlier childhood but for the familiarity of the original home, which may be tinted with the rosy gloss of idealisation.

Changes in family composition

Historically, in the West, there has been a shared notion of what constitutes a family. Social and cultural concepts of the family have commonly focused on a traditional unit comprising birth parents and children living together. But, increasingly, families have been taking different and more fluid forms in which various family constellations are possible. Children and young people may live with a new step-parent; they might have moved in with an older family member; they could move back home after having lived with a grandparent; they may no longer see one of their birth parents; a new baby may have been born; they might have to adjust to living with new step-siblings; older siblings may have moved out. The re-shaping and re-constituting of families call for internal shifts and repositioning of relationships in general, all of which may leave a young person in a vulnerable place emotionally, particularly around the time of transition.

For those who have been accustomed to living with one parent for a period of time, the introduction of a step-parent into the home can arouse mixed feelings.

Oedipal rivalries are easily ignited as the new adult stakes an emotional claim on the parent. This process mirrors in part what takes place at the time of transition when the young person has to relinquish an exclusive relationship with just one primary school teacher and adapt to moving between teachers as well as acclimatising to having to relate to a number of authority figures.

Year 7 pupils will also be faced with the way these changes affect their social sense of self as well as their perceived status. Many students will have felt known and valued by primary school staff, some of them perhaps feeling they had a special place in their school community. In contrast, at secondary school, there are many more children to compete with, and teachers cannot be expected to know the whole pupil population on a first-name basis.

If a young person has had to face major adjustments at home, needing, for instance, to establish relationships with a new live-in partner or new step-siblings or a new baby, there can be resonances with what he or she is going through at school, where there are also new competitors or new 'siblings' who are perhaps getting more attention and seem to be better liked or 'special' in some way. It may be difficult for a young person to acknowledge some of the more uncomfortable feelings of feeling pushed out or replaced by the arrival of a new partner or baby in the same way. Here, too, there can be echoes of how the young person felt pushed out of primary school, a not uncommon reaction to having to leave at the end of Year 6. Feelings of anger towards a parent's new partner or step-siblings or a new baby who have entered the young person's territory may unconsciously call to mind the way in which the student has stepped into 'someone else's space' by entering secondary school and might make him or her anxious about the imagined resentment of Year 8 pupils who were there first.

Looked-after children

As they start Year 7, children who have been fostered or adopted may be unconsciously reminded of previous moves. Being left by a mother can feel like a shame-inducing rejection that continues to reverberate psychically and emotionally throughout life if not processed. Children unconsciously take in the prevailing idea that mothers are 'supposed to' bond with babies and value them even over their own life. For those who have no contact with their birth mother and are confused about the circumstances leading to their fostering or adoption, this wound is not easy to heal. Even if a young person was looked after from a very early age, they will still have a deep hurt connected to their fantasy of why they do not live with their birth mother. In addition, those looked-after children who have experienced a very chaotic, frightening or confusing home life may find the transition to be particularly unsettling. There is the potential for a number of different transference responses to the change of school. Past experiences which may come alive and colour the present include being taken in by a new family, experiencing a placement breakdown in a foster family, having to say goodbye to significant adults or other children when being moved on to a new foster family, going through the process of being adopted by a foster family and so on. What all these have in common is not knowing what is going to happen next. During the Year 6/7 transfer process, the young person may feel bombarded or ambushed by fragments of these memories or by flashes of feeling that are hard to make sense of and difficult to put into words. The main reaction may be to try to push the pain away or get rid of it as quickly as possible so that the causes do not have to be thought about.

Like all children, a fostered or adopted child will enlist defences in order to cope with the new situation. A common defence against the fear and uncertainty of being in a new school is feigning indifference, presenting as slightly superior, rejecting or untouchable, to enable a modicum of control to be felt. Because of a possibly limited capacity to trust that relationships can offer something good, the young person may assume a 'false self' by building up a seemingly impenetrable wall to avoid being hurt or disappointed by others as might have occurred in the past. Alternatively, he or she could present as the 'perfect' child not wanting to spoil or mess anything up in an attempt to ensure he or she is not rejected. Because school is often the one constant in looked-after children's lives, when the time comes to move from one school to another, the change can provoke intense anxiety.

Feeling 'different'

All children will have the perception that their differences separate them out from their peers at one time or another. Moving to a new school and encountering a new peer group can mean that any signs of difference loom especially large for a young person. For example, if young people feel their body is the 'wrong' size or shape or that their skin colour or cultural background or religion is different from what they perceive as 'the norm', they might be particularly sensitive. Many children will have what they think of as shameful 'invisible differences' such as knowledge that a family member is in prison or that there is violence or addiction or mental health issues in the family. They may be caring for a sick or disabled family member, or they themselves might have a learning difficulty or developmental delay. Some feel shame about their family's poverty or what they may experience as their family's low status in the eyes of the world, especially if they live on a social housing estate that has a dubious reputation.

Anxieties around these differences, both real and imagined, are amplified in Year 7 when everyone feels new and, arguably, different. In primary school such differences may feel less apparent or impactful as the school community will have become more used to certain facts about children's lives. On transfer to secondary school, it is often the case that young people become much more aware that other families have significantly different experiences from theirs, and they can worry that their present and past circumstances will set them apart from others. The move up to secondary school can be even more anxiety provoking for the child who feels acutely self-conscious. In contemporary school life, social media can take centre stage, and young people who do not have images or stories to share of an exciting or even envy-provoking life outside of school, let alone those who feel they have something to hide, can feel at a serious disadvantage compared to their peers.

The role of the school therapist

When one considers what Year 7 pupils might be bringing to their experience of starting at secondary school, we begin to understand how the school therapist can be invaluable in understanding and supporting them through this transition. 'Check-in' appointments are an ideal way of finding out how they are settling in and in the process gathering important information about their background and their current circumstances. This section will explore some of the practical issues around offering such a service including ideas about how to structure this level of support as well as what may need to be fed back to the school.

Initially, the school therapist can recommend to the line manager or the leadership team that she or he offer one to three check-in appointments for Year 7 pupils who are known to be vulnerable or are causing some concern amongst staff. Most schools will agree to this kind of service being provided and to including a description of it in their prospectus as well as raising pupils' awareness of it. As the prospectus will be read by parents and carers, the description of a Year 7 check-in service can highlight that the transfer to secondary school is a significant change for all young people and that the school wants to give pupils the opportunity to talk about how it is going for them. A clause should also be included giving parents the option to opt out, such as 'If parents/carers do not want their child to have a check-in appointment please contact the Head of Year.' This approach means it is unnecessary for the school therapist or the SENCo (Special Educational Needs Coordinator) to contact home for consent, and Year 7 pupils can be offered appointments as soon as the autumn term begins.

The Head of Year or the school manager responsible for pupils' well-being, such as the SENCo, will provide the school therapist with the names of Year 7 pupils to be seen. This list can be generated from information passed on by primary schools or from what has been gleaned from meeting pupils at their interview for their place in the school or from the induction day or possibly from perceptions of staff in the first days or weeks of the autumn term. Year 7 teachers and support staff can also add to the list as the year progresses, as they are in a frontline position and can closely observe their students. The school therapist can then set aside time specifically for Year 7 check-in appointments. Additionally – or alternatively – the therapist can also use slots freed up on her or his timetable for this purpose when a regular client is out of school or cannot leave class because of an exam.

The majority of Year 7 pupils will appreciate being offered a check-in appointment and tend not to feel stigmatised by it. They may take comfort from the fact that they are not being singled out for support but, in common with many of their peers, are being given a space to think about what the transition means to them. It also offers the therapist the chance to explain her or his role in simple terms and to let students know that if things do get difficult for them either at home, at school or with their social life outside of school, they can always self-refer via a teacher or through support staff.

A suggested format for a check-in session

The therapist's aim in offering a check-in appointment is to facilitate a guided conversation, bearing in mind that she or he may see the pupils for on-going sessions at a later date if it turns out that the school has more serious concerns about them or if they themselves would like additional support. A useful way in is to explain that we know starting secondary school is a big change in every young person's life, adding that for this reason the school wants to ensure that Year 7 students feel supported as well as have the opportunity to say what is going well for them and what has been difficult so far.

The therapist can 'top and tail' the conversation with more general questions about school and discuss home life in between. She or he might, for example, begin by focusing on the pupils' thoughts about the overall experience including whether or not they chose the school, what stories they might have heard about the school (or about secondary school in general), whether they feel they have made friends and/or kept old ones, what their biggest worry was about coming to secondary school, what lessons they like or don't like, what kind of student they think they are, what they see as their strengths and what differences they have noticed between primary and secondary school. The discussion could then move on to their experience of primary school, perhaps covering whether they went to more than one, what their earliest memory of school was, if there was anyone significant they had to say goodbye to, and, looking back, how they rate their experience of primary school in general.

The school therapist might then invite the young person to think about family and relationships more generally. When one is introducing this topic it can be useful to say something like *I'd like to hear from you how things are at home as well. Most of us feel a little uncomfortable talking about our family. However, understanding our relationships is an important part of life for all of us.* Such an acknowledgement can help pupils feel more comfortable discussing different aspects of both school and home life. This section could include establishing who is in the family, who lives at home, whether any family members attend(ed) the school, and whether or not there are any relationships within either the family, the school or the social network that are causing the young person concern or difficulty. Sometimes it can be useful to draw a family map or a friendship map with pupils to help identify significant relationships. Maps can also be referred back to if sessions continue after the initial consultation period.

Throughout the session the therapist can helpfully 'normalise' the different feelings and thoughts that the young person expresses, explaining that everyone – even adults – will have a reaction to change and that all Year 7 pupils need to cope with a range of responses. These can include a desire to go back to an earlier, more comfortable stage of childhood; fear of the unknown; anxieties about finding their place in a peer group; pressure to keep up academically; concern about finding one's way around the school site; fear of not knowing the rules and getting into trouble; anxieties about knowing who to ask for help; and missing important friends, classmates or teachers from primary school. It can be very powerful for young people to discover that they are not alone and that others also have difficult thoughts and feelings during periods of transition.

At the end of the session the school therapist can either thank pupils for sharing their views or, if it seems there is more that could be usefully talked about, suggest that they meet again later in the term. If it feels more appropriate, students can also be asked if, given what has been discussed, they would like the school to consider offering them on-going sessions or support of another kind (e.g. academic help).

In addition to being attuned to the unconscious forces at work in those who have had to manage previous life changes, we also need to keep sight of those students who encounter difficulties once they start at secondary school despite having no conscious reason to doubt that they will manage the transition well. Any number of circumstances or past situations can be at the root of this. Perhaps they'd forgotten the intense separation anxiety they experienced when starting nursery or reception, and memories of this are now unconsciously triggered. Or they may have been bullied early on in primary school, and the fear that this will be repeated is stirred up by the transfer. Such students also benefit enormously from having the chance to air their feelings.

Key themes or dominant concerns arising from the check-in appointments can be fed back to the school. The therapist might make recommendations that could include a follow-up session with a behaviour mentor, input from the learning support team, or on-going counselling or could suggest that someone from the pastoral team arranges a meeting with the parent(s) to discuss home life or other concerns. Organising sessions in this semi-structured way can help the therapist to gather useful information that the school may not know and also give young people an opportunity to talk about issues of importance to them. It can ensure that very vulnerable students who might otherwise slip through the net can be picked up and offered appropriate support. In addition, these sessions provide an introduction to the therapy service in the school in a way that reduces the stigma that can be attached to accessing this kind of support. Even if the young person does not go on to see the same therapist, this initial consultation will have given him or her a taste of what one-to-one support can offer.

Conclusion

In this chapter, I have introduced some of the more difficult experiences that Year 7 students may have already gone through in their short lives and the ways these could impact on their experience of the transition from primary to secondary school. As school therapists, we are ideally positioned to offer Year 7 pupils a chance to process their ending at primary school, think about how secondary school is panning out for them and, if relevant, raise awareness amongst other school staff of difficulties or complexities at home. The very existence of such a check-in service is likely to convey to school staff the importance of managing the entry into secondary school, especially for those whose life has been punctuated by unprocessed beginnings and endings. The school therapist's sensitive intervention can make a real difference between a young person withdrawing from or engaging in school life while also conveying to students that they are being thought about and held in mind.

Study questions

- What were your own school years like? What was your experience of transferring schools? If you have children, have they been through the process? What did you learn from it?
- In check-in appointments, what do you think is important to observe about how students use their time with you?
- If you have some background information on the students you are seeing, what assumptions do you need to guard against making about their previous experience of change or about their life history? Why?
- What kind of information would you be comfortable feeding back to the school?

Reference

French, Lyn and Klein, Reva (eds) (2012) *Therapeutic Practice in Schools: Working with the Child Within*, London: Routledge.

Part III

Using creative approaches and applied therapies

Chapter 18

Applied dramatherapy techniques

Tara Richards

Dramatherapy draws from a range of key theories including Bowlby's work on attachment, Winnicott's concept of transitional space, Klein's object relations, Erikson's psychosocial model of human development and Rogers' client-centred therapy. It is also rooted in the work of pioneering theatre practitioners such as Peter Brook, Jerzy Grotowski and Keith Johnson and makes use of anthropological 'rites-of-passage' rituals, myths and fairy tales. Training in dramatherapy is offered at the post-graduate level in the UK; dramatherapists who work in schools either will be in training and working on a supervised placement or will have completed their Master's Degree and be state registered. They will bring their own particular skills to their work with students referred to them.

Some of the techniques that are core to dramatherapy practice can be adapted for use in therapy or counselling sessions with adolescents. My aim here is to introduce a number of dramatherapy approaches which other practitioners trained in related fields such as art or music therapy, counselling, play therapy or psycho-therapy can add to their 'toolbox' to support their school-based work with young people.

Beginning and ending the session

Rituals used to support the transition in and out of each session provide consist-ency and containment. The check-in used at the start offers clients the opportunity to bring into focus whatever is foremost in their mind. This could be a combina-tion of feelings, dreams, thoughts, home or school issues or significant events that have impacted in the preceding week. Or the check-in might bring up feelings or fantasies related to the 'here and now' of the session and the transference relation-ship. Whatever comes to the surface can be opened up and explored in more detail.

A check-in might take the form of a specific introduction that the therapist uses every week once the client is settled in the room such as *Let's begin as we always do with a check-in. How have things been since we last met?* Giving the opening question a label such as 'check-in' is a light-touch way to start the session while also conveying that the therapist is benignly interested.

Checking in with the use of an emotions chart

A check-in exercise can be used each week, such as a hand-drawn or computer-generated bar chart which records the dominant emotions clients have experienced in the preceding week and how they are feeling in the here and now. One chart can be used for the whole term with each week's entry dated. Clients can be invited to choose colours to represent specific emotions or to use tones ranging from light grey through to black (e.g. light grey or yellow = calm or happy; medium grey or blue = low or sad; darker grey or green = envious or jealous; deep grey or orange = frustrated; black or dark red = angry; etc.).

The grid is then filled in using scaling of 1 to 10 to grade intensity of feeling, an example of which is provided in Figure 18.1. If clients tend to focus on the same emotions each week, they can be encouraged to think about other emotions. The therapist can ask them which feelings are currently missing from their life which they would like to be experiencing and what they might be able to do to bring this about. This helps them widen their emotional range and share feelings they might previously have avoided. The chart as a whole can be reflected on at the start or end of each term to note patterns or habitual ways of experiencing emotional life, to think back on the most frequently felt feelings, to identify whether or not there have been changes and to formulate a focus for the next half term or term.

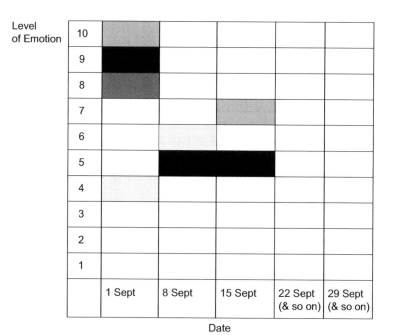

Figure 18.1 Emotions Chart

Using symbolic objects to start the session

The therapist can put together a box of miniature objects which clients can empty onto a table or even onto the floor (perhaps onto a nice piece of cloth) at the start of the session and then select those that reflect their inner state. A variety of miniatures should be offered, including people; small superhero or fantasy figures; toy soldiers; domestic and wild animals; buildings, fences and trees; stones; crystals; and other objects that might lend themselves to metaphor or symbolic thinking. The way in which clients handle the object they've chosen to represent their feelings or their current mental state can signal what they might need, either from the session or more generally – or both. It can be easier for some adolescents to explore feelings, experiences and states of mind from a safe distance, assigning painful or challenging qualities, characteristics and circumstances to miniature figures rather than to themselves.

A simple checking-out exercise

To symbolically mark the end of each session, clients can be asked to think of one thing to take away from the session and one thing to leave behind. Two small boxes which differ in colour can be used to aid this exercise, one representing what is to be left behind and one symbolizing what is to be taken away.

Directive exercises

During the first phase of work, directive exercises can be used to enable the therapist to build a fuller picture of clients, better understand their family dynamics and learn about the significant people in their lives. The therapist then hears the story from the young person's own perspective while also enabling them to thread together their life narrative, possibly for the first time. This serves to give the client the experience of being seen, known and heard as well as creating a more coherent internal picture of their experiences, which may leave them feeling less fragmented or confused.

These exercises can also be used as assessment tools. The therapist can see what clients choose to include or exclude and whether this ties in with the reason for the referral and with information passed on by the school. Sometimes significant events are revealed that may not have been previously disclosed. A guided exercise can act as a helpful starting point for forming a therapeutic focus incorporating both the school's and the client's aims for therapy.

Life mapping

The client starts by drawing a horizontal line across the middle of a piece of paper which represents a timeline that charts the years from birth (0) to the present day (for example, age 15). This line also marks a neutral emotional state. With a different colour, the client then draws a continuous line up and down recording the emotional highs and lows of their life.

They can stop the line at any point to insert words, draw symbols or place objects which label key events, including the age at which each event occurred. They complete their map in silence and let the therapist know when they are ready to move on to the next stage.

After making the life map, clients are asked to share their story and are encouraged to identify and include some of the feelings they had at the time, with help, if indicated, from the therapist. The story is then reflected on, along with what it felt like sharing it. Included in this exploration is thinking about whether or not they might have shared it with others before and, if so, with whom and what came up for them looking back at their life so far, as well as any parts of their story they may have had trouble remembering or found hard to retell.

The life map can be kept in a folder for the client and returned to at a later date. It can also be added to if key events that were previously left out come up, or it could be brought out further down the line if the client has difficulty thinking about what to talk about. The therapist might suggest adding to the map or making a friendship map or a school life map. In both instances, the same format is used, with the client charting significant feelings and events relating to the overall theme selected.

Making a spectrogram

Creating what dramatherapists call a 'spectogram' follows on naturally from the life map. The aim is either to make a drawing or to use miniature objects to illustrate family relationships and the client's wider social network. If using miniatures, the client is invited to select objects to represent themselves and significant people in their lives, such as family members, relations and friends. Pets can also be included. The client then positions the objects on a sheet of paper in an arrangement that spatially represents who is closest to whom in their life and with whom they themselves have the strongest ties. Or the client can make a picture to map their relationships, drawing or painting figures on the page in a composition that best represents who is important to them and who might be on the margins. The client selects their objects or makes their picture in silence and then shares it and reflects on it with the therapist once it is finished.

Sub-personality exercises

During adolescence, young people grapple with issues relating to all aspects of their identity and their role in life, perhaps best summed up by questions such as *Who have I been? What kind of child was I? What formed me? Who and what do I now want to be?* and *How do I become this?* To make sense of these questions, it is important for adolescents to have space to experiment and explore different roles so that they can arrive at a "reintegrated sense of self" which incorporates their own choice of what they want to be and their sexual preferences (Bee and Boyd 2013:291).

A key dramatherapy technique which can be used for testing out different parts of the self is the exploration of clients' 'sub-personalities', which represent different parts of the self that, in turn, may reflect the influences of figures from their internal and external worlds. All of us need to be able to move between a range of roles so that we do not get trapped in a single one that seems to define us. We need space to explore and rehearse the different sides of our personalities and the roles we might take up so that we continue to grow and develop. Clients experiencing role confusion can examine their different ways of relating in a range of circumstances or contexts and work on any internal conflicts that may be revealed. Integration can occur only when all aspects of our selves, both positive and negative, are acknowledged and owned.

Clients are invited to draw, create masks or choose objects to depict their sub-personalities. Each character is then introduced to the therapist, including the name the client gives to the character, a description of the character's main traits, a typical phrase the character might use, along with an accompanying physical gesture and anything else the client feels is important for the therapist to know about the character.

To encourage exploration of what a sub-personality might represent, role play can be introduced at this stage. Dramatherapists always bookend taking on a role and then transitioning out of it by counting down or using visualization techniques. Questions that can be asked during the role-play exercise might include *How can these two roles co-exist in a healthy way? What compromises need to be made in order for both characters' needs to be met? Are they each expressing healthy sides of the personality and acting in the best interests of the client? If not, what changes need to be made?*

The client's role repertoire may also be expanded by introducing new archetypal characters from myths or fairy tales or additional characters that the client comes up with. These new characters can help the client to explore and flesh out different and emerging roles and bring to light previous roles that were prominent but may have been repressed due to significant past events or to spoken or unarticulated family rules.

Role-play techniques can also be used to bring actual situations into the session. For example, if a pupil is engaged in a conflict with members of their peer group, they can play out a dialogue between themselves and their peers, reversing roles in an attempt to resolve the situation. This puts the client into their peer's shoes, helping them to develop an important mentalisation skill by revealing new perspectives on the situation under consideration as well as allowing them to express their own authentic feelings in the here and now. It can also enable them to look back on past situations so that they can see the roles they have played and can reflect on the outcomes of the choices they made.

Conclusion

Dramatherapists are trained to bring drama techniques into their work with clients. This can involve employing particular skills that school therapists from different disciplines may not have been taught. However, the techniques described in this chapter are adapted and can be further modified to suit the client and the therapist's way of working. My aim in presenting ideas informed by dramatherapy is to offer therapists from other orientations a resource to draw from in their sessions with adolescents, especially with those young people who may feel very self-conscious about exposing personal feelings and thoughts. Storytelling and the creation of characters or scenarios from the imagination offer clients the chance to explore their internal world from a safe distance using a containing structure.

References and recommended reading

Bee, H.; Boyd, D. (2013) *The Developing Child* (13th ed.). Pearson New International Edition. Harlow, UK: Pearson Education.

Gersie, A.; King, N. (1990) *Storymaking in Education and Therapy*. London: Jessica Kingsley.

Jennings, S. (1998) *Introduction to Dramatherapy: Theatre and Healing—Ariadne's Ball of Thread*. London: Jessica Kingsley.

Jennings, S.; Minde, A. (1993) *Art Therapy and Dramatherapy: Masks of the Soul*. London: Jessica Kingsley.

Jennings, S.; Mitchell, S.; Chesner, A.; Meldrum, B. (1994) *The Handbook of Dramatherapy*. London: Routledge.

Jones, P. (1996) *Drama as Therapy: Theatre as Living*. London: Routledge.

Lahad, M.; Shacham, M.; Ayalon, O. (2013) *The "BASIC Ph" Model of Coping and Resiliency*. London: Jessica Kingsley.

Further information

To find out more about training in dramatherapy or the profession itself, contact the British Association of Dramatherapists at www.badth.org.uk.

Chapter 19

Art therapy-informed practices

Lyn French

The theme of the 52nd Art Biennale in Venice in 2007 was 'Think with the Senses, Feel with the Mind', an intriguing invitation and one which artists and most therapists instinctively take up. All therapy is, to a greater or lesser extent, a creative process, relying as it does on revealing and deconstructing our perceptions of reality, uncovering and de-coding unconscious fantasies and re-shaping the stories we tell ourselves to give our lives meaning. When working with adolescents, many therapists – whether or not they are trained in art therapy – expand their 'toolbox' to include basic art resources and encourage their clients to use them, perhaps to make a picture of their family or to draw a genogram, for example, or simply to express themselves on paper if they are finding it difficult to talk. Arts therapists, on the other hand, will weave making images or objects into the very fabric of the sessions right from the start. If a client is emotionally receptive and not excessively inhibited by the idea of using the materials or too anxious about what might result, creating work without the therapist's guidance or intervention can be akin to 'dreaming when awake' as art making draws on both conscious and unconscious processes.

This chapter will not be providing a comprehensive introduction to art therapy, which is a discipline in its own right. Instead, following an exploration of how arts therapists might think about and make use of key psychoanalytic concepts such as transference, internal objects and the unconscious, some ideas will be offered of ways in which any therapist, regardless of his or her original training, can use contemporary art to open up a conversation on psychologically and emotionally resonant themes.

Key art therapy concepts

All clients will have a transference both to the art resources provided and to the invitation to make art which will include conscious and unconscious assumptions about their own creative capacities, reflecting their known – or yet to be discovered – beliefs about the state of their internal objects and the content of their phantasies. The act of creation has roots running deep into the psyche; for all clients engaging in art therapy, there will be degrees of unarticulated anxiety about whether or not their life-affirming, nurturing and reparative or 'good' parts are at risk of being dominated or eclipsed by their hostile, envious, destructive 'bad' parts. Arts therapists often give as much attention to clients' transferences to the art resources, and to how they respond to the expectation that the resources will be used, as to thinking about the content of the work made. For example, older adolescent clients who have not used art materials since primary school days may find that the suggestion to draw or paint unexpectedly and powerfully transports them back through the years to nursery or reception class. Their early experiences – whether predominantly 'good' or mostly 'bad' – will colour how they respond to an art activity that calls up those days. Anticipatory anxieties may also be aroused; along with the threat of feeling infantalised, there could be fear of being exposed as inadequate in some way if a lack of skills is revealed.

Arts therapists often work along a spectrum marked by a psychoanalytically informed non-directive approach on one end and a more directive style on the other. That is to say, the art therapist, in common with psychoanalytic psycho-therapists, may give only the least detailed 'instruction' at the start of the session, inviting the client to choose their own materials and to use them in any way they wish. This is the equivalent to the psychoanalyst waiting for the client to start the session wherever they want to begin. The aim is to allow space for the client to enter the process in a way that is most helpful to them, which could include making a mess or making something with the express purpose of destroying it.

Alternatively, if the art therapist senses that a client has a strong, anxiety-driven reaction to facing a blank piece of paper – itself potentially symbolising stepping into a void or the risk of unintentionally coming into contact with frightening psychic material – she may decide to talk about these primitive unconscious anxieties in everyday language, perhaps picking up on the general theme of 'beginnings' and naming the kinds of feelings aroused when we encounter the new or the unfamiliar, before offering some suggestions of how to proceed. If the work is shorter term or the therapist senses the client might benefit from a directive approach, starting points or ideas to work with may be provided at least until the client finds his or her own direction.

The client can benefit from the art therapist bearing witness to the unconscious material which is expressed symbolically through the art-making processes and will be embedded in the images or objects made. The blank piece of paper, for example, can be likened to an empty stage or screen onto which internal dramas will be projected. Being able to tolerate all parts of the self and building the capacity to trust that the creative act can bring about a sense of the whole, achieving some form of integration of the 'good' and the 'bad', is one of the more global aims of art therapy, a goal that is never achieved once and for all but continues to be worked on over the course of life. Overarching aims also include:

- developing the capacity for spontaneous, meaningful play so that unconscious experiences can be worked through;
- building reflective capacities through looking together with the art therapist at the work made and freely associating to it;

- translating felt experiences into visual and verbal languages;
- letting go of limiting or restrictive concepts of 'right' or 'wrong' ways of making art or of 'good' or 'bad' work (and their corollaries – 'black-and-white' and 'all-or-nothing' thinking);
- being able to tolerate the expression of, or being put in touch with, 'the bad', that is, with previously disowned feelings, mental states or thoughts;
- accepting that art making does not always yield the expected results and developing the capacity to tolerate the attendant feelings of disappointment or 'failure' as well as being prepared to learn from these experiences and being able to move on;
- bearing the narcissistic wound of coming up against one's limitations;
- developing the capacity to build narrative threads which begin to make sense of past and present experiences;
- being able to make links between the content of the image and past or present real life events, feelings or states of mind;
- being able to think about the relationship with the therapist and how it reflects aspects of past and present relationships;
- learning to trust the therapist and the processes involved in the therapeutic work.

A common assumption is that arts therapists use the images or objects produced as a diagnostic tool. This is rarely the case; instead, the art therapist is more likely to think about the art in the context of the client's personal history, what it reveals of the person's internal world and what it might say about the transference relationship. The approach taken will also be given consideration. Although the descriptions of art-making processes provided below can serve only as a blunt instrument, they do give some idea of what can be thought about.

- In *intentional art making*, the client has a clear idea of what he or she wants to make and sets about doing so with little hesitancy or uncertainty.
- *Improvisation* describes the act of creating an image with no pre-conceived idea of the form it will take or of the content. This is best conveyed by thinking of it as equivalent to 'dreaming when awake'. The result might be a narrative work based in reality, a picture that combines the real and the imaginary (that is, 'surreal'), a completely abstract work or even mess-making.
- In *play*, art materials are used to engage in uninhibited experimentation which allows the client to creatively regress to childhood years (e.g. the client might become very involved in dripping paint into the water container to see what results and begin to imagine, for example, that he or she is creating a magic potion).

It probably goes without saying that the client may roam freely across all these categories, perhaps combining a number of approaches in one piece; however, a dominant form can often be observed which may undergo transformation over the course of time or be expanded on as the client's visual language evolves. Each of the above processes can be understood to reflect an aspect of the client's psychological functioning or as an expression of the stage they have reached in their personal development. For example, a client might possess the confidence and ease to 'go with the flow' without censoring the output or trying too hard to manipulate the final result. In contrast, a client may be rigidly controlling the process, or precisely the opposite – sliding into unboundaried and chaotically random 'mess-making'. Controlling the process may serve as a barrier to keep the therapist and unconscious material at bay, while engaging in messy work might ensure that all the thinking and containing have to be carried out by the therapist in the way that a mother performs these functions on behalf of her baby. The client can, of course, move back and forth along this spectrum even in one session.

If an actual picture is created, the therapist encourages the client to talk about associations with it, perhaps asking open-ended questions such as *What does this picture say to you? / Looking at it now, what are the main feelings you associate with it? / Does it remind you of an experience from your own life?* The therapist may contribute to the conversation by offering some of her or his own ideas along the following lines: *I'm struck by the way you've drawn this figure, placing it right up against the edge of the paper. It's very faintly sketched in as if it's just about invisible. What does this suggest to you? . . .* (If the client finds it difficult to freely associate, the therapist might continue.) *I'm wondering if it captures what it feels like to go unnoticed or to be overlooked. Or perhaps it's about something else – maybe wanting that person to go away, almost pushing them out of the picture altogether. What do you think?* By providing more than one possible reading, the art therapist role-models that images can have different meanings. As the art therapist gets to know the client's story and emotional history, she or he will be better placed to make interpretations of the work that align with the client's personal experiences and convey key states or emotions that the person might struggle to own such as feeling excluded, angry, envious, lonely or humiliated.

Alternatively, the therapist could begin the conversation by focusing on the process, saying, *You selected your materials with confidence and started straight away on this picture. This is a change, isn't it – you used to ask me what I thought you should do. I can see you're developing your own ideas. / Your picture seems to me to be a record of how much you've enjoyed just playing with the paint today. What did the experience feel like for you?*

Arts therapists may choose to affirm and validate the client's art making, taking care to avoid words that imply a value judgement such as 'That's beautiful' or 'This is drawn very well'. Instead, the comments offered will reflect genuine responses such as *You've painted your picture without going over the edges – that's taken concentration. / You've used a number of different colours, which gives a strong contrast – that creates an interesting effect. / You've used that stencil creatively – by overlapping the shapes, you've come up with an original pattern. / You've mixed your own green there – it has hints of yellow which give it warmth. / You've used your imagination to draw a picture that is uniquely yours* and so on. Authentic and specific feedback such as this conveys attentiveness and builds the client's confidence.

Using contemporary art in therapy sessions

If they were to give it any thought at all, many young people would probably make quite predictable assumptions about why artists make art and what they draw their inspiration from. They might imagine that artists experience unexpected flashes of insight or that they have in mind what we would call a 'grand narrative'. Interest and curiosity can be sparked when young people learn that artists are simply trying to communicate what it is to be human, that is, their take on the complexities, ambiguities, paradoxes and pleasures of everyday life, and to capture aspects of our experiences which might be hard to put into words.

Contemporary artists are, in fact, reflecting on, commenting about and generally de-coding or de-constructing today's world. Even if artists choose to focus on overtly social or political themes, their personal and emotional experiences will be embedded in their work either consciously or unconsciously. It is not necessary – or even relevant – for us as viewers to know the precise feeling state of the artist. Instead, we can look at an image, object, photograph or installation and let it tell us what it wants to. Letting go of trying to guess what the artist intended or needing to 'have the right answer' or the 'accepted point of view', we simply allow our own ideas, feelings, questions and impressions to float to the surface. When looking at a piece of art or an image of it in a book or catalogue, we enter into a relationship with it, discovering meanings that are particular to us. Our reaction may be one of indifference or dismissal or stronger feelings – rejection or even scorn – but this, too, leaves us with something to think about: What, exactly, are we taking offence at? What does our reaction tell us? Therapists from any orientation can make this kind of creative use of contemporary art images in their sessions with adolescents. There are many artists whose work is accessible enough to lend itself to spontaneous interpretation and analysis, such as Michael Craig-Martin, Doris Salcedo, Juan Munoz, Louise Bourgeois, Jean-Michel Basquiat, Cyndy Sherman, Marina Abramovic, Damien Hirst and Kara Walker, to name but a few. Making images available in sessions can open up important conversations. As well, contemporary work often surprises young people and can instantly challenge what they might think art is 'supposed to be about' or 'meant to look like'. Experiencing a disruption of their assumptions and the opening up of new perspectives is of significant value. We all have a tendency to cling to the familiar unless we're prompted to think differently. When we do take this risk, it can be very exciting and sharpen our capacity for critical thinking. Young people need these kinds of opportunities to discover that they have their own ideas and that they can articulate them, play with them and re-shape them. Being able to make links, to connect up ideas and impressions, memories and feelings, and be at ease with these processes is at the heart of emotional literacy.

Some adolescents we see for therapy may find it difficult to take the lead. While their resistance can be reflected on, interpreted and worked with, there will be times when it is helpful to offer them a way in. Having a selection of art books to hand, or images downloaded from the internet and printed, or a box of postcards of artists' work can be useful. A simple exercise is to lay out a couple of postcards on the table, then ask the client to select one and to describe what they see before telling you what the image conveys to them. This can reveal some interesting perspectives and may provide opportunities to make links with the client's own life or with more generalised experiences or feelings any one of us could have.

A very accessible image to use in sessions is Yinka Shonibare's sculpture entitled *Dysfunctional Family*. Shonibare, an internationally recognised artist who was nominated for a Turner Prize and awarded an MBE (Member of the British Empire), was born in London but moved to Lagos, Nigeria, when he was three years old. At the age of 18, Shonibare suffered from an inflammation across the spinal cord which resulted in one side of his body being paralysed, but this did not deter him from his ambitions. Around that time, he returned to London to study art and has continued to create works which explore themes broadly relating to individual and collective identities including ideas connected to race, class, intercultural relationships, how personal identities are shaped and a sense of 'otherness', all subjects that are resonant in different ways for young people today.

A picture of Shonibare's *Dysfunctional Family* can be downloaded from the internet, a catalogue of his work can be brought to the session, or the set of emotional learning cards co-published by A Space and Iniva (the Institute of International Visual Arts) featuring *Dysfunctional Family* can be bought online from www.iniva.org. A conversation can usefully be opened up by asking the client to describe in their own words what this sculpture may be telling us. If a client finds it a challenge to speculate, the therapist might role-model de-coding an image, saying, *Perhaps this sculpture captures our experience of our family being different from other people's families. This might be triggered by a difficult family argument or a moment when we think no one's family is as flawed or as 'strange' as ours. Or perhaps a family member has a disability or mental health problem which the family believes singles them out. Others might imagine their family stands out most of the time because of their culture or religion and are left feeling that they are seen as 'alien' by others or as not fitting in.* Questions the therapist can move on to ask might include some or all of the following: *How do you see your family? How do others see it? What do you feel most self-conscious about? Can you give an example of something from your family life or your family's history that causes you uncomfortable feelings such as guilt, shame, embarrassment or hurt? Have you ever felt like an alien in your own family?* and so on, perhaps creating opportunities to note that most people feel like this from time to time as families are complex and also to identify positive experiences and family strengths as well.

A less obvious image to use with an adolescent is a still from a video by Jennifer Allora and Guillermo Calzadilla entitled *Under Discussion*, an image which is also included in the set of emotional learning cards entitled 'Who are you? Where are you going?' co-published by A Space and Iniva. Allora and Calzadilla's photograph features a man motoring across a body of water on an upturned table. Some see it as capturing the need to make an urgent escape from a real situation which may be threatening the man's very survival or as a metaphor to convey the human desire to flee from uncomfortable feelings such as shame, guilt or anxiety. Others read it as the opposite, seeing the man as someone who playfully and rather ingeniously transforms a table into a boat, perhaps creatively responding to a lack of resources by improvising. Still others view it as a reference to home, with the table representing family gatherings, seeing the image as symbolising the way in which we take our earliest and most enduring experiences of home with us wherever we go. None of these readings is more accurate than another. And none of them may bear even the slightest resemblance to what the artists had in mind, but that's not the point. The aim is to enable the client to find a way into creatively exploring differing states of mind and making sense of experiences while also recognising that others can and do share similar feelings.

Conclusion

This chapter has provided a brief overview of some of the ways arts therapists think about creative processes as well as how they might facilitate exploration of and reflection on the images or objects made in therapy sessions. When one is working with adolescents, especially in inner-city schools, using contemporary art by artists from a range of cultural backgrounds conveys important messages about difference and diversity. As this chapter has highlighted, emotionally and psychologically resonant themes can be looked at through the lens of contemporary art, opening up possibilities for collaborative exploration and creative thinking.

Resources to buy online

Emotional learning art cards featuring culturally diverse art images on the front and questions and commentary on the back (co-published by A Space and Iniva [Institute of International Visual Arts]) can be bought from www.iniva.org. Related exercises and ideas for using the cards can also be downloaded from the Iniva website.

Draw on Your Emotions by Margo Sunderland is a book of exercises accompanied by line drawings and other visual aids which can be photocopied. The exercises can be used as published or treated as a resource to give the therapist ideas of how to bring art-based tasks into the work. Visit www.margotsunderland. org to find out more.

Chapter 20

Adopting a systemic framework

Camilla Waldburg

This chapter covers different systemic theoretical concepts as well as techniques for the therapist to keep in mind when working in the secondary school setting. The ideas can be applied during meetings with parents or carers, meetings with a young person and one or more of their family members or individual therapy sessions with the young person.

Family therapy is also known as systemic psychotherapy as it is based on the idea that a family can be understood as a system, comprising relationships which are themselves embedded in a wider social context. Systemic practice looks at relationships as seen within their social context, always aiming to be respectful of diversity and difference. The interplay between societal realities and their influences (e.g. racism, oppression, social deprivation, privilege, and so forth) and the behaviour of family members is the therapist's main focus for exploration within systemic family therapy.

Generally, a system can be defined as a group with interrelating elements combining and interacting to form a complex whole. An example of this can easily be found in nature, where the ecosystem includes water, which moves through processes all of which are interdependent: rain falls from a cloud and splashes into a lake; the sun shining on the water creates condensation which, in turn, rises upwards, forming a cloud. The cloud grows in size and eventually releases rain, which falls back down to earth, repeating the cycle again and again.

Systemic work focuses on human systems with an aim of bringing out, sharing and respecting the interconnecting or even contradictory views and stories of everyone involved. A new way forward is worked towards which is rooted in forming a more coherent and integrated family narrative as well as modifying roles in which members have become trapped. Systemic practice approaches problems practically rather than analytically; it does not attempt to determine past causes in the way in which psychoanalytic therapists often do. Rather, systemic therapy seeks to identify stagnant patterns of behaviour in systems and address those patterns directly in conversation. A key feature of systemic work is not to 'unpack' or deconstruct realities or even interpret them but instead to recognise that the therapist's role is to enable systems to change themselves by introducing creative 'nudges'.

In school-based therapy, looking at the client through a systemic lens means going beyond the client's presenting issues to explore the wider context, such as the current and historical impact of oppression and poverty, discrimination and classism, to name just a few. This chapter introduces some useful systemic ideas, which the school therapist can apply in meeting with parents, staff and clients alike.

Linearity versus circularity

Systemic psychotherapy marked a significant shift within the therapy world from 'content' and the 'impact of historical events' to a focus on the processing of events within the constellation of family relationships. The linear sequential action of events, that is, cause and effect, is replaced by the idea of mutually influencing family processes. 'A does not cause B', and 'B does not cause A'; instead, they both 'cause' each other. Explanation cannot be found in the action of the parts but in the system as a whole, including its communication patterns, complex relationships and mutual influences. Here is an example.

Applying linear thinking, some might deduce that 'a damaged mother produces unmanageable and damaged children'. A description of the situation from a circular approach is as follows: 'An unhappy middle-aged woman, struggling with an inattentive husband, who himself feels excluded from the family, attaches herself to her 20-year-old son for male companionship, excluding the 14-year-old daughter. Feeling unloved, the daughter engages in sexually promiscuous behaviour with adult men, which brings her parents closer together as they both worry about her. The son is supposed to leave home to go to university, but he feels that his mother is so dependent on him that he hardly dare leave the house. Both parents are depressed about the "abnormal behaviour" of their children.'

In terms of clinical assessment, the problem is not seen as being located within one person in the system but instead is understood to be taking place within the relationship dynamics and the fixed patterns of thinking and behaviour within the family as a whole which have been established over time. These interactions may no longer fit the current life situation (i.e. the life-cycle stage of the family, the family constellation, the cultural differences between family members and so on), and the system will need to be helped to adapt to the new situation by changing ways of relating.

In a family system, each member's behaviour and particular ways of communicating will be dependent on or influenced by the actions and reactions of other members, creating a self-regulating cycle which forms a complex family system. The family therapist performs an important function by asking questions which reveal previously unexposed ways of thinking and interacting, thus eliciting new information and bringing in fresh perspectives. This can lead to greater understanding of self and other and often results in the reduction of some of the initial difficult behaviours. School therapists can make use of this concept in their individual sessions by exploring the young person's family background, especially his or her experience of family members and the way they communicate. When, for example, arguments at home are reported, it is worth finding out about the wider context, including the lead-up to the conflict and other family members' reactions.

The following questions highlight circularity and can help open up this kind of conversation (adapted from Boscolo et al. 1987):

- When your father and your brother argue, what does your mother do?
- If I was an invisible observer in your sitting room, what would I notice about your family?
- If your mother was in this room now, what would she say about it (e.g. the relationship, the conversation, the conflict)?
- When your mother gets angry at you, what does your sibling say or do?
- Who in your family is unhappiest about this situation?
- When you are having an argument at home, will anyone take your side? Who?
- What happened just before (the argument), and who might have noticed?

Genogram

The descriptive term 'genogram' brings together the words 'generation' and 'diagram', which, together, define exactly what it is – a visual depiction of family members across the generations including relationship patterns and stories that have evolved within the family network. Family members often make a genogram in a family therapy session. With family members working collectively, the joint drawing of the genogram on a big piece of paper with many different colours is an interactive and non-threatening activity. Or it can be used as an exercise with a young person. Whether created in the family context or in an individual therapy session, the process of mapping the relational system generates many opportunities for exploring and making sense of experiences. The genogram can include biological relations as well as other significant attachment figures such as aunties, nannies, other kinship carers, neighbours and important family friends. In addition, significant professionals, such as teachers, social workers and/or mentors, can be added in order to document the relationship with professionals or outside agencies. Taking the wider context of the family into consideration reflects the systemic concept of acknowledging that behaviour occurs in a context. Transgenerational patterns can be highlighted such as alcohol use, mental health issues, extra-marital affairs, domestic violence, cut-off relationships, alliances and coalitions. Ideas about gender roles, family roles, mutual expectations and resiliencies or strengths can be allocated to different family members.

The genogram allows clients to view their families within the wider historical, social, cultural and political contexts, possibly bringing to light issues of shame, undisclosed secrets, untold stories, critical life events and recent or historical experiences of trauma. Missing information can be as significant as the themes which are openly spoken about. More than one genogram can be drawn. For example, a cultural genogram records information about the family's different ethnicities, religions or faiths, stories of migration and experiences of oppression or discrimination on both sides as well as accounts of overcoming adversity. Particular rituals and celebrations might be included in this depiction of the family (e.g. mother raised Catholic, confirmed in Italy at age 11, now a Buddhist; maternal aunt practising Catholic, confirmed in Italy at age 12; maternal uncle left Catholic church, atheist; father Sikh; paternal uncle Sikh and so on.)

Genograms help school therapists to think systemically by, for example, connecting significant events and relationships to patterns of health or illness, changes in behaviour within the family (e.g. father was an alcoholic but stopped drinking and angry outbursts stopped too) and relationship breakdown. It is important that the school therapist is sensitive to and aware of different cultural understandings of family and does not privilege his or her preferred model as 'the ideal'. The changing shape of the contemporary family means that lesbian and gay families, step-families, merged families and 'families of choice' are increasingly common, especially in large cosmopolitan cities. It is important to include the wider network branching out from the core unit, whatever the composition of that unit, always focusing on what the client considers family.

An example of how to facilitate the genogram exercise

The school therapist might ask her or his client to draw a family tree or a genogram in the first phase of their work together. The therapist may introduce the exercise by saying something along the following lines: *I am really interested in finding out more about your family. I think it's a good idea to draw a family tree or genogram together so I can get a sense of who is important to you.* If it looks like the client has a reaction to this suggestion, it can be talked through: *You look a little uncertain. Tell me, what are your doubts? . . . We can all feel a little uncomfortable talking about family – it might seem disloyal or exposing in some way. However, our aim is to understand family relationships, not to judge or criticise them. You can include your biological family members, relatives and other significant people in your life. I normally use squares to represent boys and men and circles for girls and women. I suggest we place you here (in the middle at the bottom of the page), which will leave enough space to add other generations above your family line.* The therapist might then use questions such as those listed below to develop the genogram. Language creates reality – by putting experiences and thoughts into spoken words, we are giving them validity and, to some extent, fixing their meaning. For this reason, we try to support young people or their family members in finding their own language to describe themselves and their relationships.

- Who lives in your home? What adults live with you? What other children or young people live with you?
- Who are people close to you in your life? Who do you consider your family?

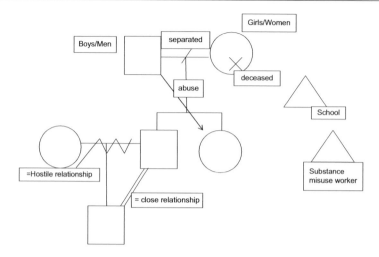

Figure 20.1 Genogram

(If we ask questions like this the young person has an opening to talk about her or his 'unusual' family constellation. In contrast, if we ask, 'Who is your mum?' or 'What is your dad's name?' we convey the message that we automatically assume the young person will have either or both.)

- What important events have happened in the past in your family? Who did these events impact most on?
- What would your family describe as significant events that have happened in your lifetime? What impact did these events have on you? On other members of your family?
- How would you describe your relationship with your parent/sibling/god-father/second step-father? Who else do you have a positive/negative relationship with? Who gets on most in your family? Who gets on least in your family?
- What aspects of your family relationships/history are you unsure about or would like to know more about? Who could give you this information?

Figure 20.1 shows an example of a genogram.

Family life cycle

All of us are born into families. Our first relationships and experiences of the world are with and through our family. We are born, develop and hopefully die in the context of our family. Embedded within the larger community, the individual life cycle takes shape as it evolves within the context of the family life cycle. The family life cycle encompasses its development across different developmental stages, each necessitating its own practical and emotional processes. The family life cycle comprises changes in relationships between family members as the need for emotional closeness declines over time and independence is developed. Rules, expectations and roles will be negotiated differently as the young person grows into a responsible young adult. Table 20.1 summarises some of these stages.

In adolescence, young people are moving through a particularly difficult transitional stage within their individual life cycle, negotiating several different emotional challenges within their families as well as in their wider social network. A healthy journey through this developmental stage is achieved when parents and carers are able to react to these transitions in a flexible manner. Difficulties can arise in transitions between different life-cycle stages if families are unable to adapt sufficiently to the emotional processes inherent in the particular transition. There might be a temptation to view these stages as normative, but cultural differences need to be taken into account. The transitional stages will vary from family to family, depending on their lifestyle, economic situation, family culture, religious beliefs and family stories. For example, families might transition through these stages at different times in their family life cycle than is highlighted in the table. Some families, for instance, believe in young adults moving out of the home to become independent as soon as possible, whereas other families will support their children until they are married and are setting up their own homes.

Table 20.1 Life Stage Transitions

Examples of some life stage transitions	Emotional processes
Single young adult: leaving home	• Establishment of own work and financial independence • Differentiation of self in relation to family
The joining of families: the new couple	• Formation of and commitment to new system • Realignment of system to include spouse's family
Families with young child(ren)	• Realigning family system and adjusting to new member • Facilitating children to make peer relationships
Families with adolescent child(ren)	• Increasing flexibility of family boundaries to permit children's independence • Midlife relationship and career issues
The empty nest: launching children and moving on	• Accepting a range of exits from and entries into the family system, such as children's new partners and deaths in older generations • Negotiating adult-to-adult relationships with children
Families in later life	• Accepting the shifting of generational roles • Adjusting to children taking a more central role in family maintenance • Valuing the wisdom and experience of the elderly • Preparation for and dealing with death of spouse and peers

Modern families, consisting of a single parent, step-families, teenage parents or inter-generational constellations, will experience challenges at different life-cycle transition stages. An example of a 'non-traditional' transition is when a grandmother takes up a caring role for her grandchild so her daughter can complete her education. The importance of this model is in the opportunity it presents to view problems within a wider context of family transitions and to acknowledge transitional stages as a potential challenge which some families will be able to work through while others will lack the necessary resources and resiliencies.

School therapists can utilise this model when thinking with their young clients about their family's life cycle. This might facilitate a better understanding of different family members' processes and the parents' struggles.

Family myths, stories and scripts

We all create myths, stories, legends and narrative scripts about our family. All are different and serve unique purposes:

*   *Family myths* are a set of beliefs that a family has about themselves, and scripts define what you do about these beliefs.
*   *Family stories* recount the actions taken in the past, and scripts prescribe the action to be taken in the present and future (e.g. how we, the Smiths, always overcome adversity).
*   *Family legends* are family stories that are re-told across generations and guide the family's future script.
*   *Family scripts* are shared understandings of the role each family member is expected to play in different contexts and interactions.

Family scripts are shaped by the family's culture, religion, parenting styles, family stories, legends and myths and in turn shape these. These scripts influence styles of parenting, ways of behaving, relationships, interaction patterns, boundaries, sharing of information and problem solving; they are often a combination of trans-generational scripts such as replicative and corrective scripts:

*   *Replicative scripts*: scenarios from childhood which are repeated in the next generation. Families with insecure relationships tend to stick to tightly scripted scenarios, as improvisation seems too uncertain and potentially threatening.
*   *Corrective scripts*: an opposite style of parenting to what one experienced in childhood.
*   *Improvised scripts*: an old script might not fit the current situation, so it is abandoned and experimenting with a new one replaces it, by observing and copying other families. In a secure relationship a new script is experienced as novel and arouses curiosity, whereas in an insecure relationship a new script might be experienced as threatening.

When meeting with parents it can be useful to help them to think about the kinds of experiences they went through at the age their son or daughter is now at. What do they remember about being 15? Who was setting boundaries and rules in their family? What mistakes did they make when they were teenagers?

The therapist can usefully comment on cultural differences in order to open up an interesting angle when discussing parenting scripts. The therapist might say, for instance, *I am not from your culture, so there are probably many things I don't understand about you. Can you explain to me what it meant to be a teenager where you grew up? What did you struggle with that you don't think your teenager has to worry about? What do you think your son or daughter is struggling with, living here in this country, that you might have not had to think about at that age? If I was speaking to your son or daughter, how do you think he or she would describe your parenting style? What do you think your teenage son or daughter would like you to understand about them more?*

Social graces (Social GGRRAAACCEEESSS)

As has been discussed, each individual family unit is embedded within its wider community and socio-political context. Factors such as race, ethnicity, social class, sexual orientation, religious beliefs, level of educational attainment and employment status shape each family's daily existence as these all define access to power and resources. These, along with family stories, beliefs and status in society, influence the family's way of 'doing family'. As therapists working with a diverse client group, we need to be aware of the inequalities and social differences between individuals and groups of people. We may be so familiar with our privileges that we assume others will automatically understand that our contribution to inequalities is unintentional, but this is not always the case.

The idea of privilege and power has been described by Michael Kimmel as follows:

> To run or walk into a strong headwind is to understand the power of nature, you set your jaw in a squared grimace, your eyes are slits against the wind, and you breathe with a fierce determination, and still you make so little progress. To walk or run with that same wind at your back is to float, to sail effortlessly, expending virtually no energy. You do not feel the wind; it feels you. You do not feel how it pushes you along; you feel only the effortlessness of your movement . . . it is only when you turn around and face that wind do you realise its strength. Being white, or male or heterosexual in this culture is like running with the wind at your back. It feels like just plain running, and we rarely, if ever, get a chance to see how we are sustained, supported, even propelled by that wind.

(Kimmel 2006, p. 63)

One way to help us become intentionally more positively aware of, sensitive to and respectful of these issues is the systemic concept of the 'Social

GGRRAAACCEEESSS'. The acronym stands for the following categories: Gender, Geography, Race, Religion, Age, Ability, Appearance, Class, Culture, Ethnicity, Education, Employment, Sexuality, Sexual Orientation and Spirituality.

The Social GRACES highlight individual differences constructed in varying social contexts and influence our position in society in terms of power, access to resources and experiences. Furthermore, these categories are lenses through which we look at the world and define the assumptions we make as well as our prejudices. In any context these categories may vary between being visible and voiced, visible and unvoiced, invisible and voiced, and invisible and unvoiced. The Social GRACES also give us a vital tool in supporting our personal reflection as well as using the concept with clients in therapeutic work. For example, school therapists can explore their practice by asking themselves about their preferred ways of working. Each of us will have our 'favourite' issue(s) to explore that are within our 'comfort zone' which we will privilege, will feel most passionately about and may be most skilled in attending to in our work. Each of us, for a variety of reasons, will also find that certain issues fall outside our 'comfort zone' which may never be brought to the surface in our clinical practice. Unless we look closely at ourselves, we may not be aware of what we might prefer to minimise, sidestep or even overlook altogether.

Conclusion

Families take diverse shapes and forms; in today's contemporary society we find same-sex parents, merged families, families with adopted children or foster children and families whose members span different generations and cultures. Nevertheless, all still exist as a system that will have particular rules with specific roles for family members and intrinsic ways of communicating, problem solving and negotiating.

Every family has its own way of 'doing family'. When one is working with young people it is important to explore with them how their family and its history have influenced and moulded them over the years. Adolescents are at an important life stage during which they are considering both consciously and unconsciously which aspects of their family's social, cultural and historical identity they relate to and which might be less relevant to them. The school therapist is in a good position to support them in sifting through their experiences and, in the process, helping them to decide what to take with them into their next phase of life and what to leave behind.

Study Questions

Answer the following questions in reference to the GGRRAAACCEEESSS (Gender, Geography, Race, Religion, Age, Ability, Appearance, Class, Culture, Ethnicity, Education, Employment, Sexuality, Sexual Orientation and Spirituality):

- Which GGRRAAACCEEESSS organise your life the most?
- Which GGRRAAACCEEESSS impact on your life the least?
- Which mean the most to you?
- Which one are you most uncomfortable with?

References and recommended reading

Afuape, T. (2011) *Power, Resistance and Liberation in Therapy with Survivors of Trauma: To Have Our Hearts Broken*. Hove: Routledge.

Boscolo, L., Cecchin, G., Hoffman, L. & Penn, P. (1987) *Milan Systemic Therapy: Conversations in Theory and Practice*. New York: Basic Books.

Burnham, J. (2012) Developments in social GGRRRAAACCEEESSS: visible – invisible and voiced – unvoiced. In I.B. Krause (Ed) *Culture and Reflexivity in Systemic Psychotherapy: Mutual Perspectives*. London: Karnac.

Burnham, J., Palma, D.A. & Whitehouse, L. (2008) Learning as a context for differences and differences as a context for learning. *Journal of Family Therapy* 30: 529–542.

Kimmel, M. (2006) Towards a pedagogy of the oppressor. In A.D. Mutua (Ed) *Progressive Black Masculinities*. New York: Routledge.

Index

Printed in Great Britain
by Amazon